Barbara Brabec

Creative Cash

How to Profit from Your Special Artistry, Creativity, Hand Skills, and Related Know-How

SIXTH EDITION

Prima Publishing

PRIMA PUBLISHING and colophon are registered trademarks of Prima Communications, Inc.

Library of Congress Cataloging-in-Publication Data

Brabec, Barbara.
    Creative cash, 6th edition: how to profit from your special artistry, creativity, hand skills, and related know-how / Barbara Brabec.
        p.   cm.
    Includes index.
    ISBN 0-7615-1425-2
    1. Selling—Handicraft. 2. Handicraft—Marketing. I. Title.
HF5439.H27B7 1998
745.5'068'8—dc21   98-26647
                                                                                                      CIP

98 99 00 01 02 BB 10 9 8 7 6 5 4 3 2 1
Printed in the United States of America

How to Order
Single copies may be ordered from Prima Publishing, P.O. Box 1260BK, Rocklin, CA 95677; telephone (916) 632-4400. Quantity discounts are also available. On your letterhead, include information concerning the intended use of the books and the number of books you wish to purchase.

Visit us online at www.primapublishing.com

Dedication and
Special Acknowledgments

I AM INDEBTED TO the thousands of men and women who have read earlier editions of this book and then sent me encouraging letters of thanks, including stories of their art or craft experiences. It is to them that this new edition is dedicated with my heartfelt thanks.

Earlier editions of this book were dedicated to my mother, Marcella Schaumburg, who convinced me as a child that I could do anything I really wanted to do; and to my husband, Harry, who inspired this dedication when he said, "Behind most successful women you'll find an encouraging mother and an amazed husband." Mother is gone now, but I will forever be grateful to her for always encouraging me to pursue my dreams, just as I am grateful to Harry for encouraging me

in all my creative pursuits during our nearly forty years of marriage.

Looking back, I now see that while I was happily experimenting with first one craft and then another in an attempt to develop new abilities, Harry was patiently tolerating such aggravations as glitter in his soup, yarn clippings in bed, and ceramic chips in the shag rug. At one time or another in the past, he has also been assaulted with the stink of lacquer thinner still in the air at mealtime, zonked on the nose by flying wood chips, and virtually overwhelmed by thirty-foot macrame cords being flung in frenzy. These days, he is thankful for the fact that I am able to express my creativity by quietly hand-stitching little teddy bears and doing cross-stitch embroidery.

Contents

Introduction

HAVE YOU EVER thought about the amazing variety of art and craft activities that take place daily in every room of the American home? More important, have you considered the amount of money such activities are generating for some people?

Today, in living rooms that share space with spinning wheels and looms, yarns are spun and weavings are done for sale through galleries and shops. In the corners of rooms once used for dining will now be found cozy little offices where creative souls are writing, designing, and developing all kinds of crafty ideas for the marketplace. People everywhere are no longer just sleeping in bedrooms, but sewing, quilting, and cross-stitching as well.

Recreation rooms used to be a place where dad disappeared to shoot pool or the kids went to play Ping-Pong. Now, the whole family is apt to go there after dinner to make handcrafts for sale at craft fairs, malls, or a holiday boutique. And do you realize how many cars in America are without a roof over their hoods because their garages have been converted into workshops for such crafts as ceramics, woodworking, metalworking, or stained glass?

And the kitchen? Ah yes, the kitchen. Granted, there's no time left to cook anymore, what with all this craft busyness going on, but all kinds of food products are being used to make handmade gifts and products for sale. Take bread dough, for example. It isn't something you bake and eat, but something you shape and paint in pretty colors to hang on a tree. Apples once peeled for pies are now carved instead, then dried to become collector applehead dolls. Macaroni that once stuck in the pan now sticks instead to a variety of box tops and containers made by children. Dried corn, seeds, and beans are used to make mosaic pictures, and eggs have become a favorite craft medium for thousands of devoted "eggers." Once served sunny-side up to contented families everywhere, eggs are often served scrambled these days because that's the only way to keep the shell intact for decorating.

Finally, we come to the smallest room in the house, only to discover that even the bathroom does double duty as a workroom. I'll bet more than one person goes to the bathroom daily to dye yarn or dip batik, and it's anybody's guess as to where the finished products go.

That leaves us with the backyard—and it, too, has become a working area for many people who use the sun as a tool to dry flowers, weeds, and herbs for a variety of products. Others make sun prints or weather their growing collection of barn siding or driftwood.

What does all this lighthearted patter prove? Simply that "arts and crafts" not only have become household words in recent years, but in many cases have actually taken over entire houses in the

process. Don't you agree that anything that takes control of one's home at least ought to contribute to its support? But how? Wouldn't it be wonderful if you could wave a wand over your home and magically transform all its *busyness* into *business?*

Perhaps this kind of magic isn't as impossible as it seems. I'm no magician, but I've pulled a few tricks out of my hat in the past and I'll bet you have, too. In effect, this book is your trick-in-the-hat, your key to success in the business world of arts and crafts. Once you've read it, I predict you'll be so inspired about your ideas and the possibilities that exist for bringing them to

Arts and crafts have not only become household words, but in many cases have actually taken over entire houses in the process. Activities such as those depicted in this imaginary cutaway house generate a considerable amount of extra income for some families, and a full-time living for others.

fruition that you won't want to sleep for weeks. Until now you may have lacked the know-how or courage to get your ideas off the ground, but no more. Through real-life examples, *Creative Cash* shows you how others have achieved success in arts and crafts businesses of all kinds. Their stories will convince you your dreams can be realized too.

I'd just like to mention that several of the people featured in this edition of *Creative Cash* were also featured in the first edition of this book, published nearly twenty years ago. The fact that they are still in the same (or related) business today says much for the satisfaction and profit that can be derived from turning a hobby into a home-based business. Further, many of the new artisans featured in this edition told me they actually launched the successful business they have today with an earlier edition of this book in hand, which says much for the value of the information you are about to receive in this all-new, twenty-first-century edition.

A Brief History of the Crafts Industry

BEFORE YOU BEGIN to make a plan for what you want to do, you will benefit from some perspective on the crafts industry. Statistics on the number of crafters in business are hard to come by, but some of the best information has come from the Hobby Industry Association's (HIA) annual surveys. The HIA is concerned solely with the trade hobby, craft, and needlework markets and, according to Susan Brandt, assistant executive director of HIA, there is at least one crafter in four out of five U.S. households, or about 70 million crafters total. "Our research shows that about 14 percent of these crafters are selling what they make," says Susan, "which translates to around 12 million people." With few exceptions, most people who now sell handmade products began as hobbyists; thus the larger the hobbycraft industry becomes, the more professional crafters it is likely to spawn.

People have been making and selling handmade goods since the early days of America, but the burgeoning *handcrafts industry* that we know today would not exist at all if someone hadn't started the *craft supply industry* back in the 1940s. Until I began this edition of *Creative Cash*, I never noticed before how closely connected these two industries really are, and how one industry's growth automatically fuels the other.

The craft supply industry that began in the 1940s on the West Coast gradually spread across the country in the next ten years, as how-to instruction books prompted the sale of supplies nation-wide. In the 1960s the first magazine for hobbyists and craftspeople was intro-duced, along with all kinds of new art and craft techniques, pattern books, and sup-plies. At the same time, hobby and craft manufacturers and publishers began to show their wares at trade shows and the industry began to receive media atten-tion. How-to craft projects began to ap-pear on television shows, and national attention was drawn to craft fairs and the thousands of individuals who were selling at them. To assist such people in their businesses, new art and craft guilds and organizations began to form.

It was good news for the craft supply industry when a Lou Harris poll in the mid-1970s revealed that two out of three Americans then participated in the arts and crafts, and many more wanted to get involved. New craft supply shops contin-ued to be opened, book publishers were releasing new titles by the hundreds, and new magazines aimed at craft consumers were thriving. In 1971 my husband, Harry, and I noticed the growing number of peo-ple who were trying to sell their arts and crafts, and decided what the world needed now was a marketing-oriented publication for crafts professionals. Although neither of us knew anything about writing or pub-lishing, we successfully launched a quar-terly magazine called *Artisan Crafts* that served an appreciative audience for five

years before it led both of us in more in-teresting and profitable directions.

During the 1980s an explosion of television how-to shows and the phenom-enal craze for *Cabbage Patch*® dolls drew added attention to both sides of the crafts industry. Like mushrooms in a forest, new art and craft fairs and consignment shops were popping up everywhere, with some of the latter going out of business almost as quickly as they opened. Clearly, both sellers and shop owners needed help in learning how to successfully run their businesses, so when a publisher asked me to write a crafts business book, I jumped at the chance. When *Creative Cash* was first published in 1979, it was only one of a dozen books on the topic of how to sell arts and crafts. None of these early books are still in print today, but many other crafts marketing and small business books have since been published for individuals who want to succeed as artists, designers or "craft entrepreneurs," and several of them are listed in the Resource section of this book.

The growth of both the craft supply and handcraft industries in the 1980s was amazing, but something much bigger was happening then. This was the decade in which thousands of individuals bought home computers not just to play with, but to run businesses from home. As millions of people joined the new *home business industry*, many did not realize they were merely joining all the artists, crafters, mail-order dealers, and independent publishers who had been working at home for two decades or more, but just hadn't been noticed yet.

In 1981 the U.S. Labor Department predicted that within the next ten to fifteen years, between 40 to 50 percent of the American work force would be working at home. A year later the IRS reported that 10 million taxpayers had listed home addresses for their businesses, stating that many of these businesses were being operated by women. (Interestingly, women also started the craft supply industry in the 1940s and more women than men have launched home-based craft businesses as well.)

In 1986 the White House Conference on Small Business placed the concerns of home-based businesses high on its list of issues and the U.S. Small Business Administration predicted that, by 2000, small firms would be producing a major share of the nation's goods and services. By the late 1990s, we were seeing these predictions come true as market research firms confirmed that more than 50 million people were working at home, and more than half this number were believed to be self-employed individuals (the rest being telecommuters and other home-workers). Industry watchers expect the home-business/home-office industry to grow well into the twenty-first century.

Without question, computer technology sparked the phenomenal work-at-home revolution of the 1990s, but I've long maintained that art and craft businesses provided the cornerstone of this industry. America had a large and well-established arts and crafts community long before it had home computers and the "home office revolution," and I am happy to have been part of its history. As new technology continues to drive the home office industry, so too will it spur craft businesses to greater success. (In a later chapter, you will see how computer technology has given creative people an incredible business boost, sparking many new business ideas and enabling long-established businesses to diversify and grow in ways they could not have imagined a few years earlier.)

Crafts' Impact on the Economy

HOME-BASED BUSINESSES of all kinds are now recognized as a vital part of our nation's economy, and many states have formed support organizations, special marketing programs, or mail-order catalogs to help them grow. For example, Arkansas, Kansas, Nebraska, Missouri, and Maine have published mail-order catalogs featuring handcrafts and home-produced food products offered by small businesses in their state. One generally gets into such catalogs by being actively involved in art or craft organizations or being known in one's community as a seller of handmade goods. People involved in economic development are often the ones who spark the publication of such catalogs. As a spokesperson for Nebraska's Department of Economic Development explains, "Helping deliver markets for the products of small and home-based businesses provides an economic boost for the entire state and sustains the viability of rural areas."

Independent research by various states suggests that handcrafts are contributing several billion dollars annually to the national economy. In North Carolina, for example, a survey of the crafts industry in 1995 revealed that craft makers and sellers were pumping $122 million annually into the economy of western North Carolina alone, giving employment to more than 4,000 part-time/full-time workers. This survey also revealed that the average income of full-time professional craft makers in that state (most of whom had an average of fifteen years' experience at their crafts) was $34,775. Multiply such figures by the number of states in the union and you begin to get an idea of just how big and profitable the handcrafts industry really is.

As you can see, a lot of money is changing hands in every area of the arts, crafts, and needlework industries, and there is a big "trickle-down" effect on the national economy. According to an article by Maria Nerius in the March 1998 issue of *Craftrends/SewBusiness,* professional crafters are spending $2 billion a year on raw craft supplies to produce goods for sale. It's anyone's guess as to how many billions of dollars craft business owners are also spending a year on office supplies and furnishings, telephone and computer systems, fax machines, and other technology. And it is because of technology that the crafts industry will continue to prosper in the future, according to HIA spokesperson Susan Brandt.

"What has spurred this industry most over the past decade has been technological advancements in the kind of supplies and materials being offered to consumers," she explains. "Photo transfer paper is but the latest example of a product that has helped to spawn a whole new industry in 1997 (making memory books, photo albums, and scrapbooks). The introduction of low-temperature glue guns suddenly made it possible for children and older people to safely use this tool. And then consider fabric paints that don't fade in the wash and decorative paints you can put on glass and safely eat from. These are but a few examples of how better supplies not only make the everyday crafter far more successful in his or her efforts, but greatly broaden the range of things that professional crafters can now make for sale."

Thus, by staying abreast of technological advances, you may suddenly discover a new business product or service you can offer, or see a new way to expand into wholesaling through better production methods, such as using a laser-cutting service instead of sawing everything by hand (see chapter 10).

One Person Can Make a Difference

THROUGHOUT THE COUNTRY, home-based businesses, many of them crafts-oriented, are revitalizing small towns and rural areas by drawing tourists into an area and providing employment opportunities to local residents. Sometimes it takes only one person to make a dramatic economic impact in a community. Take Dodie Eisenhauer, for example.

She runs her Village Designs business from her home and other buildings on the family's property in Daisy, Missouri, population fifty. Beginning in 1972 as a painter who sold her artwork at local craft fairs, Dodie later began to experiment with other crafts. One day, while playing with a piece of screen wire, she accidentally discovered a new art form around which she designed and produced a whole line of products for the wholesale marketplace. As her business grew, Dodie began to employ friends and neighbors on a part-time basis, usually during the second half of the year when she was building up her Christmas inventory. Now, however, she provides year-round, part-time employment to twelve to fifteen local workers, occasionally hiring as many as thirty during busy seasons. (When you consider this, it makes you see other small but growing craft businesses "out in the country" in an entirely new light.)

In the opening paragraphs of this chapter, I spoke lightheartedly about how a crafts business can take over one's home. "You're not kidding," says Dodie. "I started in one corner of the basement and soon took over half of it. Then I expanded into the garage and claimed the dining room for my office. In those days, purchase orders and invoices were always spilling over the dining room table and my filing cabinets were nothing more than hanging-file buckets sitting on dining room chairs. A couple of years later, when my business spread out into the driveway, I moved everything into an old house we owned across the road. A year later, when I ran out of room there, I built a 2,000-square-foot workshop and turned the old house into a storage building. At the same time, I moved my 'home office' from the dining room table (where we hadn't eaten in years) to the garage."

In 1997 Dodie turned a little house on the family property (where her grandmother used to live) into a gift shop called Village Designs at Grandma's House. To drum up business, she began to invite busloads of tourists to her gift shop and workshop. The first couple of tour groups were small and things went smoothly, so Dodie decided she could handle larger groups in the future. One December morning, two big busses arrived forty-five minutes earlier than expected, long before she was ready for them. As ninety-six people from St. Louis began to get off and stretch their legs, Dodie dashed over to open the shop and get the coffee pots going.

Generally, no more than fifty people come out at a time. Dodie takes half the group and shows them through Grandma's House, while one of her employees gives the other half a tour through the craft workshop itself, or delivers a spiel on the bus about how Dodie's business got started. "Handling nearly a hundred people at once for the first time was not easy," she said. "I never realized how much coffee this many people could drink, nor how many would need to go to the bathroom at once."

Dodie was doing okay on this particular morning until the "coffee disaster." Working too fast, trying to keep the pots going while also directing people to the bathroom, answering questions about how she makes her products, ringing up sales, and putting things in bags, she didn't notice the coffee problem until hot water and grounds start spilling out over the

table and down onto the floor. "Talk about stress," Dodie recalls. "I didn't have anything to clean up the mess and all those people crowded around me didn't help. This was one of those 'worst nightmare' days we all joke about later," she said.

Actually, this was a memorable day not only for Dodie but the whole town as well. You may recall that Daisy, Missouri, has a population of only fifty people, so everyone in town heard the arrival of those two big busses. When all those people got off in front of Grandma's House, the town's population suddenly tripled, prompting a neighbor to call Dodie saying, "We thought Daisy was going to tip over this morning with so many people on one side of the road."

This story is just one of several that gave me a chuckle as I was interviewing people for this edition of *Creative Cash*. Since a good sense of humor is absolutely essential to success in a home-based business of any kind—and craft businesses, in particular—I've included amusing anecdotes throughout this book. In between the fun and inspirational stories, however, you will also find a lot of nitty-gritty how-to information shared by professionals who have already been where you want to go. Just as earlier editions of this book have had an impact on the lives of thousands of readers, so too, I hope, will this edition lead you in exciting and challenging new directions.

Your Dreams and Goals

Those who don't look at their work through the eyes of a business person often fall short of their goals. There is no such thing as easy money, a term I've heard many times throughout the crafting industry. Setting objectives, committing to a realistic business plan, budgeting and follow through are an absolute must if one truly wants to reach an objective. Most people fall short when it comes to the follow-through stage, thinking "stuff happens" overnight.

ANNIE LANG, Annie Things Possible

SOMETIMES THE EASIEST way to turn dreams into reality is simply to focus your energies on something you really love to do. If you're ready for a challenge, now is a good time for you to do some serious thinking about yourself—what you've done in the past, what you're doing now, and what you really want to do with the rest of your life.

One of the first things you need to think about is the difference between a dream and a goal. "For goals to become reality, they must be written, they must be measurable and they must have a dead-line," stated Grace Butland in an article for *The Crafts Report*. You might dream of selling your crafts and "making lots of money"; but to state this dream as a goal, you should say something like, "This year I'm going to enter several small craft fairs and try to sell at least $2,500 worth of products." Now, with a firm goal in mind, you can plan how many hours a week you will devote to making products for sale, figure out the maximum number of products you might be able to produce and sell in a year, calculate the costs of producing this merchandise, and then figure out

1

what kind of prices you must set to actually generate this volume of sales. Of course, this automatically brings other questions to mind, which I'll be addressing throughout this book.

The most important thing to remember in setting goals is to keep them reachable. In the beginning, home-business owners need a series of small gains and achievements to keep them going. Thus you need to set each goal within the perimeter of reality, realizing it will require a certain amount of time, money and effort on your part. As soon as you achieve your first goal, set another one.

The goals of a beginner and those of a "seasoned pro" will be quite different, of course. You may start with the simple goal of just wanting to sell a few handcrafts, but your goals are likely to become more ambitious after a while. You may strive for increased sales, greater profits, or access to new market areas. Or maybe you'll dream about writing a book, becoming a teacher, opening a shop, or moving out of the crafts field entirely. Sometimes the experience people gain as a crafter convinces them they have other talents they want to develop. For example, as a result of teaching arts and crafts to preschool children, Opal Leasure is now working on a BA to become an elementary level special needs teacher. Joanne Hill, who once published business reports for crafters and spoke at home-business conferences, has become a motivational speaker and publisher of her first book, *Rainbow Remedies for Life's Stormy Times.*

Realizing Your Secret Dream

M ANY PEOPLE HAVE shared their secret dreams with me through the years. What these letter-writers didn't realize at the time was that by telling me about their dreams they were strengthening their own beliefs. By putting them in writing, they were actually drafting an informal business plan.

Years ago, when I was publishing a crafts newsletter, Karen Lyons used to write to me once a year to update me on how her business was progressing. She started selling teddy bears and other small toys in 1986, but after a while began to lose interest in her business. Later she told me this was because she was listening to what others said she should do instead of listening to herself. Now Karen is a successful toy designer who works with large toy companies to create special displays and animatronic creatures. She has also opened a studio/gallery that will feature fine art animals. "My work is my life," she says. "Thankfully, my work is fun and rewarding. Like life, it expands and grows with me."

I asked Karen what she would do differently if she were doing it all over again, and she said she would take more calculated chances. "And I'd be more confident. In the beginning I worried too much about what my husband would think."

In asking others the same question, many said they would do the same thing, only they would have started earlier. "Like many women who have turned sixty, I regret the late start to developing a career outside of wife and mothering," says Barbara Sharpe, who is now losing her eyesight and looking for a way to continue her writing and teaching in the sewing field. "I urge all women to develop a skill that will grow into a profitable venture or employment."

Rita Stone-Conwell, who began selling dolls at craft fairs many years ago, has been publishing *Crafts Remembered,* a crafts events newsletter, since 1989. She, too, wishes she had started sooner. "I let my lack of self-confidence prevent me from beginning earlier. I thought that because I have no college degrees, I would never be taken seriously. But I now serve over 3,500 subscribers and, with the expansion of my newsletter, I have diversified into doing business seminars."

"It's a big mistake to think you've got the rest of your life to get started," says Susan Young. She left a high-paying corporate job in 1992 to launch Peach Kitty Studio, the business she had been dreaming about for nearly fifteen years. In no time at all, she had built a successful business around her special passions of decorative painting, designing, and writing. "I wish I had started thirty years ago," she says.

Identifying What You Do Best

I ASSUME YOU are reading this book because you want to profit from your special artistry or creativity, but first let's make sure you've actually identified all your special abilities, talents, skills, and know-how. Many people go through life thinking they aren't artistic or creative simply because they have always taken certain life skills for granted. For example, people who say they are not artistic may forget they are using their "artist's eye" every time they set a beautiful dinner table, arrange a bouquet of flowers, or select satisfying paint or decorator colors for a room. And people who say they aren't creative tend to overlook the fact that they may be able to make a delicious casserole without a recipe, invent a game or toy that amuses a child, or find imaginative ways to use antiques as decorative items.

In other words, you don't have to be able to paint a picture to be considered an artist, any more than you need a degree in English to creatively express yourself through writing. On the next page you'll find a worksheet titled, "Identifying Special Abilities, Talents, Hand Skills, and Know-How." Take a few minutes to jot down all the things that come to mind now and, as you read the various stories in this book and realize that you could do what this or that person is doing, come back to this worksheet and add to your list. Consider not only your God-given talents but all the things you've learned just from a lifetime of ordinary living. Do not limit yourself to areas related to art, crafts, stitchery, sewing, and so on, but think in broader terms. Reflect on everything you know and do well, from raising kids or roses to managing household finances and using a computer. By the time you finish this book, you may be astonished to see how talented and knowledgeable you really are.

"You are certainly right when you say people take their God-given talents for granted," says Myra Hopkins, who started Brush & Needle in 1992 and now works full time on her mail-order pattern business. "I never thought of myself as talented. In a family that has always done for themselves, I was just one of the crowd. As a young wife, most of my endeavors were for my own needs, to decorate or make gifts, but the rave reviews of my products after I started to sell gave me

confidence to appreciate the worth of my talents. Adding the amount of learning I have accumulated to be successful really makes it exciting to continue."

The most profitable enterprises are generally built on not one but a combination of skills and past experience. Although they may seem unrelated in the beginning, they often come together in a unique way to make a successful business package. As a young adult I never could have imagined that my typing and secretarial expertise, coupled with a love of arts and crafts and experience as a musical entertainer for women's clubs, would eventually result in a successful career as a home-business writer, speaker, and self-publisher. Now I see that everything I've ever done before, and everything I've learned to this point in life, are now part of who I am and what I do for a living.

Sometimes we start doing something we think we can do well only to find out it's not our "natural bent." Bobbie Irwin has been spinning and weaving since 1976, and for several years she sold handmade items. She said it took years for her to realize—and accept—that she wasn't cut out for selling. "I have only been successful since I discovered and started emphasizing my natural talents for writing and teaching," she says. "If I had it all to do over again, I'd learn to recognize my true talents and take advantage of them sooner." Her advice to others? "If it

Identifying Special Abilities, Talents, Hand Skills, and Know-How

What do you love to do? What do you do best? Under the appropriate columns below, include things you have learned from formal education, job experience, volunteer or social activities, and a lifetime of living. Under Special Abilities, list not only art- or craft-related skills, but any business skills you may have, such as organizational or time management expertise, secretarial, accounting, sales, marketing, communication, and computer skills. Do not underestimate common life skills. Many of today's most successful home businesses are closely allied to such homemaking arts as cooking, sewing, child care, stitchery, music, art, gardening, interior decorating, and pet care.

In the box at the bottom of the page, note things you have a great interest in but know little or nothing about. (Do some research on these topics by checking the library for related books, periodicals, and organizations.)

Special Abilities	Talents	Hand Skills	Know-How
_____	_____	_____	_____
_____	_____	_____	_____
_____	_____	_____	_____
_____	_____	_____	_____
_____	_____	_____	_____
_____	_____	_____	_____

Special Interests

_____

_____

_____

_____

_____

doesn't feel right, and you don't get the positive reinforcement to keep going, you're probably not on the right track."

If you do find you're on the wrong track, remember this advice a friend once gave me: "Just because you get on the wrong streetcar, nothing says you have to stay on it to the end of the line."

"Even if you're on the right track," adds Will Rogers, "you'll get run over if you just sit there."

Leaving Your "Comfort Zone"

WHILE TRYING TO find a happy medium between work that both pleases you and yields a satisfactory profit for the time expended, you will keep coming up against the limits of your "comfort zone," that sphere of life in which you do things you know how to do, around people you know, in places you've already been. In the middle of the night when you can't sleep, you may ponder the big question: "Do I want to stay where I am now—in my comfort zone—or do I want to keep moving forward, into an area that's unknown and downright scary?" Some people will say they prefer to stay where they are now—just a hobby seller who makes a little extra money from time to time—but what many of these people are really say-

ing is that they're afraid to try something new because it means a walk through unfamiliar territory. That's understandable, of course, yet we rarely make gains in life if we aren't willing to take a few risks.

In looking back, I see that my greatest gains in life and business have come at those times when circumstances literally forced me to step outside my comfort zone to try something new—like when I was asked to write my first book, present my first workshop, or share the speaker's platform with world-renowned Howard Ruff, facing an audience of over 2,000 conference attendees. I thought that venturing into the unknown would get easier with time, but it hasn't. The older I get, the more set I become in my ways and the more reluctant I am to test new waters. Yet, although I still quiver a bit each time I try something I've never done before, I've learned the importance of doing this and I encourage you to do it too. Quivering never hurt anyone, and being a bit brave from time to time can put a lot of cash into your pockets and pave the way to exciting opportunities.

Fear of failure is often first on everyone's list of reasons why they shouldn't do this or that. But failure is simply one way of finding out what works and what doesn't. We are never weaker because we have failed at something; instead we are tougher, more determined, and much wiser. Failure is the principal research method used in all scientific, medical and industrial research. (As they say in the space industry when a rocket fails, "It's not a failure, merely an early attempt at success.")

Entrepreneurs everywhere have also learned the benefits of failure. Any kind of failure, from making a wrong design or marketing move to actually going out of business, can be profitable if it points the way to a better idea that will work, or if it reveals something important in your character that encourages you to go forth in a new direction. Since the financial failure of my first business actually became a blueprint for success ten years later, I now believe we sometimes have to fail in one endeavor to achieve success in another. I think of this process as "failure turned inside out."

When you replace the word "failure" with "mistake," it seems easier to handle because mistakes are a normal part of everyday life and a big part of home-business life. What's important is how you view them. "A man who can't make a mistake, can't make anything," said Abraham Lincoln.

Jeanne Walker, who has been sewing and crafting for over forty years, says "Creative minds are never idle. If a mistake happens, it's just an opportunity to create something new."

"I believe there are no mistakes, only adjustments," says Genii Townsend, who designs, constructs, and performs with puppets and marionettes. "Every step I took in my business was a growth, one way or another, because I learned from each mistake and corrected it."

Sometimes all you need to get past the "failure hurdle" is a little encouragement from someone you love who believes in you. Cathy Neunaber said a great encouragement for her was the day her father came to her new art studio, Lasso the Moon, with a bookmark bearing a quote by Les Brown: *Shoot for the moon—even if you miss it, you will catch some stars.* "Even now," she says, "it reminds me that others have great faith in me and it helps me to keep the faith and keep going."

© Cathy Neunaber

Encouraging Others

- -

AS A PROFESSIONAL writer, I have long been publicizing the work and home businesses of deserving individuals. Often when I write about someone, it's the first time their name has ever appeared in a book or national magazine. That gives me a kick but, more important, publicity like this often gives the person I've mentioned a "boot in the butt," making them see their activity in a more serious light. For example, a few months after I wrote about Rochelle Beach's Cinna-Minnies Collectibles in one of my columns, she told me my article had given her the confidence to move forward and become more professional. "We now have a logo and a promotional newsletter," she said. "And we've just signed a contract with a marketing rep who is looking for a manufacturer who can mass-produce a line of my products." Notes like this really make my day.

A Cinna-Minnes Collectible
© 1998 Rochelle Beach

I can't give publicity to everyone, of course, but if I happen to sense a feeling of discouragement in someone's letter, I try to take the time to scribble a short note of encouragement to them. That's because I remember my days as a beginner and all the people who encouraged me when I was struggling to become a professional writer and speaker. When Tsia-Suzanne Sullivan, a gifted Native American artist, told me how she dreamed of becoming a freelance illustrator, her

©1998 Tsia-Suzanne Sullivan "Touch the Sun Originals"

letter vibrated with feelings of insecurity. "I'm just a beginner who dreams of having a home-based business that will provide my family with a livable income." she wrote. "I want to be there for the three children I'm raising alone."

Maybe you, too, need to hear what I told Tsia: "All the world's greatest artists were once beginners too. Just keep reading, experimenting, and reaching out. Things will happen." Later, Tsia told me my letter was the confirmation she needed to seriously pursue her dream. I tell you this to emphasize how important it can be to offer a few words of encouragement to a beginner, especially if you have achieved a certain level of success yourself. Very few people today who call themselves a success got to that point without the help, encouragement and moral support of many others.

Learning New Crafts

IS THERE SOME art or craft that appeals to you that you do not yet know how to do, but would like to learn? It has

Stepping Out!

➤ Dad always told me I could do anything in life that I could imagine, and fear was not an option.

—Lyndall "Granny" Toothman, who is still demonstrating her craft of spinning at the age of eighty-eight

➤ When I first started out, I was always a little hesitant to take the next step, but now that I'm really into it, I want my business to be successful, and taking the next step is a little easier. It's still a little scary, but it's fun watching your business grow.

—Teresa Niell, The Topiary Garden

➤ I have developed my self-esteem and secured an education by never surrendering to obstacles. I have always looked for rainbows in the shadows and found opened doors. I've learned to not be too anxious when meeting potential and new avenues, and not to put all my eggs in one basket.

—Kathy Cisneros, Recreational Recycling

always been easy to learn new art or craft techniques, thanks to the many how-to books and magazines available. Now, with the addition of so many new television shows, how-to videotapes and adult education classes, it is even easier for people to explore new fields of interest, brush up on old skills and, in the process, perhaps discover talents they didn't know they had. Never assume you can't do something just because you haven't done it before.

I know firsthand the thrill that comes from learning a new skill. Back in the 1960s when I first began to appreciate the art of woodcarving, I found myself wishing I could carve wood, too. So one day I bought a little book titled *You Too Can Whittle and Carve.* That evening I retired to a corner of the living room with my new book, a small piece of balsa wood, and an X-ACTO knife. When my husband, Harry, asked what I was doing, I confidently told him I was going to carve a donkey's head. He laughed as he returned

to his reading. I could understand his skepticism because we hadn't been married long then and the only thing I'd carved to that point was a Thanksgiving turkey. But I had always done crafts of one kind or another, so I figured I didn't have much to lose by trying to learn how to carve wood. When I turned out my first piece of whittling a couple of hours later, I astonished my husband and even surprised myself—I had suddenly discovered a talent I didn't know I had. This naturally encouraged me to learn how to do other crafts. Before I knew it, I was selling my carvings and a variety of other items in local consignment shops and fairs.

It's an ideal situation if you can build a business around something you love to do and already do well, but successful businesses are just as often the result of research, training and practice. Annie Lang's story illustrates my point.

The recession years of the late 1970s and early 1980s had taken its toll of the rural community of Holly, Michigan, where Annie then lived. Her family needed extra income, but the only job skills she had were waitressing, selling Avon products, a little clerical training, and truck painting. "I had done a little freelance artwork," she said, "but I really didn't have any marketable skills for the job market."

Annie was never encouraged in art as a child, but she had taken a high school course in commercial art and later taught herself how to do tole painting by buying Priscilla Hauser's books on this art technique. She really wasn't interested in commercial art (or tole painting, for that matter), but this self-study put her on a new road of discovery that would eventually lead her to develop a unique style of art that would be in high demand twenty years later.

When Annie's youngest son was born with Down's Syndrome, it became apparent that she needed to be at home during his preschool years. When the local hobby shop advertised it was looking for someone to give oil painting classes, Annie jumped at the chance. Later, she took a part-time job with a local silkscreener doing design work and began to educate herself in the crafts business by reading my books and columns.

Years later, Annie wrote to me to tell me about the little home-based art business she had started in 1986. "I grossed $2,500 that year and felt satisfied to be earning extra money while also taking care of my children," she said. "I never could have imagined then where self-study, hard work, and confidence in my abilities would take me."

Annie is a wonderful example of how someone in a tiny rural community can take an undeveloped talent and run with it. Four years after she started, she was grossing over $25,000 a year from sales of her patterns by mail, and from the sale of country watercolors and hand-painted wood cutouts sold though a cooperative crafts shop she helped establish. Since then, she has self-published a line of design books and is exploring her opportunities on the Internet. As this book was being written, Annie was negotiating with several manufacturers about licensing her designs. Depending on how profitable these licensing arrangements turn out to be, she may be grossing $80,000 or more by the year 2000. Not bad for a "stuck-at-home mother" who used to paint business names and addresses on trucks!

Whether learning new skills or merely brushing up on old ones, it's never too late to start a home-based business. I'll never forget the fan letter I received from one woman who said, after reading an earlier edition of this book, "Thanks to your encouragement, I am now sharing my patterns with others and getting paid for it. Is there life after fifty and nine children? Yes!"

Understandably, many women who have spent most of their lives in the role of wife and mother have had to delay their dreams until they had more time. Ruby Tobey, who was featured in the first edition of this book and is still

Start a Wish Box

Annie Lang, who has always been goal-oriented, keeps a "Wish Box" on her desk that includes notes about all her goals—large, small, business, or personal.

"Every year in January, I add a bunch of new goals for that year, and every couple of months I go through the box and read through my wish list of goals, pulling those I've achieved while adding new ones," she says. "Everything I want to do, wish I had, or hope to achieve goes into the box."

Motif © 1995 Annie Lang

selling her Scribbles and Sketches, advised more than twenty years ago that "You just have to keep working a little whenever you can and the ideas and abilities will develop, and soon the day will come when you will have more time. Just don't quit completely and let your craft or ability get rusty. One day the kids will be a little older, or the other job less demanding. Or you might just learn to work your craft around the other things in your life."

Jane Wentz, who has operated From Wentz It Came since 1983, has an even better suggestion. "If I were doing it over again, I would involve my children and try to teach them what I was doing. I have in-

valuable experience they know nothing about, yet want and need to know."

When Rochelle Beach finally got serious about her Cinna-Minnies Collectibles business, she said if she could do it all over again, she would have worked to improve her artistic skills with no interruption while she was raising her children. "I have a lot of catching up to do," she says, adding, "It's true that what we do not use, we lose."

If you believe that you've already waited too long to follow your dream, look at it from Jenni Sipe's positive point of view. A quilter who makes one-of-a-kind hand-stitched applique wall quilts in whimsical folk art style, Jenni wishes she had started when she was a lot younger, but on reflection adds, "Then I think about Grandma Moses and feel better."

© Jenni Sipe

How Life Leads Us

H ave you ever noticed how life leads us in new directions when we least expect it? We get involved in one thing, sometimes accidentally, and before we know it, we're off and running in a new direction. We find ourselves zigzagging here and there until one day— Voila!—we find exactly what we've been searching for.

A step in any new direction will automatically set in motion a chain of events that could change and enrich not only your life, but the lives of your family and friends as well. Without question, a serious involvement in any art or craft will lead you in surprising new directions. As you will see from some of the stories in this book, many couples who began with just one of them producing art or crafts for

sale are now working together full time. In some cases whole families have gotten involved in a business activity based around mom's or dad's former hobby.

In observing so many home business owners through the years, both inside and outside the crafts community, I've noticed that few of them end up in the same business they started. The reason for this is that we often don't know what we can do until we actually get involved in something, and only then will we know what to do about the new ideas and opportunities that present themselves. Through experience in your moneymaking endeavor— whatever it happens to be—you will begin to learn your special strengths and weaknesses. You will suddenly discover talents and skills you've taken for granted, or didn't even know you had. You will add excitement to your life because you'll start meeting new people. The longer you work at producing and selling your products and services, the more you will understand the marketplace and your special place in it. This understanding will naturally spark ideas about new products or services you might sell, or new sideline businesses you might start.

The important thing now is to *just get started*. Then you will gradually gravitate to this or that, learn some new lessons, expand your horizons and someday land in a place you can't even imagine now. As evidence of this, I offer Kathy Cisneros's success chart, which illustrates how one thing always leads to another and proves that exciting journeys in life always begin with one step in a new direction. Kathy owns Recreational Recycling, an enterprise that began as a hobby business and quickly turned into a multifaceted career.

Kathy Cisneros's Bottle Cap Stairway to Stardom

1. In 1992 I invented some bottle cap Christmas ornaments to raise money for a little girl at our church who had a rare form of cancer.

2. While buying supplies to make more ornaments, I was hired as a bottle cap craft teacher at Ben Franklin's craft store.

3. While conducting my "bottle cap demonstration" in Ben Franklin's store, I was spotted and hired by the Sheriff's Department to teach my craft to various schools all over Orange County, Florida.

4. The Orlando Science Center asked me to participate in their annual major fund raiser, "The Winterfest Pet Fair."

5. I was invited and featured at the Orlando Museum of Art as one of Orlando's ecological artists.

6. When Ben Franklin's national craft magazine did a feature article on me, I received mail from all over the country asking if there was a book on bottle cap art.

7. The Science Center asked me if I could provide bottle cap kits for their Recycling Birthday parties. So I got a business license and began to put together craft kits for them to buy. I also got a computer and taught myself how to work the graphics. I then wrote and illustrated a bottle cap craft book titled *Recreational Recycling*.

When I learned all that had happened to Kathy in the space of only six years, I asked her to list the individual steps she had taken on her journey to success, and the things that happened as a result of each new step. She then sent the "Bottle Cap Stairway to Stardom" illustration shown on page 14.

8. The Humane Society featured me and my bottle cap business in their national children's newspaper, *Kind News.*

9. The Osceola County Library System featured my crafts for a month in their Earth Day display showcases, and the Disney Village Marketplace also invited me to participate in their Earth Day events. (Plaid Enterprises supplied me with quantities of paints and glue for each well-publicized event.)

10. While seeking advertising, I was offered my own craft column in *Flea Market News.*

11. *Pack-O-Fun* international craft magazine featured several of my crafts in various issues, including my bottle cap yo-yo and cross.

12. I got my own Web site at www.rainfall.com/caplady.

13. I teamed with a local musician and music teacher to write and produce the play "The Bottle Cap Kids," which was based on my bottle cap craft book and featured at the Orange County's Earth Day events, as well as the Walt Disney World Village.

16. In June 1997 the County Commissioner presented me with an Environmental Excellence Award for my business.

17. I recently signed a contract with Humanics Publishing to publish my book *Bottle Cap Activities.* This book will include the play.

18. I wrote more than sixteen songs, and Deep Blue Records offered me a songwriting contract to do an album.

19. My newest enterprise is Poetry Portraits, which I am promoting on the Internet at www.members.aol.com/poemsofyou/private/pt1.html.

20. In 1998 my success story was featured in Barbara Brabec's book.

Producing for Today's Marketplace

The road to success must start with the entrepreneurial spirit and a strong belief in yourself. Always be eager to read, to learn, to do, to see, to go . . . to advance yourself and build on your intelligence.

PAMELA SPINAZZOLA, Pamela's Studio One

WHAT DO YOU plan to make for sale, and what kind of supplies and materials will you use? Where will you find them? What are the problems in using commercial designs and patterns? How can you learn to develop your own designs if you're not naturally artistic? Once you've decided what you want to make and sell, how can you learn who might buy what you make? How do you figure the "right price"? Are you going to try to do everything yourself, or will you have the help and support of your family? These are just a few of the questions addressed in this chapter.

Your art or craftwork may be the best of its kind, or it may not be nearly as good as you've been led to believe. While compliments from friends and relatives are good for the ego, such praise is only an indication that your work might sell, not a guarantee. In the end, the marketplace is the *only place* to test the quality and salability of your work. If your products are well designed and well made of good materials, chances are good they will sell . . . providing your prices are right for the particular area or place in which you're selling, and a dozen other people aren't offering the same kind of products you are.

The Importance of Quality and Good Designs

RETAIL AND WHOLESALE buyers alike place a lot of emphasis on high quality. The dictionary defines quality as "a peculiar and essential character; an inherent feature; superiority in kind; a distinguishing attribute," but what constitutes "quality" in handmade products? You'll get varying answers from different people, just as you would if you were to ask them if something was expensive. That which seems expensive to me might be cheap at half the price to you or vice versa. Thus the word "quality" will mean one thing to a New York gallery owner who sells designer crafts, and something else entirely to a small town shop owner who sells a variety of local handmades.

Regardless of how well they are made, products assembled from kits and certain hobbycraft materials have little or no commercial value and are unlikely to sell outside the realm of church bazaars, boutiques, or consignment shops. (In particular, that includes all those "product kits" the mail-order scam artists are offering. Many readers have told me about all the time and money they lost when they answered such ads. See the related sidebar, "Beware of Opportunity Ads.")

Accept in the beginning that you cannot successfully sell the same kind of products that average individuals can make themselves. You may be able to work in the same art or craft mediums and use the same kind of raw materials; but to successfully compete with the thousands of professional artists and crafters out there today, you must offer products that are original in design or at least different from what everyone else is making and trying to sell. When you look around at what's being offered for sale at craft fairs, shops, and craft malls, you will notice that many people are trying to sell the same kind of products being made by the majority of the population as a hobby. According to the HIA, most craft hobbyists are involved in several different activities, with the largest percentage involved (in this order) in: (1) cross-stitch and embroidery; (2) crocheting; (3) apparel and fashion sewing; (4) crafts sewing; (5) cake decorating or candy making; (6) needlepoint; (7) home decor sewing; (8) floral arranging; (9) home decor painting/accessorizing; (10) knitting; (11) art/drawing; and (12) wreathmaking/floral accessorizing.

The more different your products are from what all the hobbyists are making just for fun, the better your chances of good sales and profits. It will take time and practice to find your own style, but with experimentation I'm sure you will find ways to add your own unique twists and touches to products made from common materials. In the beginning, Opal Leasure, The Apron Strings Lady, says her products were more "straight laced,"

but as she grew in expertise and confidence, her crafts flourished into lovely art creations. "I became a decorator of sorts, recommending products to customers, decorating entire rooms and homes with my own distinctive style."

You may already be a good artist or designer, but if you lock yourself into working with hobby materials, you will never make much money or be taken seriously by others. Barbara Otterson, who

Beware of "Opportunity Ads"

Beware of ads that begin, "$341.04 weekly possible making baby bibs at home!" or, "Make our kitchen aprons for fun and profit—$344.08 weekly!" Such advertisers say all you have to do is buy their supplies and materials, make products to their specifications, and they'll buy everything you make. Don't believe it! There is *no market* for products that come in "supply kits" offered in opportunity ads. Since this is a scam thousands fall for every year, it deserves extra attention here. These people—mostly mothers who want to stay home with the kids and make money too—are quick to believe the magazine ads that say it's easy to make money selling craft items—such as baby bibs, pot holders, aprons, jewelry, Christmas ornaments, pillows, and the like. The promoters of such schemes will guarantee your complete satisfaction and a full refund of your money, but they simply won't do this. They may offer to buy all the products you make, but they won't, and their reason will be that your work does not meet their standards. And it never will, because they have no intention of ever buying anything from anyone. These advertisers are simply out to sell you cheap product kits.

Barbara Brabec, *Homemade Money,* 5th ed. rev. (Betterway Books, 1997)

named her business DreamWeaver, is a good case in point. In 1987 she started selling jewelry made from plastic and wood beads she strung. A few months later, she moved from plastic to glass beads and inexpensive gemstones. A while later, she dropped the wood beads and switched to using polished brass and copper washers. Today she creates exquisite sterling silver and gold jewelry that incorporates semiprecious stones and lampwork glass pieces. What motivated Barbara to change materials and learn new skills?

"I've always been an artist at heart," she explained, "and I wanted my work to be taken more seriously. I liked what I was doing, but wanted to turn out a nicer quality product. Even though copper and brass was a step up from plastic and wood, I saw that my work was never going to be accepted into the good shows. I kept getting requests for silver jewelry, and tried silverplating the washers, but found it both dangerous and difficult to do."

When Barbara started looking into using silver, she was surprised to find it was not that expensive. She experimented first with silver wire (which she soldered), and then with sheets of silver from which she cut various designs, learning as she went along. "I'm mechanically inclined, so often I can look at something and understand how it's done. When I can't, I ask questions. I've picked a lot of people's brains at shows and generally found people to be open and sharing."

Eventually, Barbara built a 12 by 16-foot freestanding studio in her back yard so she could fabricate and form silver and gold and do enameling, lost wax casting, and slumping and fusing of glass, new craft skills she acquired by reading books and attending workshops. At the time I interviewed her, she was just beginning to design a new line of glass and silver goblets, offering yet another example of how one thing always leads to another.

Goblet by Barbara Otterson © 1998

As your designs and the quality of materials improve, you will find that buyers are willing to pay more for them. For example, when Lynn Smythe started Dolphin Crafts in 1995, she was selling mass-produced, easy-to-make beaded jewelry. Now her originally designed, one-of-a-kind beadwork creations sell for $50 to $450 each.

Looking back, many successful sellers shudder when they think about what they offered initially. "I'm still selling the same product, only now I'm using much better quality materials," says Teresa Niell, who launched The Topiary Garden in 1994. "Some of the first topiaries I made were so ugly, I'd be ashamed to admit they were mine." Adds Trudi Clark, who started Fire and Lace in 1984, "I'm still creating with clay, but can't believe I had the nerve to sell what I made fifteen years ago. My work has matured—gotten better, just like me!"

Buying Supplies Wholesale

P EOPLE WITH HOME-BASED crafts businesses have had problems obtaining supplies at wholesale cost for the past thirty years. One reason is that most crafters who sell on a part-time basis at the retail level don't sell enough of any one thing to justify ordering supplies in the large quantities many suppliers demand as a minimum order. No one has all the answers for the problem of how and where to buy raw materials and other craft supplies wholesale, but there are many ways to obtain supply source information:

➤ **Learn who makes or sells what you need.** Read trade magazines and other publications for artists and crafters. (Note: Trade magazines are not found on newsstands, but are available by subscription and often found in libraries. Selected publications are listed in Resources.)

➤ **Check your library.** Look for the *Thomas Register of American Manufacturers,* which lists products by category, trade, and brand names along with the names of companies that make them. When requesting a company's wholesale catalog (which is rarely free), type your letter on business stationery. Otherwise you may be perceived as a hobby business that does not qualify for wholesale prices.

➤ **Subscribe to periodicals that contain supplier ads.** One of the best magazines for this kind of information is *Craft Supply Magazine*, a trade magazine aimed specifically at the gift producer market (see Resources).

➤ **Attend trade shows.** Sponsors of the Hobby Industry Association (HIA) shows have finally recognized craft designers and "converters of craft materials for the gift market" as a legitimate market. Although such buyers no longer have to go through all sorts of machinations to gain entry to an HIA show, it is still up to individual exhibitors as to whether or not wholesale orders will be accepted from them.

"Not every supplier exhibiting in such shows is interested in dealing with professional crafters (PCs), even when they can meet minimum order requirements," an industry insider told me. "Although PCs, for the most part, order in larger quantities than small retail shops, some suppliers fear their invoice won't be paid. That's why it's important to dress and act like a business person at such shows. Don't give suppliers a reason to doubt you won't pay your bill. Don't go up to them and meekly say, 'Will you sell to me?' Instead, state firmly, 'I'm ready to place my order; are you ready to take it?'"

➤ **Join an organization.** Membership in some organizations enables artists and crafters to buy supplies in bulk with other members. (See Resources for some of these organizations; library directories will lead you to others.)

➤ **Search the Internet and World Wide Web.** Teresa Niell says she is finding the Internet to be a great way to find the supplies she needs to make topiaries, wreaths, and related items. "It's a wonderful resource tool. You can search for almost any kind of material and come up with something. Since crafters are quick to share information, message boards are also a great way to find a certain product you're looking for."

➤ **Other tips.** In the beginning, when your supply needs are small, your best bet may be to concentrate on finding suppliers who offer bulk or special-discount prices. Craft magazines often carry ads of such companies. Since retail shops everywhere are hurting for business these days, some might offer a 20 to 30 percent discount on larger-than-usual orders. In fact, if you need fabric or fur, you might come out ahead buying this way instead of at full wholesale.

"Buying wholesale requires a large-quantity purchase and minimum orders at each wholesale house," says teddy bear designer Jan Bonner. "Fabrics purchased in 20-yard bolts are expensive, and you could easily be stuck with a large portion unsold at the end of a season. Patterns in fabrics and colors also change each season. Calico in style in the 1970s gave way to chintz fabrics in the 1980s, then to dark backgrounds in the 1990s. I've decided it's better to buy some amounts on sale at 30 percent off than large amounts at 50 percent off. This enables me to achieve a variety of color for less cash output."

Jan adds that you can always find a good buy on supplies, but never can replace the capital used to buy them. "Always be careful to have an adequate supply of money on hand to make a quick move in the marketplace," she cautions.

Dollmaker Rita Stone-Conwell has learned not to buy supplies in large quantities until she knows an item is going to be a good seller. "I also learned that just because a color or style interests me, it does not mean others will buy it." After a lifetime of sewing, Barbara Sharpe says her most expensive lesson was purchasing a huge stash of fabrics for projects never started. The fabric retailers have promoted the adage that 'She who dies with the most fabrics wins.' "Wrong," she says. "Fabric does not earn interest."

Fabric does earn respect, however, as Maria Nerius will confirm. She still cringes when she relates this story: "I was fascinated with a product called lamb's fleece. When it came on the market, I immediately bought $600 worth—a big investment for me—because I was so excited about working with this wonderful new material. I forgot only one thing: I'm allergic to wool. In my excitement, *fleece* and *wool* just didn't correlate. Thirty minutes after handling the material, I was covered with red blotches and had to go to the hospital. I ended up giving all of this material to the senior center."

Using Commercial Patterns and Designs

MOST HOBBYISTS USE commercial patterns and designs for their art, craft, sewing, and needlework projects. When they start to sell, it's only natural to continue using the same patterns and designs to make products for sale. There is a problem here, however. Not only is there a limited market for such products, the commercial use of such patterns and designs may be strictly limited or totally prohibited by copyright owners. In spite of what you may have heard, every pattern and design published today is protected by copyright law and intended for *personal use only.* The fact that you've bought a pattern does not mean you have the legal right to use it to make products for sale.

Furthermore, the fact that you may not find a copyright notice on a piece of art or craftwork in no way implies that the design is free for the taking. Everything that qualifies for protection under copyright law *is automatically protected from the moment of creation,* even if the copyright owner fails to file a copyright claim or chooses not to include a copyright notice on the work itself.

Because every copyright owner has a different policy about how his or her creativity may be used by others, it is impossible for me to give you specific guidelines about the commercial use of patterns and designs. Generally speaking, however, you cannot legally *wholesale* any item made from any design or pattern in a consumer crafts magazine or book, or from any pattern or design purchased from any other source. (Note: Be careful about lifting images off the Internet because a lot of copyright problems are developing here. Sites that offer commercial clip art are one thing; illustrations taken from any other source could lead to legal problems.)

Am I saying, then, that you can use the patterns or designs in books and magazines to make products for sale at the *retail* level? Yes and no. Many designers and publishers now include a statement along with their copyright notice that spells out how designs may be used. Some restrict the number of products that may be made for sale while others allow unlimited sales of products provided they are sold only through retail outlets. Still others draw the line at selling through outlets where people other than the crafter realizes a profit. In the latter instance, products could be sold at craft fairs, holiday boutiques, or by mail through an individual's catalog, but not offered for sale in a consignment shop, craft mall, or any other wholesale outlet. How-to magazines also have varying policies about how their projects or patterns may be used. If a particular magazine doesn't regularly carry a notice about how readers can use their patterns or designs, the only way to

To Be Safe, Be Original

Never copy the designs of other crafters. Lifting someone else's designs is not only morally wrong but legally dangerous. Professional crafters tend to protect all of their work with copyrights and will not hesitate to sue anyone who steals their creativity. What you cannot know, of course, is where other crafters are getting their designs. What if the crafter you want to "borrow from" is illegally using someone else's copyrighted design? By taking it for your own use, you would not only compound the crime but put yourself at financial risk.

know for sure is to write the magazine and ask.

Developing Creativity and Design Ability

THE ABOVE DISCUSSION emphasizes the importance of developing your own line of originally designed products. Your next question is likely to be, "But what is *original?*"

Some crafters believe if they buy a pattern or design and change it in some way that it automatically becomes their "original creation." *This is not true.* You can't just lift something here, add it to something there, change its size, shape, or color and call the resulting image your own. Legally speaking, copyright infringement occurs whenever anyone violates the exclusive rights covered by copyright. If your infringement of someone's copyright affects their profits, the penalties can be severe—$100,000 or more, in fact. Since it requires only "substantial similarity" to establish copyright infringement (a point that is always debated in copyright lawsuits), this is not something you want to mess around with. In short, the sooner you begin to create your own patterns and designs the better.

You may protest that you are not an artist, that you can't draw a straight line and couldn't begin to design your own projects, but I don't believe that for a moment. I know you're an imaginative individual, else you wouldn't be reading this book. And I'll bet you played with crayons as a child, creating imaginative pictures your mother thought were wonderful. Although your drawing may still be childlike, it is nonetheless a talent you can use. Like everything else, your drawing skills are likely to improve with practice. (If they don't, just remember the high prices people pay for "primitive art.")

You *can* learn to apply your natural creativity to products you make for sale, and the first thing you ought to do is visit your library and look for books that can help you do this. Also:

➤ **Buy some design books.** You will find thousands of copyright-free designs and motifs in the *Pictorial Archive* books published by Dover Publications (see Resources). You may use the designs and motifs in these books in any manner or place you wish, without further payment, permis-sion, or acknowledgment. A few sample motifs are included here to give you an idea of what you'll find in various books.

➤ **Study museum objects.** There are no copyrights on ancient objects in muse-

The copyright-free illustrations shown above are from the following books in Dover publications Pictorial Archive Series: A. *Art Deco Designs and Motifs;* B. *Old-Time Circus Cuts;* C. *Authentic Designs from the American Arts and Crafts Movement;* D. *Decorative Art of the Southwestern Indians;* E. *Teddy Bear Cut and Use Stencils;* F. *A Treasury of Flower Designs for Artists, Embroiderers and Craftsmen.*

ums, so always go with pad and pencil in hand. Because designs in one medium are easily transferable to another, artists through the ages have studied the work of others for inspiration and ideas, adapting them for their own use. Thus one person's "original" macrame hanging may actually have been inspired by an ancient Egyptian weaving or ceramic pot, while a colorful contemporary quilt pattern may have been lifted from the design of a sixteenth-century stained glass window. Many is the time I've looked through a needlework design book and found designs that could also be used by rugmakers, handweavers, mosaic artisans, or decorative painters. In turn, designs on ancient ceramic pots, Indian baskets, or African masks (all neatly captured in Dover's *Pictorial Archive* books) lend themselves beautifully to needlework and such crafts as jewelry, paper-mache, woodcarving, weaving, macrame, beadcraft, and so on.

➢ **Develop a "seeing eye."** Designs are everywhere for the taking—you need only train your eyes to see them. Nature is full of intricate patterns that can be translated into images that could be used on craft projects. Begin by looking more closely at the designs to be found in seashells, leaves, flowers, and snowflakes. Notice how things look in silhouette or when the setting sun casts a shadow of bare branches, then try to sketch what you see. When I began to do this years ago, I found "pictures" in the strangest places. Once when I looked out the breakfast window I spotted a funny old woman hiding in a clump of snow on the tree and grabbed a pencil to transfer my vision to paper. Harry thought I was a bit daft because he couldn't see a thing.

Another day, while baking cookies, I noticed the design my electric beaters left in the dough and saw not cookies but a "kookie owl" perched on a branch, surrounded by swirling leaves. The cookie baking had to wait until I captured this rare bird on paper for a future piece of needlework. The interesting thing about the designs pictured here is that I couldn't have created them without the help of an outside spark of nature. I'm just not an artist, you see.

In summary, to become more creative you must first open your mind to the possibilities. As an unknown poet once said, "The universe is full of magical things patiently waiting for our wits to grow sharper."

Doing Market Research

CRAFTSPEOPLE TEND TO make products that please them, then look for people who might want to buy them. But that's backward thinking if you're serious about making money. Instead, first do market research to discover what today's marketplace wants or needs, then try to produce it. Otherwise you'll have to create your own market, and this is difficult to do.

Kathy Wirth has been designing needlework projects since 1991, contributing to numerous consumer magazines. In earlier years, however, she and her partner designed and sold their own self-published needlework designs. Kathy

Thoughts on Creativity

➤ I have learned that we women are made of untapped sources that can take us to any height we aspire to. Most of us don't know what we want, which is where the imagination comes into play. Ideas spark ideas. The thing is not to turn off that crafty idea before it gets a chance to be born. As kids, we were told, "Oh, it's just your imagination," and we turned it off. Now we have to give ourselves permission to tune in, just like a child. It is a gift to us and we don't have to copy anyone else. We can "do our own thing."

Genii Townsend, Out of the Gourd-inary

➤ Many craftspeople stifle their own God-given creativity by trying to be like everyone else and create items like the guy or gal down the street. Don't let others dictate to you what your area of creativity should be. If you want to write, paint, direct a play, create crafts, design wooden shelves, sing to the mountaintops, or simply raise your children to see God's beauty in a flower, you have achieved creativity. Now have the faith and trust in yourself, your talents and ideas by selling what you make as a craftsperson in a world where only the sky is the limit.

Opal Leasure, The Apron Strings Lady

➤ You have an unlimited ability to be creative. If you spent every minute of every day for the rest of your life, you could not exhaust your resources. Whatever direction your creativity leads you, you will do it differently than anyone else in the world. You have been touched by the hand of God in the same way as Shakespeare and Da Vinci.

LaVerne Herren, Publisher, *Show Business*

said one of their most expensive lessons was producing what they thought was attractive and artistic, instead of what the public wanted to buy. "You have to do market research to find out what will be salable," she cautions.

Market research is nothing more than interesting detective work. To take some of the mystery out of selling, you must first discover who your potential customers are, where they are located, and how you're going to reach them. While doing this, also consider the various sales outlets open to you, the methods you will use to make sales, and whether, in fact, you have a salable product at all.

To begin, ask yourself a few questions. Do people really need what you're making?

If so, how many people? What kind of people? Where do they live? Can they easily get what you make from someone else, perhaps at a lower price than what you would have to charge to make a profit? If people don't really *need* your product, do you think they might simply *want* it? For example, no one really needs another ceramic coffee mug, more hand-woven place mats, or another picture for the wall, but there will always be people who *want* such things. In fact, most people today buy handcrafts not because they need them, but simply because they want them and prefer them to mass-produced merchandise.

You may think your products are unusual, but the only way to know for sure is to look around and see if anyone else is selling the same things you are. In addition to browsing local fairs, boutiques, and craft malls, check out consumer craft magazines and national mail-order catalogs to see what type of art or handcrafts are being offered. If you're online, you've probably already checked out the various Web sites of artists and crafters who now have a presence on the World Wide Web,

either on their own individual sites or in one of many online craft malls and art galleries. Knowing what products others are selling and the prices being asked for them will give you clues on how to present and price your own products.

Barbara Deuel makes books, photo albums, scrapbooks, and journals sold under the name of Homebound Books. Her market research convinced her she could build a business around her ideas. "Nine years ago I was working a dead-end job and making books as a hobby and for my own use as an amateur photographer," she says. "The only books I could find in stores had plastic pages, which are ugly as well as harmful to photographs. Friends began to notice my books and ask if they could buy them. I did some research and found that the only comparable books in stores were priced very high, usually as one-of-a-kind art objects. The first store I approached placed a $200 order. Because of the nature of the business, I was able to get started with only about $300 in capital, my main expense being a sturdy paper cutter. Within six months I was working on the business full-time and it has grown steadily since. Now I work full-time and sell mostly at wholesale through sales reps."

You can get a lot of market research information simply by listening to your customers, says Jan Bonner, who sells mostly to collectors. "Today, collectible

Are You Changing with the Times?

Craft shows have changed greatly over the past ten years. Are you currently changing along with them, or are you behind the times? Many crafters find they have a great product and get so locked into it that they forget the times may be passing them by. It is easy to say you know what your customers want because of their past buying habits, but remember your customers are always changing too.

There are many more shows now than there were ten years ago. Because of that, our competition is much keener. We need to consider whether our sales are going down because of too many shows, or because of our lack of change or knowledge. Our customers want more sophisticated products, displays, and uniqueness. Because of this, promoters are required now to also do their homework. They must have more enticing shows, better quality vendors, and the vendors must present much better booth displays to be accepted in the better shows. Once accepted, we must really go to work to produce sales above and beyond our competition.

This is where all the business knowledge comes into play. Things that can make or break your sales include (1) your product—its selling price, color, usefulness, uniqueness, and packaging; (2) booth display—colors, use of signage and props; (3) your personality and ability to network; and (4) your business management and marketing skills. All of these things combined can make you money, but falling down in any one category can ruin your business.

Marsha Reed, Publisher of *Craftmaster News*

bears need to be dressed with a lot of details. The current market prevents a plain bear with a simple ribbon from being attractive to the average buyer," she says. "I now have hundreds of designs I rotate, compared to two sizes of two designs when I started. The fur styles of bears were featured in the beginning; now it's a theme or personal outfit and more imported mohair, which was not available in the early years."

Your market research must also take into consideration the trends of the day, from which colors are currently popular to what collectors are currently seeking. "I've learned to use large department stores as my personal research company when it comes to color and fad changes," says Rita Stone-Conwell. "They pay big bucks for research, so why not take advantage of it?"

Pricing Insight

KNOWLEDGE ABOUT PRICING increases with time and experience, but it is always a challenge, even for professionals who have been selling for years. There are pricing formulas product makers can use, but they must always be used in conjunction with common sense and an understanding of what buyers want and are currently willing to pay for certain items. As a jeweler–craftsman once told me, "After using my formula to set a price, I usually throw the whole thing out and figure what I can get." A kit manufacturer says she always looks at the wholesale price she has calculated, then adjusts it according to what her common sense tells her the item will actually sell for. Here are some other things you need to consider when setting prices.

PERCEIVED VALUE FACTOR

Beginning sellers have a hard time accepting the fact that most buyers don't care how long it takes to make something, or how much it costs to make. Their only concern is whether the asking price matches the size of their pocketbook and their estimation of what a product is worth. Remember that all buyers, including yourself, have preconceived notions about what any item should cost.

"Customers today are price smart," says business writer and professional crafter Nancy Mosher. "They know what they expect to pay for an item before they look at the price tag. If their idea and the actual price match each other, then you have a sale. If too many crafters have the same or similar product, the customer will expect the price to be similar. The more unique your product, the more you can play with pricing and perhaps even get a higher price for it."

One of the first things all professional crafters learn is that certain items must be priced higher to compensate for others. Often, an item that takes a lesser amount of time and effort to produce can be priced higher than something that may have been twice as difficult to make and took three times as long besides.

Always try to find out what "the going prices" are for items similar to those you produce, and never feel guilty about taking a larger profit on something you have produced easily and quickly. Higher profits on some items will help balance lesser profits on other products you may love to make, but can't sell at higher prices. Or, as one crafter puts it, "My 'bread and butter' items—my guaranteed sellers—enable me to spend time on more creative but less profitable items."

SELLING AREA

Where you live, or the area in which you are trying to sell, has everything to do with the prices you can get. The same item might sell for $25 in one area, $50 in another, and $100 in another, depending on the economic stability of the area and the demand for that particular type of product at that time. If you move to a new area, don't be surprised if some things sell better or worse there than they did before.

Joyce Roark lived in California for a while before moving to Michigan and later to Baton Rouge, Louisiana. "The products that sell here are much different from other parts of the country," she says. "The majority of people here prefer country, wood, and rustic items. Victorian designs don't do as well here. Learning the likes of the people in the region where you sell your crafts is very important."

Each community is different, and when you can't get the prices you need to make a profit, you have four choices: (1) You can continue to sell locally and take whatever price you can get, even though you feel cheated in the bargain; (2) you can make the effort to find more appre-

ciative buyers in other parts of the country; (3) you can develop a different line of products that might sell better; or (4) you can quit selling altogether and simply craft for your own enjoyment.

COST OF SUPPLIES VS. TIME

Many crafters price their products simply by multiplying the cost of materials times two or three to get the retail price:

Cost of Materials × 2 or 3 = Retail Price

This pricing formula has a serious flaw, however, because it doesn't take into account the amount of time it takes to make one item. For example, let's assume you are making a product that costs $2 to make. If you set a $4 or $6 price based on a doubling or tripling of the cost of materials, you would end up with a gross profit of $2 or $4 per item. This is great—*providing you can make more than one item per hour.* If it takes an hour to make this particular product, however, using this formula to set prices would result in your earning less than the minimum hourly wage.

Using this simple pricing formula without taking into account the time you spend making a product (or the fact that buyers may perceive it as "art" instead of "craft") is likely to cause you to seriously underprice a product. For example, if you are offering a collectible doll or fine wood sculpture whose material costs are only $10, doubling or tripling the cost of materials would result in a retail price of $20 to $30. Such items, however, might actually sell for hundreds of dollars in the right market. Pricing on the cost of materials alone may work for hobby sellers, but it's totally impractical for craft professionals or serious artists.

The Value of Your Time

SINCE TIME (LABOR) is a critical factor in setting prices, you will have to give serious consideration to the value of your time somewhere along the line. Who you are and what you do affects not only the prices you are likely to charge for products or services, but what you are willing to pay for the products and services of others. The decision as to what your time is worth is a personal one that may be influenced by a number of factors, including your education or degree of skill, your age, reputation in your field or industry (the "ego factor"), previous salaried job experience, where you live, the demand for what you make or do, and your need for money.

Do you have the right attitude for financial success in a business of your own?

There's a big difference between working for economic necessity and working for extra money, "just for the fun of it." People who look at their art or craft as a way to earn a living do not have the luxury of merely pursuing artistic ideas, doing a couple of shows a year or consigning work to a local shop. Profit, to most people, translates to money, so when your financial security is at stake, your attitude naturally changes. You suddenly take a hard look at what you're doing and begin to realize the true value of your time.

Once, in a study of sixty home-business owners in my newsletter network, I came up with some interesting figures for the number of hours people work. Half the businesses were part-time; the rest indicated the home business was their livelihood. Almost without exception, people reported the hours they worked in variable terms of from twenty to thirty or sixty to eighty. I learned that mothers, for example, tend to work shorter hours in the summer because the kids are around. Writers and publishers like myself have periods when we have to glue ourselves to the desk or computer to meet a deadline. Craft producers may put in forty hours one week and eighty the next, depending on how many shows they've entered, or whether they've just gotten a big purchase order from a wholesaler. And the business that's just gotten a

The Nostalgia Market

To get higher prices for your work, you must offer the public something it cannot easily get anywhere else at a lower price—something different and appealing. If your basic product is rather ordinary, then your designs must be exceptional.

For instance, thousands of people decorate eggs, and many who paint designs on them are fortunate to get $10 to $20 apiece. But I recall one egg artist who had no problem getting $75 and more for her hand-painted eggs because she understood her market and the value of nostalgia. Sharon's basic product—an egg—was ordinary, but her "Santa Over Chicago" design (Santa in his sled with the Chicago skyline in the background) was unique, and she couldn't produce them fast enough.

There seems to be no limit on what people will pay for nostalgic items that strike a special chord in their memory or fit into a special collection they may be building. So to increase your profits, always offer at least a couple of items for collectors. As soon as you see a new collector trend on the horizon, start dreaming up new products that will appeal to that market.

wave of publicity may be inundated with mail or orders for a while and have to put in a lot of extra hours accordingly.

In short, people who work at home— particularly craft business owners—must "go with the flow." My research indicates that people in part-time businesses (in any field) work an average of twenty-five hours a week, while those who say they work full time put in nearly fifty-three hours a week on their business. But as some have told me, "That doesn't count

brain-wave time" or, "When I'm not working, I'm planning or studying." One woman who said she worked eighty-four hours a week stated, "I'd work more if I could stay awake." A mother with an infant said she could squeeze in only about ten hours a week, while a mother with older children, aged nine and ten, noted that her business has grown with the kids. "The progression seems to be, the older they get, the more time I can spend on the business."

A fellow who filled out my data sheet for the business he and his wife run said: "Wife works overtime with husband who works around the clock. Hours? Incalculable." Another couple in business for about a year said, "We find we spend most of our time either working on the business or thinking about it. We average about sixty hours a week on the business. We enjoy working, and find that our biggest problem is allowing ourselves time to relax and take a break. We are both 'Type A' personalities who have to guard against workaholism. The stress generated by living and working in the same place is often overwhelming, so we constantly have to remind ourselves to take time off."

One couple summed up the feelings of many: "Since we enjoy our business so much, it's hard to define hours spent at it. We work at it every day and most weekends. Business is both our livelihood and our pleasure."

In surveys I've done at crafts marketing workshops in the past, I've learned that most crafters who sell primarily at craft fairs figure they're getting between $5 and $10 an hour for their time. Some, however, make practically nothing at all for labor, while others with "high-end" products may be making $20 or more an hour for their labor. What's interesting is that very few part-time artists and crafters know for sure what their profits are be-

cause they don't keep track of how much material and labor goes into each of their products and, further, they don't seem to care. To them, what's most important is the enjoyment they get from making and selling things to appreciative buyers.

A weaver once dubbed this the "love factor," saying, "Most of us would continue to produce if we never sold another piece, simply because we love what we do. I use no formula to price what I make because love goes into my work. It is design and pattern, informed with sensitivity. But I am not a dreamer either, so I put realistic prices on items that are for sale."

A decorative painter adds: "I love to paint and I'd rather paint and sell it than paint and look at it. My husband and I both figure our costs by time and materials and take that into consideration when pricing our merchandise. We are often told that our prices are too low, but we feel we are getting a fair return and we are selling."

If you are doing what you want to do, on a schedule of your own making, you may be content to accept a lower hourly rate of pay than you might demand if you were working for someone else. If you're trying to generate serious income for yourself or your family, however, you may need to make an attitude shift and look at what you're doing in a different light. While many crafters settle for less than what they feel their time or products are worth, others have learned how to command higher prices for everything they sell and have shared special tips in other chapters of this book.

Make It a Family Affair

FINALLY, HERE'S A special tip on how to maximize your time and relieve your stress at the same time: Get the support of your family before you start your business, or figure out how to involve them now if you've already started. As indicated earlier, a home-based business has a sneaky way of gradually taking over one's home, making the business a family affair in the process. You may plan to be the sole owner and worker in your business, but if your family has at least an emotional involvement in what you're doing, they may not mind so much when dinner is late or they run out of socks because you were too busy to do the laundry.

Artist Ruby Tobey has successfully worked with and around her children for over twenty years. "Attending the annual War Eagle show in Arkansas is now a family tradition," she says. "My kids went with me when they were small, now one of them is bringing his kids and spending time with us every year."

"Make your children an active part in the goings-on of your household and crafts business," advises a retired businesswoman who ran a shop out of her home for many years. "Chores will make them aware that they belong and that they're important to the functioning of your home or family." Many craft couples find jobs their children can do and then pay them for this work instead of just giving them an allowance. This brings the family closer together while also giving the business a sweet tax deduction.

Although even young children can be a big help to a crafts business, it's even more important to get the help and support of your spouse. In many businesses started by women, spouses provide hours of unpaid support in processing and packaging orders, doing shows, keeping the books, writing advertising copy, designing printed materials, and so on. In some cases when fellows have lost their jobs or been forced into early retirement because of corporate downsizing, this has been all the push they needed to join their wives full-time in business. You'll meet some of these couples in this book.

"If I were doing it over again, I'd try to get more support from my husband and involve him more in the business," several women told me. What's the trick in getting spousal help? A little loving coaxing seems to work best. I turned my musician-husband into a typist thirty years ago by sweetly asking him one day if he could possibly "hunt-and-peck" some address labels for me on the portable typewriter because I didn't have time to do the mail and all the writing, too. Although Harry had no office experience or any previous contact with a typewriter, he quickly became an accurate typist and office helpmate. I dubbed him my "Three-Finger, Two-Thumb Wonder" because that's all the digits he's ever used to type about thirty-five words a minute. Now retired from the music business, he still opens and processes all our business mail, handles bank deposits, puts out mailings, and much more. His help through the years has made all the difference in what I was able to accomplish as a writer and publisher.

Rita Stone-Conwell used a slightly different maneuver on her husband, Tom, who is well-versed in the use of computers. "Honey," she said, "you know I don't understand this computer stuff. I need your help." So he set up her Web site and now maintains it for her in the evenings or on weekends. In effect, Rita's business has now become Tom's new hobby. When he's not at work or slaving over the computer keyboard for Rita, he tries to find a little time for his other hobby of wood-carving.

The most interesting "couple story" I've heard so far has to be Gary and Rita Villa's. In 1985 Gary had a good job with Hallmark and Rita was making about $10,000 a year selling dollhouse furniture, cutting all the little pieces herself. When Gary would come home from work, Rita would coax him into helping her cut the wood pieces. This naturally increased their production capabilities and the business grew. Eventually, Gary had to quit his job to work full time with Rita. Hired three employees. Bought a $92,000 laser machine to do all the cutting, then another one at $120,000. Hired more employees. Expanded their product line. Bought a third laser. Started offering laser-cutting services to others. Today, Gary and Rita's business—Smidgens, Inc., in Lima, New York—is generating nearly a million dollars a year in sales of products and services. All because Rita once said, "Honey . . . I need a little help here."

Hey, you fellows out there! If you happen to have a clever and creative wife who has just started what you think is a "little crafts business," listen up. What she's doing could be the start of something BIG! And if you happen to be the one with all the creative ideas, be sure to ask for your wife's help and creative input. Two together can always do more than one alone.

P.S. "Family" doesn't mean only spouses and young children, of course. Successful craft businesses have also been formed by sisters or brothers working together, by granddaughters working with grandmothers, or fathers working with sons. More common, however, are mother–daughter teams. As I was writing this chapter, I got a note from Genii Townsend, who said she was then merging her Out of the Gourd-inary puppets and marionettes business with her daughter's business, Fantasymakers. "Since we are both performers and teachers, I sus-pect this new mother–daughter team will have many interesting adventures in the future."

In later chapters, you'll meet Genii again, along with many others mentioned so far in this book. (If a particular individual or business interests you, check the index to find other page references to them and Resources for their address.)

Nitty-Gritty Legal and Financial Stuff

You can call it a hobby, but making it a business on paper will set you free. You become free to explore ways to increase the return on your investment, ways that are not available to the hobbyist. If you continually complain about how difficult it is to make money at crafting, think about how you are treating your endeavors. Put it in perspective. Do those few things that will make it more of a business and it will set you free to be more profitable.

NANCY MOSHER, business consultant and owner of NanCraft

CREATIVE PEOPLE RARELY want to hear this, but a certain amount of "nitty-gritty legal stuff" goes hand in hand with even the smallest home-based business. This chapter briefly discusses important laws and regulations on the local, state, and federal levels, answers common questions of home-business beginners, and explains the consequences of not doing what is legally and morally right in various situations.

"But I just want to make a little extra money," you might say. "I don't want to mess with all this legal stuff." If that's how you feel, you might as well close this book and go back to your knitting, or whatever it is that you love to do, because the goal of this book is to help you generate *meaningful income from a real business*, whatever its size. Even if you make only a few products and sell only at a couple of fairs, shops, or holiday boutiques, you will make more money and realize greater profits if you approach your activity in a businesslike manner. (And doing things honestly and legally will pay rewards far greater than money.)

You've heard it countless times: *Ignorance of the law is no excuse.* As soon as you begin to sell what you make, the same laws and regulations that apply to "big businesses" begin to apply to you. On the surface this sounds frightening, and it might be enough to stop you dead in your tracks if you haven't had any business experience in the past. Before you get discouraged, however, let me remind you that it's easy to be a law-abiding citizen *once you know what the laws are.* Due to space limitations, this chapter cannot

When "Business" Actually Begins

Are you going to be "in business," or do you just want to sell what you make as a hobby? The choice is yours. The IRS defines a hobby as an activity engaged in primarily for pleasure. Losses sustained in the pursuit of a hobby are not deductible. If hobby income is under $400, it should be entered on your 1040 tax form. If hobby income is more than $400, however, you must file a Schedule C (1040) tax form. This allows you to deduct related expenses up to, but not exceeding, the amount earned from the hobby. When a hobby business shows a profit, taxes will be due on it. Making a profit, however, does not automatically put you "in business." Your activity becomes a business in the eyes of IRS only when you begin to make regular business transactions with the idea of profit in mind, and actually make a profit in three out of five consecutive years.

If you claim to be in business but fail to make a profit in three out of five years, the IRS may question your tax return and disallow certain deductions unless you can prove your case. If you have maintained complete records for your business, that will be a strong point in your favor, as will the amount of advertising and promotion you have done. Your overall expertise and business image may also influence your case. In the end, the question of whether your art- or craft-related activity will qualify as a business for tax purposes is a complex one. No one factor, such as failure to achieve a profit in at least three out of five years, can be used by the IRS to disallow your deductions.

begin to address all of the tax, legal, and financial issues that affect individuals in small businesses, but there are plenty of sources for such information when you're ready for it, such as my book *The Crafts Business Answer Book* (Evans, 1998). This and other helpful books are listed in Resources, so you can look for them in your library or bookstore. Additional discussions of some topics introduced in this chapter will also be found in other chapters of this book. (Check the index to find page numbers.)

Note: All the information in this chapter is directed to individuals who plan to operate their business as a Sole Proprietorship. This legal form of business is preferred by most crafters because no government approval is required to start, and the business ends automatically when its owner stops running it. Business profits (or losses) are taxed as personal income. The sole proprietor is fully liable for all business debts and actions, which means that one's personal assets are not protected in the event of a lawsuit. (See "Insurance Tips" later in this chapter.)

If you are thinking of going into business with a partner, or believe you need to incorporate your business, first do some research on each legal form of business by reading business books listed in Resources. Then consult with an accountant or attorney to make sure you're moving in the right direction. The pros and cons of partnerships and corporations are far too complex to discuss in a book of this nature.

Be Different — Start Professionally!

IN HER CRAFT business seminars, Nancy Mosher has learned that many crafters who have been selling for some time still haven't registered their business name locally or gotten a resale tax number. "For some reason," she says, "some crafters think that doing such things is going to draw unwanted attention to them or that they will have to deal with paperwork they don't want to mess with. They want all the advantages, but they aren't willing to do what's legally necessary to get them."

I agree. Many crafters who say they are "in business" haven't taken care of half the tax, legal and financial matters that need attending to, so beginners aren't the only ones who need the information in this chapter. Other things crafters tend to overlook is the importance of a separate checking account and telephone number for their business. They may start to sell from their home without checking local zoning laws, or accidentally violate a federal law or the legal rights of others because they haven't done their "home business homework." Many so-called craft professionals send poor signals to buyers by their unprofessional behavior at shows or their use of inferior printed materials. Some literally advertise their unprofessionalism by selling at fairs and not charging sales tax on purchases, or insisting on cash only, which tells bystanders they are probably cheating on their income taxes.

It's never too late to make changes in your life or business, never too late to set higher goals or strive for more professionalism in everything you do. If you learn from this chapter that you have forgotten to do something important, take care of it as soon as possible. If you have unknowingly violated a law, don't panic—it may not be as bad as you think. You may be able to get on the straight and narrow merely by filling out a required form or paying a fee of some kind. (Actually, the fear of being caught when you've broken a law is generally worse than doing whatever needs to be done to set the matter right.)

How much do you know now or need to learn or do? Here's a little test. Read each question below and check the box if you don't know the answer:

❑ Is your home-based business likely to violate local zoning ordinances?

❑ Do you need any kind of license or permit to legally operate a business from your home?

❑ What's the penalty for selling products to consumers without charging sales tax on them?

❑ Why is it so important to have a separate telephone number and business checking account for your business?

❑ Why must you register your business name locally, and what could happen if you don't?

❑ How do you get merchant status for your business so your customers can pay with a credit card?

❑ How will having a small business at home affect your homeowner's or auto insurance policies and the amount of coverage you now have?

❑ Do you need personal or product liability insurance?

❑ What kind of bookkeeping system is required by the IRS?

❑ What deductions can a home-business owner take to lower the amount of profit on which self-employment taxes will be due?

❑ When do you need a lawyer's advice, and when can you safely operate without one?

❑ What federal regulations apply to artists and crafters in business?

Unless you can answer all of the above questions, you need to read this chapter carefully, with highlighter pen in hand. This is a lot of information to swallow at one time, so remember that old saying— the only way to eat an elephant is one bite at a time. To make your work easier, I've included a handy checklist at the end of the chapter to remind you of the various things you need to check on or take care of.

Taking Care of Business

H ERE ARE SIX important things most people try not to think about when they begin to sell their art or craft. If you want to get started on the right foot, however, or correct an uncomfortable situation in your present business, take care of these "details" as soon as possible:

1. ZONING LAWS, LICENSES, AND PERMITS

In years past, artists and crafters rarely had to be concerned about zoning laws, licenses, and permits, but the home-business boom of the 1990s changed everything. Many communities that see home-based businesses as a source of extra revenue have updated their zoning ordinances and require all home-based business owners to get a license. (Yes, even craft fair sellers are considered home-business owners.) Depending on where you live, a business license might cost from $15 to $200. Before calling City Hall to find out what you need to do to be legal, you might want to visit your library and look at a copy of your community's zoning ordinance. (Find out what zone you're in, and then check the section that pertains to home occupations.)

In many areas where antiquated zoning laws are still on the books and home-based businesses are popping up everywhere, zoning officials are simply looking the other way because this is easier to do than change the law. If home-based businesses are prohibited in your area, you have three choices: operate underground, fight to get the law changed, or move. If you choose to operate underground, as so many others do, don't annoy your neighbors—one complaint about too much noise or too many people coming and going could put you out of business. And don't draw attention to your business with ads or publicity in your local paper. Zoning officials probably will never check on you unless you give them a reason to do so.

2. COLLECTION OF SALES TAX

If you are working at your art or craft as a business and selling to consumers at the retail level—at a fair, holiday boutique, home shop, or by mail—you must collect sales tax and file regular reports with your state unless it is one of the few that does not have a sales tax. *Hobbyists are not exempt from this law, regardless of how few sales they make.*

Since each state operates differently (some now require the collection of taxes on sales in states other than your own), you must call your state's Department of Revenue, Sales Tax Division, for detailed information on this topic. Simply ask what you need to do to apply for a resale tax number (also called a "tax exemption certificate" or "retailer's occupation tax registration number"). If you emphasize that yours is a small business, you may qualify for annual filing, which will keep your paperwork to a minimum.

Even if your state doesn't have a sales tax, you still need a tax exemption certificate or resale tax number to buy supplies and materials at wholesale. This number identifies you as being qualified to buy goods in the wholesale market without paying sales tax, and anyone who agrees to sell to you will ask for it. Likewise, crafters who wholesale to shops and stores must get their buyers' tax numbers for their files.

Don't ignore this law. All states have become aggressive about collecting sales and use taxes, so it is not unusual to find sales tax officials browsing the larger craft fairs to catch offenders. If caught, a crafter could face severe financial penalties. In my state, for instance, anyone caught violating the sales tax law is subject to a penalty of 20 percent over and above their normal tax obligation and could receive, *for each return not filed,* from one to six months in prison and a fine of up to $5,000. (If that doesn't get you scurrying to get your resale tax number, nothing will.)

3. BUSINESS TELEPHONE

Although you can receive business telephone calls on a residential line and make outgoing business calls as well, you cannot legally *advertise* a residential phone number on your business cards or stationery, in an advertisement or press release, or on any other promotional or advertising materials. To do so could result in a fine; and if you can't advertise your telephone number, your business cannot grow.

Telephone companies were among the first to recognize the profit potential of home-based businesses, so they have come up with a variety of creative, low-cost options designed with people like you in mind. Call your local telephone company now, explain your situation, and ask them to suggest an affordable solution. A separate line for business becomes all the more important if you plan to buy a fax machine or go online with your business. Initially, I hesitated about buying a fax machine because I didn't plan to use it often and couldn't justify the cost of a second business line for it. A "flexline" proved to be perfect for my needs. After paying a small installation charge, my only monthly cost is for the actual time I use the flexline to send or receive faxes (five cents a minute). Your phone company probably offers a similar service, though it may be called by a different name. Another affordable solution offered by most telephone companies is separate rings that can be assigned to one phone line so you can identify incoming business calls.

4. BUSINESS CHECKING ACCOUNT

Many crafters use their personal checking account to conduct the transactions of their business. You must not do this because the IRS frowns (to put it lightly) on anyone who commingles business and personal income and expenses. To do so may cause the IRS to rule that yours is not a business but a hobby. This, in turn, could cost you all the business deductions previously taken on earlier tax returns.

You can save money on your business checking account by calling several financial institutions and comparing the charges they make for such things as im-

printed checks, deposits, checks written, bounced checks, and so on. Some banks charge extra for each out-of-state check that's deposited, an expense that adds up quickly for active mail-order businesses. For this reason I have always done my business banking through a savings and loan association, which operates under a different set of rules than a bank. I've never paid a monthly service charge for my business account and have always received interest on the balance. The only problem here is that many S&Ls went out of business a while back, so there may not be any left in your area. In addition, S&Ls do not offer business loans, commercial lines of credit, or merchant card services—things a growing crafts business is likely to need at some point in the future.

In the beginning, when your business income and expenses are low, you may not be able to justify the cost of maintaining a business checking account (or even have enough money to put into one.) In this case you might open a separate personal checking account and dub it your "business account." Ask your bank if it will allow you to imprint the name of your hobby business on these checks until such time as you can afford to open a regular business account. If not, at least you will be able to satisfy IRS requirements by depositing all business income to this second account, and paying all business bills from it. (If you need your crafts business income for living expenses, first deposit it to your "business" checking account, and then write a check on this account for deposit to your personal checking account, calling it "owner draw.")

5. REGISTERING YOUR BUSINESS NAME

When you operate a business under any name other than your own, you are using a fictitious or assumed "trade name." State laws require local registration of trade names because they cannot legally be held responsible for anything. Thus if your name is Nancy Brown and you operate under the name of Brown's Bears and Dolls, you must file a "Fictitious Name Statement" with your city or county clerk. On legal documents, and on paperwork at your bank, your name would read, "Nancy Brown, DBA Brown's Bears and Dolls." (DBA means "doing business as".)

The registration process and fee varies from state to state. In most states, you will have to place a legal ad in a general-circulation newspaper in your county and run it three times. (When you register, you will be given the correct wording to use in this ad.) If by chance you are operating your business in violation of local zoning laws, or simply don't want your

Start a Business Diary

When Yvonne Ward started her Country Garden Designs business, she wisely began to keep a calendar record and diary of all her business and creative activities. "It contains a record of everything I do, who I call, what I make, what I buy, and so on. By recording everything, I no longer have to hold all this information in my head. I just refer to it when I need to recall something."

By starting a calendar or journal of every step you take as you launch or expand a business, you will have an invaluable record that will give you a motivational boost each time you look back and see how much you've accomplished in so short a time. If you ever need to write a business plan, it will provide all the essential information for it.

neighbors to know what you are doing at home, the ad you run in the paper does not have to be placed in your home town paper but can be run in any newspaper in your *county.*

Once you've protected your name by local registration, you may register it with your Secretary of State to prevent its use by any corporate entity in the state. To protect a name on the national level, you will need to trademark it. Additional information on how to do this is available from the Patent and Trademark Office.

What happens if you don't register your business name? In my state, and probably others as well, it is a Class C misdemeanor to operate a business that has not been properly registered. In case you've been operating illegally and are now shaking in your boots, let me ease your mind by telling you that no one goes around checking to see if all small business have been registered. If this is something you haven't done yet, just do it now.

Some people who have operated unregistered businesses for years with no one being the wiser may wonder why they should bother to register now. If being lawful doesn't matter to you, maybe this fact will: *Unless you register your good business name, it can be stolen by anyone who wants it.* If someone else registers your name, he or she can legally force you

to stop using it, no matter how long you've been operating under that name.

Furthermore, you may not be able to open a business checking account without a DBA registration form. And without a business checking account, you probably won't be able to place a wholesale order for supplies at a trade show, says Nancy Mosher. "Suppliers are naturally suspicious of small craft businesses to begin with, and may ask to see a business check as evidence that a crafter is really in business and entitled to wholesale prices in the first place."

6. OFFERING CREDIT CARD SERVICES

Although you are not required to accept credit card payments, you will probably find it important to do so when your sales reach a certain point. If you regularly participate in fairs and shows where most crafters accept credit card payments, or you offer higher-priced products than others, you may lose business if you can't accept this form of payment. Many professional sellers say their sales have increased by 25 percent or more after they begin to accept credit card payments, justifying the extra cost of working this way. The problem is that small home-based businesses cannot always get merchant status from a local bank and have to look to other sources for this service. Although many Independent Sales Organizations (ISOs) now offer credit card services, their lease, application and service fees are too pricey for most small businesses. The least expensive way to get started seems to be through membership in one of the organizations now serving the needs of home-based business owners. Most now offer credit card services as a special member benefit (see Resources). The technology related to taking credit card sales at off-site locations is changing all the time, so start to research this topic now to learn about the newest equipment and costs of operating this way. (Articles on this topic appear regularly in craft business magazines, and I've discussed it at greater length in *The Crafts Business Answer Book.*)

Insurance Tips

A S SOON AS YOU start a business in your home, your insurance needs change dramatically. For starters, you need to talk to the insurance agents who handle your homeowner's or renter's insurance policy and car insurance. As your business grows, you may want to buy coverage for all the merchandise you have on display in craft malls or at fairs, or you may need a product liability policy in

order to wholesale to certain markets. Here's a brief look at each type of insurance and what you need to check on.

HOMEOWNER'S OR RENTER'S POLICY

The policy you have on the personal possessions in your home will *not* cover business equipment, office furniture, supplies, or inventory of finished goods *unless* you obtain a special rider. Such riders, called a "Business Pursuits Endorsement" by some companies, are inexpensive and offer considerable protection. Your insurance agent will be happy to give you details. (Be sure to compare the cost and benefits of this type of insurance with the special in-home business policies now offered by some of the home-business and art/craft organizations listed in Resources.)

If you have a costly computer system, don't list it under a rider attached to your homeowner's policy because everything insured under the rider would be figured on a depreciable basis instead of what it would cost to replace it (even though you may have replacement-value insurance on all your other possessions). An in-home business policy or a special policy from a company that specializes in computer insurance will offer better protection.

AUTO INSURANCE

When you talk to the agent who handles your car insurance, explain that you may occasionally use your car for business purposes. Normally, a policy issued for a car that's primarily used for pleasure or driving to and from work will not provide coverage for an accident that occurs during business use of the car, particularly if the insured is to blame for the accident. *Ask questions to be sure you have adequate coverage for your needs.*

INSURANCE ON CRAFTS MERCHANDISE OFF-PREMISE

Craft fair sellers and those who consign products or place them on display in a craft mall or rent-a-space shop always run the risk of losing goods to fire, theft and other types of damage. Shop owners cannot offer insurance protection for consigned merchandise or goods placed on display through a rent-a-space program because such merchandise is not owned by them. In the event of fire or other loss, sellers will be the losers unless they have their own insurance. (Exception: Shops and stores in shopping malls are mandated by law to buy liability and fire insurance whether they own the merchandise in a store or not.)

Membership in the American Craft Association will give you access to property and casualty insurance that offers some protection on property at fairs and shows (see Resources), and American Family Mutual Insurance offers an "Arts, Crafts, and Hobby Stores" business policy that offers protection against fire on merchandise consigned to stores. (See your local phone book for an insurance agent near you.)

PERSONAL LIABILITY INSURANCE

Personal liability insurance protects you against claims made by people who have suffered bodily injury while on your premises. The level of protection you may have on your homeowner's policy, however, is unlikely to be sufficient if someone injures themselves on your property while doing business with you (attending a holiday boutique, for example, or stopping by to pick up an order). This is something you need to discuss with your insurance agent. Ask if you can extend your personal liability coverage with a business rider or "umbrella policy."

Many businesses incorporate to get the limited liability benefits of this legal form of business. However, a corporation does not provide "blanket protection" against lawsuits. In some cases, it might be less expensive and just as safe to buy liability insurance. "A corporation will not shield you from personal liability that you normally should be responsible for, such as not having car insurance or acting with gross negligence," says Bernard Kamoroff, CPA and author of *Small-Time Operator.* "If you plan to incorporate solely or primarily with the intention of limiting your legal liability, I suggest you first find out exactly how limited the liability really is for your particular venture. Hire a knowledgeable lawyer to give you a written opinion."

Product Liability Insurance

Liability insurance offers protection against lawsuits by consumers who have been injured by a handmade product. As soon as you enter the marketplace with products of any kind—even as a hobby seller—you can be held personally liable for any damage, injury or sickness caused by one of your products. If a child swallows part of a craft toy, if a fiber wall hanging enflames or a ceramic casserole cracks and spills its hot contents into the lap of its user, the maker of the product can be

Record-Keeping Tips

➤ Except for petty cash purchases, pay everything by check or a credit card so you end up with a "paper trail." This will please the IRS and make your bookkeeping a breeze.

➤ Before filing each paid bill, note on it the date and amount paid along with the check number. If you accurately post to your checkbook stub what each bill is for, you'll never have to look at the individual receipts again. Simply post your books from information on your check stubs, and do this work periodically to avoid year-end pile-up and panic.

➤ Keep tax records and returns at least six years after returns are filed. This period will cover the federal income tax statute of limitations and the statutes of various state and local taxing authorities. (Some business records, such as journals, ledgers, copyrights, licenses, and so on, should be kept indefinitely.)

held responsible. (Selling through a shop that carries product liability is not the answer to this problem since if a customer sued a shop, the shop's insurance company would undoubtedly turn around and sue the craft maker.)

Liability insurance is so expensive that few crafters ever buy it. Most simply produce and sell products that comply with the consumer safety laws discussed below under "Important Federal Regulations." Some things that have caused injury and court cases in the past, which you can easily avoid, are lead-glazed pottery, stuffed toys with wire or pins in them, knitted items made of yarn or fiber that burns rapidly, and jewelry that might injure the wearer or another person because of sharp points.

Although the relative safety of most handcrafts makes the chances of a lawsuit slim, the need for product liability insurance will increase in direct proportion to the number of products one makes for sale. Sooner or later, wholesale sellers will find that some buyers (particularly mail-order catalog houses) won't deal with any supplier who doesn't have product liability insurance. One way to get a minimal amount of coverage at reasonable cost is to join a national organization that offers an in-home business insurance package. Such policies generally include at least a million dollars' worth of product and personal liability in-

surance. For more information, request brochures from the national organizations listed in Resources.

Bookkeeping and Tax Returns

IN ADDITION TO the detailed tax information you can get directly from the IRS, many accountants and tax attorneys have written helpful books available to you in your library (see Resources). Here are a few tips to get you started.

BOOKKEEPING SYSTEM

Good records are vital to the success of any business, so unless you are totally inept with figures, you should keep your own books. Working with all the income and expense figures of your business and preparing your own financial statements will tell you more about the health and profitability of your activity than anything else you do. One nice thing about the IRS is that it does not require any special kind of bookkeeping system. Their primary concern is that you devise a bookkeeping system that clearly and accurately shows all the money coming in and going out of your business. Sole proprietors need nothing more than a business checkbook, a cash receipts journal, a

A Humorous Tax Audit

Two years after filing her annual tax return, the IRS questioned Beverly Durant about her miscellaneous business deductions, which they said seemed higher than they should be. They said she had to come into their office and bring with her all her tax receipts for that year. At that time Beverly didn't have all her receipts beautifully organized and filed in monthly envelopes, as she does now, but had just dumped them loose into a file drawer. Naturally irritated that her small home-based business was being audited in the first place, she just pulled all those receipts out of the drawer and dumped them into a big brown box. When she was called into the IRS agent's office, she plunked the box down in the center of his desk.

"With the box between us, I couldn't see him and he couldn't see me," Beverly said. "He opened the box, looked in, and said 'Them's your records?' I said, 'Yep, that's them.' And then he sat back down, filled out a bunch of forms, handed them to me, and said, 'Sign here.' And that was that. I'll never be afraid of the IRS again," she concluded.

Note: This might not work for everyone. It's possible that Beverly had a little divine intervention. You must consider that in the crafts industry she is known as "The Angel Lady.'"

Barbara Brabec, *Handmade for Profit* (M. Evans, 1996)

cash disbursements journal, and a petty cash fund.

If the whole idea of keeping books is upsetting to you, obtain a copy of Bernard Kamoroff's *Small Time Operator* (Bell Springs Publishing). Updated annually, this classic business and tax guide explains complicated topics in easy-to-understand language and includes all the ledgers and worksheets you will need for a year's worth of bookkeeping. If you'd like to do your bookkeeping on computer, a variety of easy-to-use software programs are available.

ACCOUNTANTS AND EAS

If you decide to hire someone to help with your annual tax return, avoid using a commercial *tax preparer* because their area of expertise does not include home-based businesses and the many special deductions to which they are entitled. What you need is an accountant, certified public accountant (CPA), or an Enrolled Agent (EA). Although I have used all three in the past, I now use and prefer an Enrolled Agent. EAs are licensed by the Treasury Department to represent tax-payers before the IRS. Although they have more tax training than a CPA and are qualified to answer complex tax questions and prepare annual tax returns, their fee may be lower than that of an accountant or CPA. (Call 1-800-424-4339 to get a list of EAs in your area.)

In addition to filing necessary tax forms and handling your annual tax re-turns, any of these professionals can assist you in making business decisions about such things as the best legal form for your business, when you ought to purchase equipment, and what kind of outside help to hire. Regardless of which professional

Reporting Cash Sales

Some people who are paid in cash may be tempted to "forget" to report such income on their annual income tax return, but I hope you will think three times before you do this. Intentional tax evasion or falsification of federal income tax returns can lead to severe financial penalties; but even if the IRS never catches you, your conscience will demand its own price. I recall one woman who told me she was "secretly selling" at one craft fair each year and not reporting her income because she just didn't want to take that step from being a hobbyist to being "in busi-ness." Eventually, she became so worried about what she was doing that she started waking up in the middle of the night imagining that IRS agents would soon be knocking at her door. In the end, she "went legal" when her fear of being caught was greater than her fear of being in business.

Your goal as a new business owner should be to show a profit on your Schedule C form that grows larger with each passing year. Watching your business grow on paper will be very satisfy-ing to you and, someday, this kind of "track record" could make a big difference in your ability to get a loan, finance a special project, or buy a new home. Because there are so many legiti-mate deductions available to home-business owners, it is always more advantageous to de-clare all business earnings than to try to hide a portion of them.

you hire, they all charge by the hour, so go to meetings well prepared. Dumping a sackful of receipts on someone's desk at tax time could prove to be very expensive. Ideally, you will gather all essential information on paper and the accountant or EA will put the right figures on the right lines of each form, saving you a ton of stress. (Unless there is a question about a particular expense, accountants rarely need to see expense receipts.)

When you get your return from the accountant, be sure to double-check all the figures. Even professionals can make a mistake, and several times in the past I have found errors that could be corrected before the IRS computer ejected our return and considered it for audit. If you ever are audited, having a good record-keeping system will at least enable you to substantiate any deductions you have taken.

SELF-EMPLOYMENT TAXES

When your business shows a net profit of $400 or more, you must file a self-employment form (Schedule SE) along with your Schedule C form and pay into your personal Social Security account. The amount of self-employment taxes due on one's business profits at the end of the year often comes as a shock to home-business owners. If this is your first year in business and your income is growing,

be sure to consult with a tax adviser to see when you need to begin making quarterly estimated tax payments to avoid a penalty when you file your annual return in April.

SOCIAL SECURITY INCOME

If you are a senior who is starting a home-based businesses to supplement Social Security income, remember there is a limit on the amount you can earn before losing part of your Social Security benefits. Since the amount one can earn without losing benefits changes every year, figures are not included here. The good news is that individuals past the age of seventy can earn any amount of income desired without losing any of their Social Security benefits.

Call your local Social Security office for details on this topic. (To get that number and other information about your account, call the Social Security Hotline at 1-800-772-1213.)

Home-Business Deductions

- -

A COMIC ONCE SAID that nothing has done more to stimulate the writing of fiction than the itemized deduction section of the income-tax forms. In truth, home-business owners are not as likely to lie on their tax returns as they are to overlook legitimate deductions to which they are entitled. You may deduct any expense that is *ordinary, necessary, and somehow connected with the operation and potential profit of your business,* including:

➤ Cost of goods (all supplies, materials and delivery costs)

➤ Labor costs (including wages paid to family members)

➤ General business expenses (telephone, auto expense, postage, printing, advertising, Internet/Web site expenses, printing, insurance, professional services, bank charges, repairs, show fees, travel expenses, and so on)

➤ Business education costs (memberships, books, subscriptions, seminars, and so on)

➤ Major purchases (computer system, office furnishings, equipment, tools, machinery, and the like, which may be depreciated over time or expensed according to IRS regulations)

➤ Expenses related to the use of your home for business (known as the "Home Office Deduction")

HOME OFFICE DEDUCTION

As a home-business owner, you may deduct many expenses that aren't available to ordinary taxpayers. Because your home is your place of business, you are entitled to the "Home Office Deduction," which can greatly reduce the amount of income on which self-employment taxes must be paid. For example, you could put a new roof on your house or install a new furnace and take a deduction for a portion of the expense (depending on the percentage of space your business occupies in your home). The same percentage also applies to the deductions you may take for utility bills, rent or mortgage interest, and real estate taxes.

WAGES PAID TO FAMILY MEMBERS

Merely by moving money from one family pocket to another, you can legally gain a tax deduction for your business and shelter a certain amount of income from state and federal taxes as well. As a sole proprietor, you can hire children as young as seven years of age to work for your business and pay them a salary instead of an allowance. You can also hire your spouse and establish an employee benefit plan that will enable you to deduct 100 percent of your family's medical expenses and insurance premiums on your Schedule C form. (These are complex topics you should discuss with an accountant or tax adviser.)

A variety of free tax booklets related to running a business at home are available from your local IRS office. One in particular that you should request is *Business Use of Your Home* (#587).

Legal Assistance

WHILE A SOLE proprietorship can be started without legal assistance, it would be folly to enter into a partnership of any kind without the guidance of an attorney. Although a number of books explain how to set up a corporation without legal help, I'd think twice before I'd try this. Few creative people could handle all the details here without going into "stress overload."

You don't need a lawyer to register your business name or get a sales tax number, but don't sign a contract without having the fine print checked by an attorney or other qualified professional who knows the ins and outs of the particular industry involved. While most attorneys can offer general advice on the fine print of any contract, book publishing contracts, royalty arrangements with manufacturers and licensing arrangements can be tricky. In such cases what's important is not only what's *in* a contract, but what *isn't*.

You don't need legal assistance to file a copyright claim, but your chances of getting a trademark will be better if you have the help of an attorney who special-

izes in patents, copyrights, and trademarks. Artist Sammie Crawford, who has become known as The Fairy Gourdmother, secured a trademark for this descriptive name in 1996 without an attorney's help but almost wound up paying the registration fee twice because she omitted one little description about the drawing on her application form. Joyce Roark, a jeweler who has trademarked her Loving Thoughts line of jewelry with the help of an attorney, says to try to do it on your own is asking for complications. "Even using an attorney, I had problems," she told me.

You will certainly need legal assistance if you ever have to defend an infringement of one of your copyrights or registered trademarks. The only time I've ever needed an attorney's advice for my home-based business was when someone tried to steal the name of my *Homemade Money* book and attach it to a sleazy make-money-from-home magazine. Although it had never occurred to me to trademark my book's title, an attorney who specializes in copyright and trademark law successfully defended my common-law trademark claim to that name with a few letters that cost very little for the benefit gained.

When looking for a lawyer, ask friends for a reference—just as you would do when shopping for a good accountant or new doctor—remembering that lawyers have specialties, just like doctors. If you need an attorney but cannot afford one, you may be eligible to receive free legal service from the Volunteer Lawyers for the Arts (VLA), a nonprofit organization with chapters all over the country.

Learning more about legal matters is something you can do gradually by reading the legal columns in small business periodicals and occasionally adding a few business or legal books to your business bookshelf. As your small business grows, you will be wise to put special information resources high on the list of things you can't afford to be without. Your ultimate financial success may depend on them.

Important Federal Regulations

M OST OF THE legal things you need to take care of on the local or state level can be handled with a phone call, a visit to City Hall or the filing of a required form. By following the simple guidelines above, you can safely offer your products for sale on the local level and have the comfort of knowing you are operating your crafts business in a legal and professional manner.

Although your products may never cross state lines, you must be concerned with a few federal laws and regulations as

well. This section lists categories of laws applicable to the sale of various handcrafted items. Write to the individual government agencies named in each section to obtain complete information about individual laws and regulations (shown in italics) that apply to the products you make and sell. Addresses will be found in Resources. You can also get information from these agencies on the World Wide Web.

CONSUMER SAFETY LAWS

The Consumer Product Safety Act of 1972 protects the public against unreasonable risks of injury associated with consumer products. The Consumer Product Safety Commission (CPSC), establishes and enforces mandatory safety standards for consumer products sold in the United States. One of the Commission's most active regulatory programs has been in the area of toys and consumer goods designed for children. If you make and sell toys, be sure to obtain complete information from the CPSC about what you must do to insure that your products are safe for children and that your risks of a consumer lawsuit are minimal or nonexistent.

The CPSC also enforces the Flammable Fabrics Act. Most fabrics comply with the regulations set forth in this act, but if you intend to wholesale children's clothing or toys and want to be doubly sure that the fabric you are using is safe, ask your supplier for a "guaranty of compliance with the Flammability Act." Most fabric manufacturers test their fabrics for compliance and issue a guaranty of compliance that is generally passed along the chain of distribution by using an invoice statement that reads: "Continuing guaranty under the Flammable Fabrics Act filed with the Consumer Product Safety Commission."

Tag and Label Laws

The Textile Fiber Products Identification Act requires that all items made of any textile or fiber (garments, quilts, stuffed toys, rugs, etc.) have a securely affixed label or hangtag that includes (1) the name of the manufacturer or other person marketing the textile fiber product; (2) the generic names and percentages of all fibers in the product in amounts of 5 percent or more, listed in order of predominance by weight. Examples: "100 percent combed cotton"; "92 percent cotton, 8 percent other fibers." If the item contains wool, it falls under the Wool Products Labeling Act of 1939 and will require additional identification. Information about both Acts is available from the Bureau of Consumer Protection.

Most sellers like to design their own labels, but standard fiber content and care labels are readily available from companies that advertise in craft magazines. Examples of both standard and

custom-design labels are shown on page 57 (furnished by Widby Enterprises, USA). Labels may include a combination of fiber content and care labeling instructions (see "Care Labeling Laws" below), but if the maker's name is not included on such labels, a second label (generally a "designer label" with the manufacturer's name and logo on it) would probably be added to the product being offered for sale.

The Federal Trade Commission (FTC) requires an additional label or tag on all wool or textile products that indicates when imported ingredients are used, even if the product is made in the United States. Thus the label for a shawl woven in the United States from imported fibers would read, "Made in the USA from imported products" or similar wording. Items whose materials originate entirely in the United States need only state "Made in the USA," "Crafted in USA," or similar terminology. (These regulations are also applicable to the copy used to describe such products in mail-order catalogs sent to consumers.)

Care Labeling Laws are part of the Textile Fiber Products Identification Act. If you make and sell any textile, suede or leather product in the form of a finished article of wearing apparel, or any textile product in the form of a finished household furnishing, you must permanently affix a label that provides instructions on the care and maintenance of the item.

(This includes all wearing apparel, household furnishings, piece goods, yarn, and rugs.) More information on labeling laws is available from the Federal Trade Commission.

Note: Crafters may design and print their own hangtags or order custom-designed tags and labels that comply with the various regulations above. Many craft magazines carry ads of companies who offer such tags and labels.

Finally, I will briefly mention an aggravating state labeling law that may never affect you, but which you should know about, just in case. Originally intended for manufacturers of pillows, mattresses, and other bedding items, the Bedding and Upholstered Furniture Law is being applied to crafters in only a few states who make items that contain any kind of stuffing, such as teddy bears, dolls, quilts, pillows, and padded picture frames. Information on this topic is sketchy at best, but one source told me that bedding officials in Pennsylvania have recently begun to visit craft fairs in search of toy sellers (calling anything with stuffing in it a "toy"). When discovered, crafters in this state must buy a license ($25/year) and place a special label on each "toy" they sell. Because this law is arbitrarily enforced in only twenty-nine states at most, crafters generally ignore it altogether unless they are challenged by authorities. The only penalty for breaking it seems to be the removal of merchandise from store shelves or a fine if a seller refuses to comply with the law after being notified of it. So just forget I ever mentioned it, okay?

TRADE PRACTICE RULES

Several booklets are available that define the trade practice rules for all industries. Some of possible interest to this book's readers are: *The Jewelry Industry, The Hand Knitting Yarn Industry, The Ladies' Handbag Industry,* and *Catalog Jewelry and Giftware Industry.* The FTC also has regulations about the selling of products by mail, specifically the Thirty-Day Mail-Order Rule and Truth in Advertising Rule. If you always ship orders within thirty days of receipt, and never make false product claims, you are not likely to have any problems with these laws. Free booklets on both of these topics are available on request.

Note: When an FTC rule has been violated, it is customary for the agency to order the violator to cease the illegal practice. No penalty is attached to most cease-and-desist orders.

COPYRIGHTS, TRADEMARKS, AND PATENTS

If you have created an original work of any kind and want to protect it from theft by others who would profit from your creativity, specifically request these free publications (and any others available) from the Copyright Office: *The Nuts and Bolts of Copyright Law* (Circular R1); *How to Investigate the Copyright Status of a Work* (Circular R22); and *Trademarks* (Circular R13). The Patent & Trademark Office also offers free information about patents and trademarks. (Other discussions of these topics will be found in other chapters.)

Business Brings Its Own Benefits

D ON'T LET THE information in this chapter stress you needlessly, but do reflect on it with your long-term goals in mind. If you dream of having something more than just a hobby business, and you care about doing things right (professionally and legally speaking), the basic information in this chapter will get you started on the right foot or enable you to correct uncomfortable situations that may now exist.

The idea of being in business and having to cope with all the stuff I've just dumped on you may seem frightening now, but with time and experience you will gain confidence and your business fear will at least become manageable.

When I asked a number of people how they had changed or grown since they started their home-based business, many expressed surprise that they had been able to do what they had done, given their lack of business experience in the beginning. Almost all pointed to an increase in self-confidence.

A few years after she had started her business, From Wentz it Came, Jane Wentz said she was still struggling with fear, even though sales of her applique garments and table linens were good. She said then that her greatest problem usually was herself and fears related to lack of knowledge or the guts to try. "As my confidence grows and I risk a failure, I grow and gain much in the way of new customers and the courage to step out again and try something else." When I contacted Jane for an update on her business, now fifteen years old, she said "I amaze myself at some of the things I say, do, and believe today. Most of this, I think, comes from running my own business profitably, and some just from reaching the age of 50-plus years."

"If I'd known then what I know now, I might not have started," says Sue Cloutman, who has operated Color Me Creations since 1995. "Yet each step seemed to come at a time when I was ready to learn it, and my confidence has had amazing boosts along the way. Every few months I find myself doing something, such as speaking in front of a group or approaching potential customers, that I feel I never could have done a few months prior. I've learned so much! If I could do it over again, however, I would get a larger loan, go right for the boxes and bar codes, and make a more aggressive start."

Self-esteem is another byproduct of being self-employed. "I feel better about myself," says artist Julia Morrill, who started a part-time business when she no longer had the stamina or mobility to do work outside the home. "Now I plan to use my thirty years of paintings and drawings in new and exciting ways. I'm looking forward to more Web page/ Internet involvement and computer-generated products."

You may protest that you're the world's worst person at organizing things, but a business of your own will help you become better organized while also forcing you to place a greater value on your time. "I've become more organized as I've forced myself to create and meet deadlines," says Merrilyn Fedder, a designer of primitive needlework patterns. Barbara Deuel, who makes photo albums, scrapbooks, and journals, says, "I've become more confident and organized—out of necessity and against my nature—and I've also become more creative working in this field." Susan Nelson, a rehabilitation

WORKSHEET

Checklist of Legal and Financial Things to Do[*]

- ☐ **Call or visit City Hall or County Clerk**
    - ☐ to check on local zoning laws (info also at your library)
    - ☐ for information about need for a license or permit
    - ☐ to register a fictitious business name

- ☐ **Call local telephone company about need for a business telephone or separate line for fax or Internet access**

- ☐ **Call local financial institutions**
    - ☐ to compare cost of a business checking account
    - ☐ get a safe deposit box for storage of valuable business papers

- ☐ **Call insurance agents**
    - ☐ about business rider on house insurance (or need for separate in-home insurance policy)
    - ☐ about benefits of an umbrella policy for extra liability insurance
    - ☐ about car insurance (using car for business)
    - ☐ about product liability insurance (if you think this might be necessary)

- ☐ **Call state capital**
    - ☐ to register business name on state level (if such protection is desired)
    - ☐ about resale tax number/collecting sales tax (Department of Revenue)

- ☐ **Send for or otherwise obtain free information (mentioned in text) from these government agencies:**
    - ☐ Internal Revenue Service
    - ☐ Consumer Products Safety Commission
    - ☐ Bureau of Consumer Protection
    - ☐ Federal Trade Commission
    - ☐ Copyright Office
    - ☐ Patent & Trademark Office

- ☐ **Ask friends for names of a good attorney, accountant, or EA**

- ☐ **Check out local office and computer supply stores and mail-order catalog suppliers**

[*]See Resources for addresses of government agencies.

counselor by trade and a designer of cat-motif items part-time, says she has learned organizing improvements through trial and error. "I've also gotten a tougher skin on my ego and invested creations."

In addition to the financial profits of a well-run home-based business, many other benefits come within the territory. Janet Burgess, who has operated her Amazon Vinegar Drygoods shop and mail-order catalog since 1982, says she has learned not only self-confidence, but patience, something she didn't have before she started. "It takes an incredible wad to stress me out now," she says. "After nearly twenty years in business, I can take almost anything." If she could do it over again, Janet says, she would start her business in a more business-like fashion, with a computer. "Amazon started as a hobby and I have never caught up," she says.

Until you make a genuine commitment to the idea of crafts as a business, you will find true financial profit an elusive thing. Taking care of the "legal stuff," learning more about managing a business with computer technology, and getting serious about pricing and marketing are just some of the things you'll need to do as your business grows. The checklist on page 61 will help you keep track of the nitty-gritty details. Just remember that all of the successful craft business owners quoted above and throughout this book were once hobbyists who felt intimidated by all the "nitty-gritty legal stuff" they had to contend with in the beginning. Clearly, it was worth the effort for them, and I believe it will be worth the effort for you, too.

Selling at Fairs
and Shows

Success, to me, is being looked at as a professional with the ability to be able to get into any of the large shows I apply to. It's the network of friends I've developed over the past fifteen years and the growth I've experienced as an individual and businessperson.

NORMA RUDLOFF, Rose Petals

BEGINNERS AND PROFESSION-ALS alike *love* to sell at craft fairs and shows, and most seem to prefer this method of selling above all others. If you haven't yet begun to sell what you make, entering a local crafts fair is the best way to break into business with a minimum of splash—meaning you can get your feet wet without committing the rest of yourself.

By personally offering your wares to the public, you will get immediate feedback (a form of market research) on whether people are interested enough in your art or craft to actually buy it. Craft fairs are an ideal way for beginners to test prices and gain confidence in selling, but professional sellers also use craft fairs to test prices and see customers' reactions to their products.

Craft fairs provide an excellent opportunity for all sellers to meet and network with others who share their interests. If no one comes to your booth, then you should make the effort to reach out to others. A good ice-breaker is to comment on the quality of someone's work and ask if they've done this particular show before.

In talking with several people at a show, you will gain information on other shows that might be profitable for you. Although you will need to subscribe to some show-listing publications, seasoned fair sellers confirm that the best source of information about shows will always come directly from sellers themselves.

How to Find Good Shows

AMERICA IS UNIQUE in all the world for both its abundance of fairs and its number of selling craftspeople. No one knows how many craft fair sellers there are, but industry watchers believe there are at least 10,000 art and craft fairs each year in the United States. (If you counted every little street fair and church bazaar, however, you might come up with as many as 20,000 events.) Most shows will have an entry fee ranging from a few dollars for a small local show to a few hundred dollars for a large juried event that might have several hundred exhibitors and attract thousands of shoppers. Generally, shows fall into one of the following categories:

➤ local fairs (street fairs, flea markets, church, school, and community events)

➤ juried art and craft shows (held everywhere nationwide)

➤ mall shows (held in shopping centers nationwide)

➤ period/costume events (Renaissance, Pioneer/Heritage, Ethnic, Native American, Living History, Shaker, and so on)

➤ collector/special interest/trade shows (dolls, teddy bears, miniatures, candles, dog shows, and so on)

➤ craft guild/association shows (annual, for members only)

➤ holiday shows (held in public buildings—Christmas, Easter, Valentine's Day, and so on)

Although there are exceptions, most shows are held on weekends because everyone figures the best buyers are people with jobs who have discretionary income for art and handcrafts. This is great for sellers, too, many of whom need to be at home during the week to take care of children. To find good shows, you must subscribe to publications that announce upcoming events months in advance. Several people now publish show-listing periodicals or calendars that list hundreds of events per issue. Some of these publications focus on shows within a specific region, while others list events nationwide. A subscription to one or more will keep you informed of events in your region and alert you to major shows that might be worth driving some distance to attend. Some show publications list only basic information such as event's name, date of show, and who to contact for entry information, while others include special evaluations of shows based on reports from exhibiting craftspeople. You may need to sample several publications to find the ones right for your needs (see Resources).

Be wary of shows that appear to use artists and crafters as a drawing card but seem to be promoting other things, such as antique shows, concerts, outdoor picnics, horse races, or carnival-type attractions. Look instead for shows that emphasize arts and crafts for sale, and try to get into shows where the number of sellers per craft is limited. This will automatically cut your competition and entice buyers, who will have a wider variety of crafts from which to choose. Serious craft fair sellers participate mostly in juried shows. ("Juried" simply means that certain standards have been established for each show, and exhibitors must meet those standards to be accepted into the show.)

SHOW PROMOTERS

Sunshine Artist is America's premier show and festival publication, in publication since the mid-1970s. In talking with editor Amy Detwiler, I learned the secret of this publication's success and its benefits to subscribers. "After so many years of publication, we have quite a network of state reporters, stringers, and craft show auditors who regularly send us reports on all the shows listed in the magazine," Amy explained. "Anyone who is just breaking into art and craft shows would do well to study our listings carefully to find shows that are right for their products. Each show is good for somebody. The trick is finding the right fit."

Don't hesitate to call a show promoter to get his or her opinion as to whether your products are a good fit for their show. Ask about other exhibitors who have already signed up. "Sometimes the nicest thing I can do for a crafter is reject them from a show when I feel their work won't sell," says a show promoter. A craft seller who frequently calls show promoters prior to sending in an entry form agrees: "Most reputable promoters aren't going to let a crafter come into a show if their work doesn't fit."

"Professional show promoters (about 200 in the country) tend to be regionalized," says Amy. "Once you've connected with a promoter you like and trust, there are advantages to signing with them to do all their shows. You'll always know what to expect and you won't have to send slides

Entry Fee "Rule of Thumb"

There has long been a rule of thumb in the craft fair industry that a profitable show is one that generates sales ten times the amount of the entry fee. While this seemed to work for years, long-time craft fair sellers now say this is getting difficult or impossible to do because of the increased number of shows and sellers in some areas.

In her business workshops, Rita Stone-Conwell says she tells people that the "ten-times rule" is ideal, but the higher the booth fee, the less likely this level of sales will be reached. "So much depends on the market, where you're selling, and what the people are looking for. If you're paying only $20 to get into a show, you could very well see ten times the booth fee. If you're paying a $400 booth fee, however, it's unrealistic to expect $4,000 in sales."

Several other professional crafters I spoke with agree with Rita. In trying to figure the profitability of a show, many simply compare costs versus income. "We count it a successful show if our expenses are no more than half the gross," says Bob Gerdts, who emphasizes that "expenses" include not only the entry fee, mileage, motel, and meals, but the cost of goods in products sold.

or photos for each show. You may also be able to limit your deposit to a minimal amount." (Some juried shows require entry fees months in advance. Normally, they are payable half with registration and the balance a month or so before the show.)

Some people figure anything will sell if the audience is large enough, but that isn't true. The number of people attending a show is not nearly as important as the *interests* of the people attending a show. Knowing where a show promoter plans to advertise an event will tell you much about the kind of people who will attend a show, so don't hesitate to ask this question when you call a show promoter. (Reputable promoters will always give you this information. If you can't get it, pass on the show. You may be dealing with one of the few sleazy promoters out there who are only interested in filling a building with

The Advantages of Doing Local Shows

As a work-at-home mom in Bronx, New York, Yvonne Ward sells the products of her Country Garden Designs business mostly on the local level, doing street fairs and craft shows at schools and churches. While some might see this as limiting her market, Yvonne sees it as invaluable networking.

© 1998 Yvonne M. Ward

"It's important to stay connected to your community," she says. "I have become well-known here by doing so many local shows. Whereas I once had to do a lot of marketing legwork, buyers now come to me. People who were initially just customers are now friends. I've made valuable business connections at shows that have led to sales of a different nature, such as doing wreaths for local shop owners. My mailing list is growing, and I get a lot of word-of-mouth advertising."

bodies and could care less about whether anyone sells anything or not.)

DISTURBING TRENDS

A number of professional crafters interviewed for this book mentioned two disturbing trends in some craft shows. In their zeal to make money, some promoters are practically doubling the number of spaces for exhibitors while doing nothing to increase the size of the buying audience. You don't have to be a mathematician to see that twice the number of

sellers working the same size audience means diminished sales for every exhibitor in a show. Show promoters who do this sort of thing won't long survive, but they'll hurt a lot of crafters before they exit the scene. If the number of exhibitors in a particular show is substantially greater than in years before, check to see if advertising for the show has also been increased to attract a larger crowd.

The other trend is one called "buy–sell," where exhibitors buy commercial goods or imports for resale at craft shows. Some show promoters who are having trouble filling shows are relaxing their entry rules and accepting such exhibitors, which hurts the sales of other sellers. While there is nothing wrong with adding a few commercial items to your line of handcrafts if the products are compatible and help overall sales (craft shops do this all the time), people who sell commercial goods do not belong in shows that are being promoted to the public as featuring only handcrafted work.

"People have to be taught the difference between handmade and buy–sell," says potter Trudi Clark. "There is so much of the latter, even at the best shows. Promoters must put a stop to people selling imports at craft shows. Integrity is a word all craftspeople should learn the meaning of."

One show promoter says such products are sometimes sneaked into a show. "That's why I always hold the photos or

Renaissance Fairs and Fantasy Shows

Lois Boncer is a soft-sculpture artist who specializes in mythological figures and fantasy creations such as dragons, unicorns, and Pegasus sculptures. "I've quit trying to compete with Taiwan, Korea, and Mexico," she says. "I no longer make 'cutesy stuff' for the toy market, but am focusing instead on selling to adults interested in art. If I were doing it over, I would target a higher-level market and not do craft fairs, street fairs, city park fairs, and swap meets where people are looking for cheap. The most profitable advice I ever got was to focus on doing Renaissance fairs and science fiction and fantasy shows for collectors of unusual stuffed animals and dolls."

© Lois Boncer

Lois says some of the Renaissance shows are advertised in regular art/craft fair calendars; but to find shows in the science fiction and fantasy industries you must search out trade publications in these fields and look for ads from promoters. "Once you find one show," she says, "you can network with other exhibitors to learn about other shows."

slides my exhibitors have sent me. When the show opens, I check every booth to see if people are actually selling what they said they were going to offer. If not, I will remove their names from my list and not give them entry to future shows."

Learning How to Sell

I F YOU'RE JUST getting started selling at fairs, go to your first show hopeful that things will sell, but don't be too discouraged if they don't. Making things and *selling* things are two different things entirely. It's rather like the person who, when asked if the fishin' was good, replied: "Oh, the fishin' is easy, it's the *catchin'* that's hard."

Success in selling does not come overnight, and profits may take a while to materialize. "My very first sale at a show was for $8 and the customer gave me a hundred dollar bill," says Janet Middleton, of Caned Canines & More. "The sale came quickly and I received a false sense of encouragement. For a moment I thought, 'This is going to be easy!' I then sat for hours with very few sales, and reality set in."

In the early days of her Country Garden Designs business, Yvonne Ward sold a little of this and a little of that at flea markets, not yet sure what she wanted to focus on. "I've learned that selling is an art that develops with time," she says. "After I felt more at ease with the business of selling my crafts and saw that I was selling well, I eliminated flea markets and started participating in craft fairs and craft shows. I narrowed my product line to concentrate on making crafts I enjoyed most and had a talent for. Now I sell personalized quilted photo albums, recipe, telephone address, and guest books, hand-painted pots, country-style wreaths, and Christmas ornaments with a folk art or country theme."

Beginners everywhere naturally lack confidence when they first begin to sell what they make. Some people avoid contact with the public because they are shy or lack confidence in their work. Others don't want to hear discouraging remarks, such as, "Oh, I can do that myself," or any of a hundred other comments made by thoughtless people. Negative feedback is one of the few disadvantages of direct selling you must learn to accept.

One of the hardest things to learn is not to take rejection personally. "In the early days, should someone pass my booth without purchasing, I would be crushed," recalls Rita Stone-Conwell. "Now I realize that my product is not the problem, it's just that I'm offering something that doesn't interest buyers at the time." In thinking about her early days of selling at fairs, Rita remembers that her booth held too many different crafts and looked much too busy. "After a couple of years, I decided to focus on the crafts I enjoyed doing most. Soon I was doing only dolls made from a product called Paper Twist. Currently, my doll line has over thirty-five different styles."

For every person who has immediate success with selling, hundreds of others struggle for it on a trial-and-error basis. Although you can read a book to learn something about the art of selling, the only way to get over the *fear* of selling is to grit your teeth and step forward. "My first party plan presentation was hilarious with my stuttering and nervous twitch," says Opal Leasure, who first sold her wood crafts at fairs but later found party plans the perfect way to go. She not only developed her own successful style of selling but went on to help others achieve success by publishing a party plan guide. "In the beginning, I was ill-prepared and literally shaking in my shoes. Looking back now, however, I find this very humorous. As my self-esteem grew, so did my business."

Part of selling is learning what to say and what not to say when someone appears interested in products. Bob Gerdts, of Bob & Carol's Egg-Art, Ltd., says the one thing you never want to ask anyone is, "May I help you?" because the answer will always be "No, thanks, I'm just look-

ing." What works best for them, he says, is just to open the door to conversation with a simple remark such as, "Good morning! Lovely day, isn't it?"

Everyone has bad selling experiences where sales are not as expected, but if your first selling experience is a disaster, you may have to do some serious talking to yourself before you can muster the courage to continue. Janet Middleton sells a line of wooden animal silhouettes by mail and at dog and cat shows. The first show she entered (the Newfoundland Club of America National Specialty show) was a disaster from start to finish. Held in different parts of the country each year, this particular four-day show was 300 miles from Janet's home.

"I worked two months to build up my inventory with all kinds of 'Newfie' items I felt collectors would love, but my sales didn't begin to cover the cost of doing this show," she recalls. "On the way home, I did some serious thinking about what I was doing and whether it was worth continuing or not. Although I was discouraged, I decided I believed in myself and my product and wanted to keep going. When I did my second show a month later, I got a good response and the boost of encouragement I needed."

For Janet, giving up simply was not an option. With time, she has become stronger and more self-confident about selling. "I am no longer bothered by

A Typical Crafts Couple

Jean and Steve Belknap are typical of many couples who do craft fairs on a regular basis. "She's the boss," says Steve, who has a full-time managerial job, "but the business has been a team effort for the past seven years."

"Steve has always been my greatest supporter," says Jean, "As the business grew, he was just naturally drawn into it—ordering supplies, building display stands, doing customer mailings, and helping me sell at shows."

Jean designs soft sculpture animal dolls appropriate to her Noah's Ark logo. Her product line currently features growing families of giraffes, zebras, alpacas, and llamas, plus angels, Santas, and Christmas ornaments. Her business began, however, with one rabbit offered for sale at an Easter show in 1991. Within a year, sales of her dolls, toys, and Christmas ornaments were so good that Jean quit her secretarial job to work full-time on her business, named The Country Spirit.

Although the Belknaps do mostly retail shows on weekends, they do some wholesaling too. (They will never forget their "big wholesaling experience" when they got over a thousand orders for Jean's "Tyler the Giraffe" doll for the QVC Home Shopping Show—see chapter 7.)

Jean and Steve exhibit mostly in their own state, but occasionally go farther distances for special shows in other states. "The main benefit of traveling to other areas is that you get a wider cross-section of buyers and a greater knowledge of what will sell in different areas of the country," says Steve, "but we also benefit by selling at local shows because it gives us a sense of community. We enjoy seeing our neighbors and fellow crafters at such events."

Prior to doing a local show, the Belknaps, like most successful fair sellers, send out mailings to all their customers in surrounding communities. "We've found that many people will drive an extra distance just to see us at a local show," says Steve. "We also send a mailing to our entire list twice a year—in early spring for shows running through July, and in August to announce our fall and Christmas shows."

seeming rejection," she says. "I feel good about the things I offer and appreciate the many nice comments I receive; but even without them, I believe my work has value."

If no one buys what you offer, you might mistakenly think your products aren't worth much when in fact you may simply be trying to sell them in the wrong place, to the wrong audience, at the wrong time, or at the wrong price. As you will learn, all of these things have a bearing on whether something will sell or not. Sometimes, as in Janet's case, there is no real explanation for why things don't sell. In talking to other exhibitors at that particular show, Janet learned that many other exhibitors fared badly, too, and no one could figure out why. When you run into a blank wall like this, the best thing to do is follow the advice in that old song— "Pick yourself up, dust yourself off, and start all over again."

Your Personal and Professional Image

THE WAY YOU look, act, speak, dress, and respond to people who show an interest in your work has everything to do with your ability to get sales. "Your customers are interested in more than your product," says veteran seller Jane Wentz.

"They want a trustworthy relationship with *you*. They want to deal with an honest, dependable, confident fair vendor. The manner in which you display yourself and your products is just as important as your product itself."

Here are some things you can do to "spiff up" your professional image and maximize your opportunities for sales.

MANNER OF DRESS

Look neat and dress in keeping with your art or craft. If rustic or country crafts are your specialty, jeans and a plaid shirt or other homespun costume would be appropriate. If you do an ethnic art or craft, a costume related to the country of origin will attract extra attention. If needlework, quilting, or macrame happens to be your specialty, incorporate your needle skills into a blouse, skirt, jacket, or vest. When there are two or more people in a booth, something as simple as matching aprons, shirts or hats can be a great attention-getter.

PRINTED MATERIALS

Use nicely printed business cards, flyers, brochures, and order forms. This not only makes you look more professional, but increases your chances for follow-up sales. People who buy something at a fair, as well as those who seem interested but don't purchase anything, may decide to order by mail once they get home and have a chance to read your sales materials.

Business cards do not always have to be "cut and dried" designs, as cloth doll designer Tiffany Wall illustrates with her clever card. She first drew a large picture of some of her products, then had a printer reduce it to the right size for a card, pictured below. "The pictures of my products on the card make my business more memorable to customers," says Tiffany. "I've made numerous sales from people who have seen it."

The addition of classy hangtags to your products will also increase sales. Fiber artist and author–publisher James Dillehay offers this interesting example of the power of a good hangtag: "Sometimes the customer sees 'cheap' on a lower price tag and rejects the work as inferior. I once wove a series of shawls with cotton and mohair yarns, pricing them at $65 each. For several months, they just didn't sell. I replaced the hangtags with new ones emphasizing that the

pieces contained pure Angora mohair, and raised the price to $85. They all sold the first time on display. This success inspired me to make more pieces emphasizing the expensive materials which also sold at the higher price."

Jewelry designer Joyce Roark has recently trademarked her "Loving Thoughts" name, and now uses both a self-stick label on boxes and a tiny heart-shaped hangtag on jewelry items (shown here in actual size). "The use of professionally printed tags has made a difference in my sales," she says. "I've also increased sales by selling my products in boxes and packaging them in bags that contain my trademarked logo."

Joyce also sells a line of gift boxes from jewelry size up to the china vase size. "I started doing this when I noticed that most crafters at fairs package sales in plastic bags they get at the grocery store. Now their customers come to me to buy boxes for items they want to give as gifts."

Yvonne Ward has also increased sales with the use of professionally printed stationery, cards, and bags printed by NEBS, a mail-order catalog company in Groton, Massachusetts. "They offer a variety of standard designs, one of which was perfect for my business. I order 500 white plastic bags at a time (about 15 cents each) imprinted with a flower design and my Country Garden Designs business name. Many people who see these bags think I have a store," she says, offering a good example of how something as simple and inexpensive as an imprinted bag can change a customer's perception of one's business.

BOOTH BEHAVIOR

Sellers who sit in their booth with arms crossed, staring at the crowd with a bored expression (or worse, reading a book) are *not* radiating interest and friendliness. As one buyer commented, "These actions almost dare customers to stop, and they usually don't. It takes action to get attention. Paint, whittle, tie knots, move about—*but do something*."

I loved this story from Mary Lou Highfill, who once sold $125 worth of pincushions at a show without ever setting her goods out for sale. "I was in a living history show at the Chisholm Trail Museum in Kingfisher, Oklahoma," she recalled. "I had asked for two tables but received only one, so I displayed only my bonnets, putting my box of pincushions under the table. Some of the other reen-

actors wanted to see the pincushions and bought some. In a little while, visitors came by asking if they could see the pincushions, wanting to buy. People were curious about others sitting in a chair behind a booth going through a box under the table and then buying items, so they would ask if they could look, too. This is similar to a show I did in my early days of making and selling everything—you said to be busy in your booth, maybe doing whatever you made—so I was putting together a small cookie cutter angel doll. Before I had it together, three women bought an unmade doll (in pieces) for full price."

DISPLAY

The average craft fair display is about ten feet square, although this will vary from show to show. Depending on what you're selling, you may or may not want your customers walking within this area, so your first design consideration will be how you're going to direct the flow of traffic in or around your booth. Ideally, your display will show enough work to demonstrate the range of items available and allow shoppers to browse without being overwhelmed by too many choices.

Ingenuity is the key to good display planning, along with originality and practicality. Emulate but do not duplicate the successful-looking displays you see at other shows. If your product line is limited and your budget is slim, you can do indoor shows with something as simple as cloth-covered tables, hinged panels (pegboard or fabric-covered), or shelf arrangements. When displaying products on a table or counter, experiment with different shelf arrangements and display devices so all products are not on the same eye level. Use interesting accent items to hold or give contrast to different products. Maybe your wares would look great heaped in a handmade basket, stuck in an old jar, or leaned against a marvelous chunk of driftwood. Small expensive items, such as jewelry or miniatures, may require special glass-enclosed display cases.

Display Tips

"Your first display will never be the ultimate because many things change as your business grows," says teddy bear designer Jan Bonner, who has been selling at fairs and shows for more than twenty years. "A good display fixture must be portable, modular, easy to set up, neutral in color, and durable." Although Jan's first display was attractive, it proved to be too heavy for her to transport alone and took up too much space in her van. Now she uses break-apart bookshelves that fit along the inside wall of her van. "You should be able to place pieces without having to think," she says. "Time wasted sifting through parts like a jigsaw puzzle may make the difference in your mood when you open."

Jan also emphasizes the importance of customer safety and maintaining your booth as it naturally deteriorates from constant setting up and tearing down. "You will be held responsible if something should fall and injure a customer or another's property, so make sure your booth is durable and unlikely to cause injury to anyone. I always carry a tool kit with me so I can do whatever is necessary to ensure safety."

While your goal in designing a booth should be to attract attention, be careful not to overdo it. "It should also carry out the theme of your crafts, but never compete with your products for attention," says Jan. "An effective display should offer contrast and give the eyes comfortable resting places."

If you plan to do outdoor shows, you will need to invest in a display unit. Since your work may actually be judged by the overall quality of your display, make it as sturdy, functional, clever, and eye-catching as you can. Many sellers design and build their own booths, but commercial craft fair canopies and modular displays are available from several companies who regularly advertise in craft business magazines.

Demonstrating Your Art or Craft

THERE IS NO doubt about it: You will sell more products if you demonstrate your art or craft at a show. Old-time crafts such as chair caning, cornshuckery, lace-making, tincraft, and woodcarving lend themselves especially well to demonstrations. Although you may be selling small or medium-sized products, the bigger your demonstration product, the better. Woodcarvers in the Ozarks, for example, may sell small carvings and sculptures, but they are often working on a large item during a show, such as a wooden figure, bear, or carousel pony.

"Our sales are always higher when we demonstrate at a show," says Bob Gerdts. "Carol and I sell decorated eggs, some with musical movements and semi-precious stones, for $50 to $55. We demonstrate by carving an egg with a Moto Tool. When we don't have a site with electricity, we use a battery-operated unit. It's slow, but it gets the idea across. We spend most of our time on our feet talking to people, explaining our craft. If we sat in the back of the booth with a book, like so many sellers do, we wouldn't sell anything."

Yvonne Ward agrees. "I sold all my hand-painted pots for Mother's Day last year simply because I was demonstrating sponge painting, tying on raffia ribbons and gluing on special trims of buttons and seed packets. My buyers loved being able to choose their own colors and trims."

If you can't actually demonstrate how your art or craft is made, perhaps you can demonstrate how it is used, or add to the impact of your exhibit with oversized exhibit items. Genii Townsend designs, constructs, and performs with puppets and marionettes that retail for $39 to $79 each. She does only indoor shows, taking custom orders and selling her patterns and kits. Her booth walls are draped in black to make her brightly colored dolls stand out, and buyers are lured into her fantasy-themed booth by a couple of six-foot gourd dolls positioned out front. At the center of her exhibit is a little stage with a black drape Genii stands behind to demonstrate her puppets. Around the outer edge of the booth are several tables, each featuring a particular gourd doll or puppet. A larger version sits on top, with smaller figures underneath. "Each one is like a little theater in itself," says Genii, who never forgot an article she once read on effective displays. "It emphasized that we have only about fifteen seconds to catch a buyer's attention, so we've got to use our imagination and theatrical techniques. I have soft music playing in the background, and the overall effect is very dramatic—full of color, lights, and glitter."

© Genii Townsend

"Oh my goodness!" is a comment Genii often hears when people walk into her booth. "I try to make the booth very happy and uplifting so people are glad to be there and don't want to leave," she says. "If they do, they want to come back."

Action does sell, but not every seller can demonstrate, especially when doing a show alone. Artist Geoffrey Harris, who does hand-colored linoleum art prints, has solved this problem by creating a special three-dimensional framed display box that shows each of the steps involved in creating his art. About 16 by 36 inches, it contains (1) a block of linoleum with six carving tools beneath it and sample cuts on the linoleum to show what each tool does; (2) a carved, inked block; (3) a copy of a black-and-white "linocut" print pulled from the block (see example on page 78); and (4) a print that has been hand painted with water colors, matted, and framed. Beneath the first three examples are typed explanations of each step in this art process. "This display has helped me sell my work," says Geoffrey, "because people who have never seen this art form before can understand the work involved in it, while others who used to do linoleum block carving in grade school gain a new appreciation for the difference between craft and art."

Geoffrey's business, Harris Collectibles, has been his livelihood for the

© Geoffrey Harris

past six years. He does between twenty and twenty-five outdoor art fairs a year (no craft shows), paying an average entry fee of $200 per show. His art sells for between $100 and $300, depending on how it's matted or framed. "My work is always changing, but some of my most popular pieces have been sports art (baseball, golf, and football), music pieces, and lighthouses," he says. Geoffrey's business card is a postcard that he prints several times a year. "I just go to Kinko's and create it on

How to Keep Cool at a Hot Show

Veteran crafts fair entertainer Lyndall "Granny" Toothman always wears a long dress and bonnet when she demonstrates the art of spinning, and this kind of costume can get mighty uncomfortable on a hot day. Once when she was doing her spinning on the *Old Tucson* movie set in Arizona (a job she got simply by suggesting the actors might enjoy a little entertainment between takes), she learned how to keep her cool on a very hot day.

"I was sitting on a porch doing my spinning in 110-degree temperature when one of the fellows on the set brought me a box of dry ice," she said. "I put two pieces of it in my bonnet and set the box under my long dress and spent the rest of my spinning time there cool as a cucumber."

a computer so they can print up a batch for me. It lists upcoming shows for the next two or three months."

Get a Gimmick

ONE WAY TO increase sales and profits is with a good gimmick, which Webster defines as "an important feature that is not immediately apparent" or "a new and ingenious scheme or angle." A gimmick can be something as simple as using raw materials that seem unusual to buyers. I recall a weaver who accidentally discovered her gimmick when she began to weave with fur strips cut from old fur coats. People not only liked the idea that she was into recycling, but loved to watch her demonstrate a weaving technique unfamiliar to them.

Sandy Mooney accidentally discovered her gimmick while demonstrating batik at a local fair many years ago. At that time she was making charming character dolls, pillows, scarves, aprons, and "whatever else I could think up that could be translated into batik," she recalls. One customer, amused by her colorful display of life-sized stuffed batik dolls, remarked, "They're great, but you should make some of them into hookers." Sandy thought that sounded like fun, so she made one a few weeks later. "For some reason," she said, "she looked like the great grandmother of

all the madams instead of the beautiful sexy gal that I had in mind. Someone bought her (perhaps as a gift for a grandfather), and after several more tries, I finally came up with a good-looking sexy lady."

Sandy no longer makes her unusual "Ladies of the Evening," but she says they played an important role in the development of her current business, Sandy's Wearable Art. A seller at art fairs for thirty-five years, Sandy is currently doing clothing and coats. "I put my son through four years of college with the money from my hand-dyed, screen-printed coats," she says. "Now I'm working on wearable art that is more time-consuming, complex, expensive, and more interesting for me to do." Sandy adds that she has had many funny experiences at shows and may someday write a book about them titled *Camping Out in Your Good Clothes.*

Liz Fye and Maryn Wynne are a mother–daughter partnership that designs and manufactures costumes for pets under the name of Flytes of Fancy. Although they now wholesale exclusively, they got their start selling retail at dog shows, displaying costumes first on stuffed animals, and later on special display dogs with wood heads and leather ears. "Our gimmick was that we would let people try our costumes on their pets. Once they did that, a sale was guaranteed."

Like so many other professional sellers, Liz and Maryn fell into wholesaling accidentally the day a sales rep approached them at a show. Because they had been savvy about pricing from the beginning, they were able to quickly move in this direction. "In just a couple of months, that rep sold more at wholesale than I had sold all year in dog shows," says Maryn, "so we changed directions."

How Product Lines Change and Grow

AFTER SELLING AT a few fairs, your product line will gradually change in response to what craft fair buyers have told you or indicated through their purchase choices. Marie Slovek lives in South Dakota, where she says the rolling prairie is dotted with tiny white churches and little one-room schoolhouses. She sells her Prairie Moon Originals in local craft fairs ("local" meaning forty-five to seventy miles away), in nearby shops, and by mail to stores in other states. "I continually change from sewn items, to wood, to yard signs," she says. "Where I live, it's important to watch upcoming trends and market to them."

"Many people give up when they find they aren't selling their work," says bread dough artist Norma Rudloff. "Being willing to explore other types of craft ideas, however, will lead to many different opportunities and experiences." Norma started making dolls for sale in 1982. When the Cabbage Patch Kids® doll craze hit the market, she moved from doll making into salt dough ornaments and later switched to bread dough. She kept practicing her craft until she learned the secret to making miniature roses that look so realistic a bee would try to pollinate them. "I haven't found any competition after doing this for the past eleven years," she says. "My customers are intrigued with the realistic-looking bread dough rose arrangements I create. As more women work, they don't have time to create, but they do want to decorate their homes with handcrafted objects. I've learned that, to succeed in selling, you have to find your own niche and be different from everyone else."

Mary Lou Highfill has certainly found a great niche. At the age of sixty-four, she has become an authority on sunbonnets and pincushions—and you may be surprised to learn how much in demand she and her products are. "I started out making teddy bears, soft animals, pot holders, a sunbonnet or two—just a little bit of everything—until a show at the Kirkpatrick Museum in Oklahoma City," she says. "I had several sunbonnets among the teddies, so the Kirkpatrick center listed me as a heritage craftsman when the Harn Museum asked for a list of historical craftspeople. After doing a show there, I sold sunbonnets to their gift store until it closed. Then the town of Purcell asked me to demonstrate the sewing of sunbonnets at their heritage craft shows. Because the economy was bad in Oklahoma, and Barbara said in her newsletter that people buy practical items during hard times, I added some low-priced pincushions to my line. The Lace Guild bought all of them and asked me to join their group."

Today, Mary Lou sells to lace guilds all over the country, does sunbonnet programs all over the state, and says she feels like she is preserving an important piece of Oklahoma history. She is additional

proof of the message I pounded home in chapter 1, about how life leads us and why we have to take that first step if we want to get anywhere. In looking back, Mary Lou says she is amazed at how the "finger of fate" has kept pushing her along in new and exciting directions. Her pincushions, which once sold for $2, are now collectibles—a croaking "Victorian Bug-Eating Frog" best seller goes for $34.

© Mary Lou Highfill

Note: The addition of a sound can be a great sales-boosting gimmick. Mary Lou's pincushion line also includes dogs that bark and cats that meow. The noisemakers, coupled with her unusual choices of fabrics, have people grabbing them as fast as she can unpack them at a fair. "I can't begin to keep up with the demand for these products," she says. (I am currently encouraging Mary Lou to put her pincushion designs in pattern form so she can make more money in the future without working so hard.)

Craft shows that prove profitable tend to attract the same sellers and buyers year after year. When you return to a show that has been successful in the past, you must have something new to offer people who are familiar with your work. If you can't add new items to your product line, then you must at least change your colors, patterns, designs, or booth display so your work will look fresh and different to those who know you.

"Most of my customers are true collectors of my dolls, so I try to surprise them with new animal, angel, and Santa designs each year," says Jean Belknap, who diversified her line of full-size soft sculpture dolls with miniature versions that can be worn as pins.

"Each year you see the same faces and get to know the families," says doll maker Maria Nerius, who has done some shows regularly for the past fifteen years. "Many buyers who have my original work now add to their collections each year. Beginners need to be reminded that when they sell at a fair, they are not just selling a product, they are selling a little piece of themselves. When people buy from me, they're investing in me—they own a piece of me, not just a doll—and they have actually contributed to my success. I sell myself. I'm proud of what I do and I want to share that joy with someone else."

"Make yourself memorable to customers by giving them the best service you can," advises crafts seller and business writer Barbara Massie. "A satisfied customer does more to promote and build your business than anything else." Barbara says her wreaths always sell because the designs are unique to the materials used. What's amusing to her, though, is how wreaths she has designed and road-tested for decorating cars and trucks are sometimes purchased for placement in a cemetery because of their durability in all types of weather. Recently, a fireman asked her if her wreathes were weatherproof, and when she said yes, he bought one for the front of the fire engine. Now *that's* creativity!

Earlier I stressed the importance of always having something new to entice old buyers to buy again, but as your business grows, you're going to find that some items will just sell and sell, with little or no changes. Although Barbara Massie says she always finds something new to freshen her inventory, she has one item that has sold for ten years with no changes—the "Candy Mouse Container" pictured on page 83. It's about eight inches long and five inches high and sells for $5. Made of burlap, this product is always lined in a red and white patterned fabric appropriate either for Valentine's Day or Christmas. "I sell it filled with red and white candy," says Barbara, "but some people like to put miniature pine cones in it or use it as a flower pot holder.

It makes a great gift for a teacher or for someone in a nursing home or hospital."

© Barbara Massie

Barbara's mention of selling candy reminds me of a story Joyce Roark told me. She decided to expand her Loving Thoughts® line of sterling silver and gold-filled jewelry with the addition of jewelry boxes and other decorative boxes priced at $10. "We sold a few but there wasn't a lot of interest," she says. "So I decided to sell one jewelry box as a candy box. I put a dollar's worth of miniature candy bars in it, attractively arranged, and increased the price to $15. They sold at once, and I even had people fighting over the last box. We laugh every time we talk about the box that wouldn't sell for $10, but sold at $15 with the addition of a dollar's worth of candy. People sure are funny!"

Lessons Learned

THE MORE YOU sell, the more you learn. These craft fair sellers point to pitfalls you may be able to avoid:

"I underestimated the actual costs of doing my first show and overestimating the sales I would earn from it," says Susan Nelson, Cats 'N Stuff.

"From Barbara, I learned the importance of making a profit," says Rita Stone-Conwell. "In the beginning, I figured if I went home from a show with any money in my cash box, I was doing well. I never took into consideration product costs, time to produce, booth fees, and so much more. Now I include all that and always make a profit on every item I sell."

"I've learned not to believe everything I hear," says Jan Bonner. "The show banter from other crafters used to pressure me to do more and feel incompetent—basically stress. Now I try to positive-talk to myself to prevent panic attacks before large shows and I try to talk to, lunch with, and surround myself with positive friends. I also make more time for family."

"I've learned not to overproduce items when I am unsure as to whether there is a market for them or not," says Janet Middleton.

Norma Rudloff has learned to stick with her main supplier of dried materials because they sell only the best. "In trying to cut corners," she said, "I bought eucalyptus at a good price only to find it wormy."

"Don't count your eggs before they're hatched," says Trudi Clark, who makes

Custom Orders

Many craft fair sellers commented on the losses they suffered by not asking for a deposit on custom orders or special commissions. If you decide to take a custom-design order, remember that some people will order something, then decide later on they don't want it—after you have spent several hours and perhaps many dollars in materials. Either ask for a down payment sufficient to cover your actual costs (to be kept if the customer cancels later on), or make sure your custom-designed item is such that it can be easily sold to someone else.

"I've learned to always be paid up front," says Sondra Lucente, who creates custom "Family Portraits" of wood dolls dressed to represent a family. "I had a couple of orders that I completed with no money down. How foolish! I put many, many hours of love and creativity into each custom order, which did not have a market elsewhere. Now I simply express the need to be paid up front."

"When doing custom orders, be sure to obtain the customer's *signed approval* of the design," says laser engraver Ernie Ziegler, "and be sure to charge for any product samples you provide. Get at least a 50 percent deposit on all custom orders." Ernie also emphasizes the importance of charging what your product is worth—not what will be a bargain to a buyer.

hand-thrown clay wall pockets with inlaid lace designs. "Never count on money you haven't made yet, and don't think the next show is going to be as good as the last. Always save money." Trudi, who has worked full time at her craft since 1984, says she has learned not to get upset when no one is buying her work. "I'm just happy that I'm free to do what I want and don't have to be tied to an awful nine-to-five job."

Honing Your Sense of Humor

I F YOU DON'T have a good sense of humor before you begin to sell your crafts, you'd better hone it now because you never know what's going to happen at a crafts fair. "One *must* learn to laugh," says Marie Slovek, "or you'll never survive outside craft shows that feature lightning, wind, and rain." Rita Stone-Conwell recalls an unforgettable craft fair held on a farm. "The different aromas experienced at this show is something I will never forget!"

What most crafters recall, however, are the crazy things shoppers say to them or about them at a show. Susan Young, who paints custom ornaments and signs, remembers the woman who spent a lot of time at her booth browsing. As she was walking away, Susan heard her say, "I was doing this stuff when I was six years old." What's funny is that she later returned and bought $213 worth of products.

Once when Kay Owings was selling her macramé, a woman asked her to take a piece apart and put it back together again so she would know how to do it. Says Kay, "I sold her the piece and told her to take it home and take it apart herself."

"You've got to keep your sense of humor," says Bob Gerdts. "At a difficult-to-do show that included long hours and a rough load in/load out, Carol got upset when a browser said to her friend, 'Artists do this because they are lazy.' Some well-educated, advanced-degreed friends of ours encountered a woman who in front of them told her children, 'You better get a good education or you'll wind up like those people.' Another woman said di-

rectly in front of me, 'They need a better artist.' My favorite involves a lady who was looking at some of our eggs and asked if I had any less expensive ones. When I pointed some out, she replied, 'Yes, but they are not as nice as those more expensive ones.'"

Some shoppers insult craft sellers, others make them laugh. Cathy Neunaber, whose business name is Lasso the Moon, had a good laugh the day a customer wrote a check and made it payable to "Lassa the Mooso." Vicki Stozich designs and sells patterns and clothing for cement geese (the market for which is larger than you might believe). "I kept thinking this was a trend that would die out, but it just keeps growing and growing. I get a kick out of watching people's reactions to my designs at craft shows." she says. "Sometimes when they see one of my geese dressed up, they double over laughing." (Is this what you call getting a giggle from a gaggle of geese?)

When Dodie Eisenhauer isn't tipping over her town with tour buses from St.

Things to Ponder
Before Entering a Show

1. What expenses will be incurred for the show?

2. Can you sell enough to cover your expenses and make a profit? If not, will the experience you receive compensate for any financial loss?

3. How many people are expected to attend the show, and is your art or craft a "good fit"?

4. Do you have a wide range of products priced to fit everyone's purse?

5. How will you respond to inquiries from shop owners or other wholesale buyers?

6. Are you going to encourage custom orders?

7. What aspect of your art or craft could you demonstrate at the show?

8. Will you wear something to the show appropriate to your art or craft?

9. How are you going to keep track of sales at the show, and what kind of payment will you accept?

10. How are you going to wrap or package purchases?

11. Do your printed materials encourage bounce-back mail-order sales?

12. Are you set up to collect sales tax?

13. If your display is to be left overnight for any reason, have you considered the possibility of theft or damage? Do you need to buy any insurance coverage?

14. If exhibiting outdoors, will you be prepared for wind or rain?

15. If the show is a bomb, can you "pick yourself up, dust yourself off, and start all over again"?

Louis, she does an occasional retail fair to do some market research and get people's reactions to new products. She sells originally designed angel creations and other products made from screen wire that is first painted, then cut and creatively formed by hand. At a crafts fair in Missouri a woman commented, "I didn't know that plastic stuff came in all them colors." Dodie's daughter, who was manning the booth, patiently explained that it was screen wire, not plastic. "The painting is done with an air compressor that uses forty pounds of pressure," she emphasized. "It's difficult to paint because the air has to blow the paint through the screen wire so it doesn't get caught." After listening to this detailed answer the woman said, "Do you sell the air compressor?"

I'll close with a story of my own. Back in the 1970s, when Harry and I were attending a lot of traditional craft fairs, it seemed that everyone in the world was selling the same kind of pottery or ceramics and Harry was really getting bored with nothing but pots, pots, pots. At about the same time, we attended a play whose story line happened to be about a company that sold ceramics. As the owner was trying to explain the enormous diversity of the company's product line, actor Robert Morley interrupted with a line that brought the house down and had Harry laughing so hard he cried.

"Spare me the details," Morley quipped. "There are only two kinds of pots: those with handles and those without."

There is great healing power in laughter. It refreshes us, gives us hope, helps us overcome anger, releases pent-up emotions, and softens the blows life sometimes deals. It benefits our body by reducing muscular tension, and thus stress. A hearty laugh exercises the respiratory system and can even reduce physical pain because it releases endorphins, the body's natural painkiller. Without question, laughter provides important balance in our lives, and we can never get too much of it. So count yourself lucky if you're an art or crafts fair seller. Even when sales are bad, a show is bound to be good for laughs.

CHAPTER

CHAPTER
5

Home Shops and Sales

The one rule we always had in our house was *no clutter!* No one could leave anything lying around, whether it was school books, toys, or clothes. This is still an indispensable rule for the working mother. It lifts your spirit. Without clutter, a house always seems to look clean, even when you know that up on that third shelf you could probably write your name in the dust.

CAROL BERNIER, home-based shop owner, now retired

SELLING AT CRAFT fairs is a way of life for many artisans, some of whom spend much of their time on the road going from one fair to another with heavy stints of production in between shows. But what if you can't or don't want to travel to shows outside your area, don't want to wholesale, and can't find enough retail outlets for your work? Many sellers have found the perfect solution is to set up shop at home. This gives one the fun of retailing without the financial responsibilities and worries of a regular retail shop.

This chapter discusses how people generally sell out of their homes through

➤ a private studio or workshop (open to the public full time or by appointment only)

➤ "open house" sales (specific hours/ days one or more times a year; public invited, or by invitation only)

➤ home boutiques (one- or two-day events held one or more times a year; public invited)

➤ home parties (in owner's home or homes of others, by invitation only)

Private Studios and Workshops

MANY PEOPLE SELL from private studios and workshops in their home or an outbuilding on their property. Where zoning laws permit, individuals may elect to open year-round retail shops in their homes or other building on their property to sell their wares and possibly other products as well. (See the sidebar "Home Sales and Zoning Laws.") A full-time shop in your home, however, is not always a good idea. First, it may be difficult or impossible to attract enough shoppers to justify keeping a shop open all day every day; second, it will certainly disrupt your family life. "I sold from a home shop for awhile," says needlework designer Merrilyn Fedder, "but it interfered too much with family life so I eventually closed it and moved into mail-order selling instead."

Some people don't like to enter a shop in someone's home because they feel they are invading their privacy. If you live in a rural area, it may be difficult to attract buyers from town. As Kimberly Stroman Doffin learned, a shop's success or failure can turn on whether the roads are good or not. For over five years, she successfully operated a gift and craft supply shop in Hoskins, Nebraska. When she ran into lease-renewal problems, she decided to move the shop to their farm, putting it in a renovated granery. "That was a big mistake," she says. "I thought I could just continue business as usual, but for the first three years we had nothing but rain, and our muddy roads kept customers away. I finally closed the shop because it just didn't work."

The most successful home-based shops seem to be open to the public by appointment only. After college, when Charlene Anderson-Shea moved to Hawaii, she was doing cross-stitch as a hobby and eventually got seriously involved in weaving. For the last seven years of the nineteen years she lived in this state, she had a home-based studio and weaving shop open to the public by appointment only. "No one else in the state was selling weaving supplies," she says, "so I decided to sell my products and a line of weaving, spinning, knitting, and dying supplies as well. My ads indicated that people should call before coming, but this didn't seem to turn anyone off. In fact, people seemed to like getting the personalized attention I offered."

Joy Crouch used to sell products from their home, but now The Sheep Station is housed in a small warehouse on their farm. The Crouch family has been selling sheepskin products by mail since 1982—everything from sheepskin slippers, caps, and ear muffs to "Lamb Chop Puppets," "Thank Ewe Notes" and hand-carved leather belt buckles ornamented with sheep heads. "We raise sheep, and our business is the best way we have to both promote lamb and wool while at the same time make extra money," she says. "I do several shows a year, give talks here and there, and sell through a local craft mall, sharing a booth with a couple of other people who offer products compatible with mine."

From the middle of November through Christmas, Joy has what she calls a "Boutique by Appointment or Chance." "If I'm not here, one of the kids will open the shop," she says. "They've all grown up with the business."

When there isn't sufficient room to work or sell out of the home itself, people may turn garages into workshops or have a structure built on their property. Susan Young designed a 12 by 16-foot wood structure to be built in her back yard,

dubbed it The Peach Kitty Studio, and equipped it with all the comforts of home. (Because the structure is considered impermanent, she didn't need a building permit.) She works in her studio every day and visitors may stop round most any time, so long as they call first.

Susan publicizes her home shop with promotional newsletters to her local customer list and attractive flyers that include a map of where her shop is located and a list of items readily available year-round. "I post flyers locally and also hand them out at fairs," she says. "I also have a sign that can be hung on doorknobs in the neighborhood." (The easiest way to hang a sign on a doorknob is to punch a small hole in it and insert a rubber band through it, looping it through itself to form a hanger.)

Home Sales and Zoning Laws

Although some communities may prohibit any kind of shop in one's home, one- or two-day events such as an open house or holiday boutique may not be a problem since they are generally perceived in the same light as a garage sale. You don't need to hire a lawyer for advice, but do contact local zoning officials before you make plans to sell directly from your home. One boutique owner told me about a problem she encountered when she began to check into the legalities of home shows. The lawyer she contacted told her that as long as she used a private invitation and served only cookies and punch, such a sale in her home would be within the law. But she decided to go one step further. "Since I hold an occupational license to make and sell my crafts and greeting cards, I decided to get a final word from the zoning folks who issued the license," she told me. "Am I ever glad I did! I learned that in Caddo Parish in Louisiana, a home sale is totally against the law. If I had been caught holding such an event, I would have lost my business license. I can hold such a sale anywhere else (a public building), but not in my home."

Open House Sales

MANY SELLERS SUPPLEMENT their shop-by-appointment sales with one or two open houses a year. This is a great way to sell to friends and customers you've been dealing with for years. Depending on how you operate and advertise the sale, it can also be a good way to attract new buyers. The big advantage of an open house is that it can be held at your convenience in your own home, and it need be nothing more elaborate than setting up a special room as your display area and inviting a few friends over for cake and coffee. When I first began to sell, I invited a dozen friends over one evening in December and was amazed when they bought $100 worth of crafts (a lot of money in those days). That was all the encouragement I needed to walk into a local shop soon afterward to show the owner what I had to offer.

Lynn Smythe has sold her one-of-a-kind beaded jewelry this way in the past, in addition to selling through a few galleries, craft shows, and one open house a year. "Sales slump in the middle of the year, so I've found an open house to be a good way to move certain items in May and June," she says. She hands out her Dolphin Crafts business card at shows and sells year-round from her home-based studio by appointment only. (By printing a map on the back of her card that tells people how to find her studio, Lynn probably saves herself hours of time on the telephone giving people directions.)

China painter Ruby Tobey, who has had a lifelong involvement in art, has been selling her work at fairs, in consignment shops and her own annual open house for thirty years. Ruby now sends promotional newsletters to her customer list telling them which fairs she will be in and announcing the dates of her open house, usually held during the third week of November. She offers her newest drawings, watercolors, china pieces, jewelry, note cards, and the "Scribbles and Sketches" poetry books she has published over the years.

"This is just a special showing for customers, friends, and anyone they want to invite," says Ruby. "I move the couch out of the living room, set up a couple of folding tables and some extra display props, use my kitchen table as a pay station, and then sit nearby painting while people look. I might have only four or five people one day and maybe twenty-five or thirty the next. I'm open usually from 11 A.M. to 5 P.M. Friday and Saturday, and maybe one Sunday afternoon."

Holiday Boutiques

HOME BOUTIQUES PROVIDE an interesting and profitable alternative to selling at fairs or through local shops, and they can be held at any time of the year. Most people tie their events to a major holiday season, however, with boutiques around Christmastime being the most common and most profitable. This kind of sale, which costs little to arrange, is almost always a financial success— even in its first year, when everyone is learning as they go. A few sellers working together over a weekend can ring up a surprising amount of sales the first time around, and each time the show is repeated, sales will increase. (A boutique that features outstanding handcrafts quickly gains a great word-of-mouth advertising base, so every customer's name

Home for the Holidays

Holiday boutiques are generally presented by a group of crafters; but if you have a large inventory of finished products for sale and a nice house you'd like to show off, consider presenting a holiday boutique all by yourself. What makes this idea different from a simple open house is the volume of merchandise displayed, the amount of room occupied by the sale, and the kind of displays and decorations used.

After presenting their first Christmas boutique, Jean and Steve Belknap sent me a videotape of how their beautifully refurbished 117-year-old house looked all decked out for the holidays. I couldn't believe my eyes! My first thought was how long it must have taken to set up this display of Jean's beautiful creations and all the special Christmas decorations and lights in all the rooms.

"A friend and I worked on the house for about three weeks before the show," Jean told me. "We decorated seven Christmas trees, had lights strung everywhere, and we must have put a hundred nail holes into our walls. Crafts were displayed throughout the living and dining rooms, kitchen, halls, and upstairs bathroom. We closed off our bedroom and my workroom, however."

One reason it took so long to prepare the house for the sale was that everything personal had to come out of each room, lest people think these items were being offered for sale. "I emptied all my cabinets and shelves so I'd have room to display crafts," says Jean. "I think I must have carted at least ten boxes of dishes upstairs to the attic, including my large collection of Precious Memories figurines."

Steve manned the study, where people paid for purchases or just chatted over refreshments of cookies, brownies, cider, hot chocolate, and coffee. The sale ran for two weekends from 9 A.M. to 9 P.M., attracting over a hundred shoppers. "Sales were great," says Steve. "We sold nearly a thousand dollars worth of products and it was like a big family and friends party for two weekends. We placed an ad in the local paper and distributed flyers three streets over and two streets back. The response was so good that we expanded a few blocks for the second week. We're definitely going to repeat this event in the future."

on the group's mailing list adds to the profit potential of the next show.)

© Carol Carlson

Selling Through Boutiques Organized By Others

Some boutiques feature the work of a select group of individuals who have agreed to work together to put on a great show in one person's home or another. Often, however, such groups allow other crafters to sell in their boutique in return for a small entry fee (to cover advertising and overhead costs) and/or a percentage of sales, turning it into a temporary consignment shop.

Julie Peterson, Minnesota Naturals, designs and sells natural accessories made of birch bark and other nature items she gathers. "I find boutiques a perfect way to sell. I don't have the personality for selling at fairs," she says, "with all the hauling, setting up and sitting there for days. With a boutique sale, I just drop off my stuff and go back home to work."

Work-at-home mom Jana Gallagher agrees. "Since I have young children, I have found that sitting all day at the local craft fairs and arranging for babysitters can add unnecessary holiday stress for me and my family. Also, the atmosphere of the home shows is exceptional. There is nothing quite like walking into a home with the smell of cider and cookies flowing through the air and seeing beautifully handcrafted items just waiting to be taken home."

Jana designs and makes a variety of crafts and craft kits while also managing her information-based Web site. She sells at three boutiques each year, two at Christmastime and one in the spring. She was invited to participate in these shows because her work is unusual and complementary to the products of other sellers. "The nice thing about these boutiques is that there is no duplication of the type of products being offered, which means no competition for sales. As a result, my boutique sales are generally higher than they would be at a crafts fair of the same duration."

What sells best for Jana are products priced between $5 and $15, including sewn and painted items, gifts for teachers (who seem to especially like holiday boutiques, she says), and holiday decor. She pays an entry fee of $20 and a 10 percent commission on sales. Boutique sellers must complete an inventory sheet describing all items for sale, with prices noted. This is later returned with an indication of what has sold. "I've been averaging about $800 for a two-weekend show, but think I may be able to double this amount if I bring in more inventory in the future," she says.

PRESENTING YOUR OWN BOUTIQUE

Several things must be considered when you take the responsibility for presenting a boutique in your own home. First is the amount of extra work this will entail. If you're already too busy just making crafts for sale, be sure you have the time it will take to put on a great show. Even when you're working with several other people, it's easy to underestimate how long everything is going to take if you haven't done this kind of thing before.

Also consider the impact this kind of event will have on your family. If the boutique will be private (by invitation only) instead of open to the general public, you won't have to be as concerned about strangers walking into your home, some of whom could have less-than-honest motives for being there. Either way, you'll need to devise a good traffic plan to channel people in and out of your home without letting them walk *through* it. All personal items (except for furniture and lighting used to display products) should be moved out of rooms open to the public and the rest of the house sealed off from view.

Once time and family matters have been considered, you'll need to set up guidelines for the type of products that will be offered for sale, think of a clever name for the event, plan how to advertise it, decide whether crafters outside your group will be invited to participate, work out commission arrangements, figure out how to take payment, handle sales tax, keep records of inventory coming in and going out, wrap sold items, capture names for next year's mailing list, and so on.

© Carol Carlson

Legal Note: Boutiques usually have interesting names that lend themselves to publicity. If zoning is a problem, however, you may have to forego publicity or paid advertising in the local paper or on radio and attract buyers with a mailing to a select group of people, suggesting they bring along a friend. (See sample boutique invitation post card on page 96, available from E&S Creations.) If you want to distribute flyers to homes in your area, you can roll them up and stick them through a door handle or beneath a mailbox, or hang a sign on the doorknob, but do *not* put flyers directly into people's mailboxes. This is strictly against the law.

© Eleena Danielson

In planning and presenting a holiday boutique, there are no cut-and-dried rules for how it must be done, so you should develop your own plan based on how others operate, and the wishes of your group as a whole. Each event will be a learning experience of things that should have been done, not done, or simply done better. Expect conflict or disagreement within the group and resolve problems as quickly as possible, laying the groundwork for more successful shows in the future. Put maximum emphasis on creating a high-quality show because this will ensure good word-of-mouth advertising, the professional crafter's best marketing tool. At some point a successful holiday boutique is likely to outgrow its home environment and have to be moved into a community building such as a church or school. When this happens you'll have to look anew at what it costs to present the boutique and make any necessary adjustments in entry fees or sales commissions.

Keeping Neighbors Happy

The trouble with home sales is traffic tying up neighborhood parking places. This can annoy some people, so anytime you're planning a gala event likely to draw a crowd, do your best to placate residents and neighbors who may be temporarily inconvenienced. One boutique presenter suggests placing "No Parking This Side of Street" signs and giving special early-entrance passes to nearby neighbors. Subdivisions with deed restrictions may not protest a boutique or open house sale if it incorporates a benefit event, such as a raffle for one of their subdivision activities (pool or security fund, for example).

Seasonal Boutiques

ALTHOUGH HOME BOUTIQUES and open house sales are generally most profitable when held at Christmastime, such events do well throughout the year, whether tied to a holiday or not. Such sales do not necessarily have to be held in your house, either, as some of the following examples illustrate.

A SUMMER SHOW

Because there is such a glut of Christmas boutiques in her area, Susan Nelson decided to have a boutique in July in her sun room, which has a separate entrance. "The first year I invited seven craft friends to display with me, but the second year I decided to ask three friends only. I don't take a percentage of their sales, but they contribute to the advertising costs. With a mailing of 20 invitations to our best customers, a few signs, and a classified ad under 'Arts and Antiques' in the local paper, we attracted nearly a hundred shoppers, netting each of us about $100 for the weekend."

Some of the products offered were handwoven baskets, jewelry, cloth weavings, paper mache bowls, and beeswax candles, plus Susan's line of products for cat lovers, including pillows, tote bags, vests, and dolls. After being in charge of all the organizing details for this show, Susan said she felt "empowered—very much like I'd completed a college course on Introduction to Applied Retail Sales." Since this boutique wasn't given a special name or theme, I suggested that Susan try a "Christmas in July" show next time around, promoting it as "A great way to get a head start on this year's Christmas shopping."

© Susan Nelson

Note: Susan learned something from this event I've never heard about before. A friend who got her flyer told her she would be violating the law if she didn't post a sign at her "cash station" stating that sales tax was being collected on all sales. "I don't know if this is a city or state regulation," says Susan, "but it sounds like something people in other areas should check on."

A FRONT YARD SHOW

For the past six years, Yvonne Ward has presented her unusual summer open house in front of her house and on the driveway under a big tree. "We live on a busy avenue in a nice suburban neighborhood," she says, "and I simply sell to passersby and to friends and former customers who have received my invitation to stop by. I set up here exactly as I would at any craft show, using my canvas market umbrella to attract attention and displaying my products on beautifully decorated tables. The wrought iron fence in front of our property is great for hanging things and tying on balloons."

Illustration by Yvonne Ward

Yvonne is open from nine to five, and sets up chairs for people who want to sit and chat or have a cup of coffee with her. "This is a stress-free event for me because I can be at home with my son while I'm selling," she says. "There are no holiday boutiques in my area, and no one else around here does anything like this, so people always seem delighted by my display and my sales are always good."

Yvonne offers a variety of products priced from $1 (for bookmarks) to $50 for custom-designed albums or wreaths. She encourages custom orders, and smiles when she recalls some of the unusual things people have asked for. The owner of a bagel restaurant who admired her country wreaths asked if she could design a special wreath for them, so she dried and varnished a bunch of bagels and designed a unique wreath that now hangs in the store. Recently, a woman brought Yvonne a swatch of fabric and asked if she could make a fabric-covered diary, phone book, and photo album to match her living room couch. "You just never know what people are going to ask for," she says. "Being able to fill their special requests makes my work doubly enjoyable."

BOUTIQUE IN A BARN

Milo and Ruth Tuma have been presenting holiday boutiques on their New Prague, Minnesota, farm since 1979. They started with a small sale in their home and later moved the business to the barn. Their sales run on weekends over an eight- to ten-week period, and they move a considerable volume of merchandise taken on consignment from over 200 crafters. Because the Tumas live on a busy highway and advertise aggressively, they often attract up to 2,000 shoppers each weekend for both their Christmas and spring boutiques, the latter of which begins about the middle of March. "Our typical customer is a young married couple with two incomes," says Ruth. "Some people spend as little as $15 or $25, while others may buy up to $400 worth of furniture or decorative accessories."

BOUTIQUE IN A BLACKSMITH SHOP

Merrilyn Fedder designs primitive needlework inspired by Early American art, selling both finished pieces and a line of patterns called Hand Dids. After presenting several open house sales, Merrilyn changed gears and began to work cooperatively with nine other craftspeople to present three boutiques a year.

"We sell in a historic blacksmith shop in Meredosia, Illinois, that is owned by the father of one of the crafters in the group," she says. "Our sales are held in the spring, fall and at Christmas. Named Salute to Summer, Fall Festival, and Christmas at the Blacksmith Shop, the first two events are one weekend in length, the third, two weekends."

Merrilyn says these sales attract a lot of men because of where they are located. "Amidst all the antique tools displayed on the walls of the blacksmith shop, we display in gift-shop fashion a variety of primitive and folk art crafts that include needlework, patterns, dolls, candles, floral, dried, and herbal items. We gather tumbleweeds from the field, string lights, and add generous amounts of greenery.

The blacksmith sells some of his work and demonstrates in an area separate from the showroom. People really enjoy coming to a special place like this."

Don't discount the profit potential of this kind of sale if you live in a small community. Merrilyn says that each of their sales have grossed between $7,000 and $12,000. This is all the more impressive when you consider that Meredosia is a small river town "on the way to nowhere," as Merrilyn puts it. Word-of-mouth advertising coupled with ads in the local paper and a few flyers posted here and there is all it takes to draw a crowd and put tidy profits into these sellers' pockets.

AN ART RUMMAGE SALE

"It just kinda happened without us trying," says fiber artist Sandy Mooney about the Art Rummage Sale she and a bunch of friends started sixteen years ago. "We do this show every two years, and people just love it. We have cars up and down the road for miles with people standing in long lines to pay for items they have purchased."

The idea for this sale was born of necessity. Originally, ten artists had a bunch of stuff they couldn't sell at fairs and wanted to get rid of. Now Sandy says the group has grown to twenty-five. "We all have unsold items, things we're not going to make any more, things in outdated

Your Mailing List — Money in the Bank

When selling from your home, your mailing list will become an invaluable business asset and the key to continued success. Capture buyer's names from checks and ask visitors to sign a guest book with their names and addresses. The mailing list should be computerized and kept up to date with regular mailings. Keep a record of what individual customers have purchased, since this will signal buying trends and give clues about what to offer next time around. When making a mailing to announce a boutique, open house, or other home sale, estimate that about 25 percent of those mailed will actually show up. (Those who do come, however, are likely to bring a friend if you encourage this in your mailing.)

colors, things that don't have a market anywhere else. So we mark all these leftovers down 50 percent or more and people literally mob in here to buy them at prices from $1 to $200."

This outdoor show is held over a weekend in August or September, in and around Sandy's back yard and garage. "I put up my craft fair canopy alongside the garage, which is where everyone pays for the merchandise displayed inside. I print 3,000 postcards or more, giving a supply to each artist in the group for handing out at fairs. We also mail to our huge pooled mailing list of buyers. People hang on to the postcard invitation for dear life because we have a rule that you can't get into the show the first night without an invitation in hand. We probably had a thousand shoppers at the last show and grossed around $18,000."

Not bad for a bunch of "leftovers"! Sounds like a great idea that crafters, as well as artists, could duplicate almost anywhere with similar success.

Home Craft Parties

DURING THE 1980s, manufacturers began to market their craft and needlework kits and supplies through individual crafters via home parties, working similarly to the way Tupperware operates.

It didn't take craft sellers long to realize that handcrafts could be sold this way, too.

In addition to being money-makers, home parties (also known as party plan selling) can be a lot of fun and a great way to break the monotony. "My demonstrations are usually on a week night," says one seller, "so my husband stays home with the children. It gets me out of the house to meet new people, talk about my favorite topics, have cake and coffee, and a good time in general."

BASIC HOME PARTY CONCEPT

Generally, a crafter arranges for a party to be held by a friend, who in turn suggests the names of other people who might like to hold a party. The party hostess supplies refreshments, receives a nice hostess gift, and earns an agreed-on commission on sales (in cash or credit toward purchases). Special bonuses are given for any additional parties booked. The crafter plans the presentation, brings products for sale, and supplies any necessary game or door prizes.

The success of this type of selling depends on being able to continually find new hostesses who will bring in new guests to buy the merchandise. The amount of money that can be made with the party plan method will vary depending on (1) the kind and price of merchandise

being offered for sale; (2) the number of people in attendance; and (3) your sales ability (demonstrating is easy—skillful selling takes practice). One party plan professional told me it took at least ten people to make a sales demonstration profitable for her, but whether this will hold true for you depends on the price range of your products and how readily they sell.

If you run out of people to host parties, think in broader terms. I recall one party plan seller who expanded by presenting parties for fund-raising groups, schools, scout groups, and churches. A group would host a party open to the public and receive a percentage of the crafter's sales of finished items and kits she manufactured.

SELLING OUTRIGHT OR BY SAMPLE

Selling outright at a home party is the preferred way to operate. "You sell the item, collect the money, and go home," says one party plan presenter. "Women like the idea of outright sales and, having been prepared by the hostess, always come ready to buy. By selling outright, you make the work easy for your party hostess, who won't have to deliver orders to buyers after the party."

Legal Note: The only problem in working this way is that letting people walk out of the house with merchandise in hand might be a violation of local zoning laws. (In some communities sellers may take orders for later delivery, but are not allowed to make direct sales in the home. Be sure to check on this point.)

If you decide to supplement your sales by taking orders for products made by other crafters, be careful to work with reliable people who can fill orders on time and duplicate the display samples they have given you. When you sell by sample, you must later deliver orders to the hostess, who in turn will deliver it to buyers, collecting any money due. (Most sellers ask for a 50 percent deposit on custom designed or personalized orders that can't be sold to other buyers.)

BEST PRODUCTS TO SELL

Trudi Clark creates hand-thrown clay wall pockets with inlaid lace designs. "I tried home parties with little success," she says. "It was backbreaking work, hauling products in and out—like setting up for a craft show, but for three hours only. Even then, it might have been worth the effort if enough people had come, but more times than not, a hostess would promise that thirty people were coming, and I'd arrive and find only five people there. I also had little patience with people who came to the parties more for the fun and games aspect than to actually buy."

Ideally, in addition to offering proven sellers at a home party, you will offer products that can be easily transported. As Trudi's experience shows, there's a big difference between moving a few cases of jewelry items or other lightweight products and setting up a heavy display of pottery. The selection of party hostesses is important, too. Make sure they understand that a crafts home party is not the same thing as a Tupperware party. Emphasize that the main "fun aspect" of your presentation will be an entertaining talk or demonstration with an opportunity to place orders for custom-designed products or buy merchandise on display. If you're going to play games, at least devise some that draw attention to your products. (See the sidebar "Crafty Home Party Games.")

HOME PARTY OPTIONS

If you like the party plan concept but lack sufficient products to sell or professional crafters with whom you can work, consider working with companies in the craft, needlework, and scrapbook industries who sell a variety of products through home parties. (Check the yellow pages under "Hobby-Home" to see if any companies are listed under "Home Demonstration Merchandise.") In deciding which

Crafty Home Party Games

While working on your crafts, I'll bet you've often muttered under your breath that people have no idea what goes into the making of one of your products. If so, this could become the basis for an interesting home party game.

Consider making up a list of questions relative to your work, and give prizes to those who give you the best answers. Begin by selecting a particular item and passing it around the room. Ask people to write on a slip of paper their answer to a specific question. For example, if you sell beaded jewelry, you might ask people to guess, simply by looking at the product for a moment as it is passed around, how many different kinds of beads (or total number of beads) you have used to make the product (like guessing the number of jelly beans in a jar). If you sell colorful items, such as stitchery, quilts, or painted products, ask people to guess how many different colors of threads, fabric designs, or paints you have used. At the very least, this will make people see your work with new eyes.

A home party game could also be used to gather market research information. Crafters are often too close to their work to see things that are obvious to their buyers. Getting just one new and innovative use for an old product could enable you to sell it to a whole new audience in the future. Select one of your items—a lovely container of some kind, perhaps—and ask people to list all the ways they might use it in a home or office setting or as a gift. To excite their creative imagination, offer the product itself as the prize.

You might also bring a new product to the party that you haven't yet named. First explain the many ways you envision people using it (emphasizing all your product benefits in the process), then ask people to write on a slip of paper a clever name for the product and award it as the prize to person who gives you the best name.

By devising creative games such as those above, you will not only get new ideas but help people gain a greater appreciation for your handcrafts.

products to sell, be sure to compare the offers of several companies, noting especially (1) start-up costs; (2) cost of promotional catalogs, brochures, delivery bags, and so on; (3) when party merchandise must be paid for; and (4) local competition (ask if there are other dealers in your area).

Home Party Success Tips

OPAL LEASURE, KNOWN as "The Apron Strings Lady," wrote the book on home parties—literally. She began her successful Apron Strings Country Home Parties business in 1993, at a time when her family needed extra income and she needed to be at home with her five children. Earlier, Opal had explored craft fairs and malls as outlets for her products; but, surrounded by competition, she figured there had to be a better way than this to sell. She liked the idea of selling through home parties but, lacking a definitive guide on how to sell crafts this way, she first had to devise her own operating methods. She never imagined then that her business plan for home craft parties would become the outline of a how-to book she would write and publish a couple of years later.

"I sold thousands of my own products at hundreds of parties over a five-year period," she says. "Initially, I was doing eight to twelve parties a month, then it calmed down to where I was doing only one or two a week. I never gave less than four parties a month." Since Opal lives in Madera, California, a place she calls "a little country town," I wondered how she could find so many people who wanted to host parties without eventually running out of both hostesses and buyers.

"It was easy," she says. "Some church ladies held the first parties, and because they were so pleased with the unusual hostess gift I offered, everyone wanted to have a party. In time, many of the people who came to my parties became friends with one another, and every time I scheduled another party, they wanted to come again because they knew I would have new products they could afford to buy. I can think of at least thirty women whose houses are literally filled with my crafts and floral items."

Okay . . . finding party hostesses is no problem, but how can you give a dozen parties a month and still have enough product to sell? "This wasn't so easy," says Opal. "My smallest child wasn't in school yet, and I had to keep my priorities straight, giving time to my family when they needed it. That usually meant working after everyone was in bed. I was so tired all the time because I would often plug in my glue gun at 6:30 a.m. and be up until one the next morning finishing up a batch of products. I couldn't have done it without my husband's help. After coming home from his job, he would often work until midnight designing and cutting out the wood shapes I needed for my various projects."

© Opal Leasure

Opal's product line included a wide variety of country-painted novelty wood items, birdhouses, wreaths, and floral arrangements. She tried farming out some of the work, with little success. "The products didn't look the same," she said. "My customers knew my style and didn't want to buy anything unless I had personally made it myself." Although nearly 80 percent of Opal's sales were for custom-designed items, she never charged extra for this, reasoning that different colors or a little personalization didn't take any more time. "It was this personalized service that made my sales so good in the first place," she says. "By letting people look through my thick photo albums with descriptive information and prices, they could literally design their own products to fit special decorating or gift needs, picking favorite colors or having someone's name added to a gift item."

HOSTESS GIFTS AND SALES COMMISSIONS

Opal believes women wanted to present her home parties because she offered a great hostess gift. "It was usually a big floral arrangement few of them could afford to buy," she says. "Although it had a perceived value of $30 or more, it cost me less than $4 in materials. To get the gift, however, the hostess had to buy at least $15 worth of my products during the party and generate at least $110 in sales for me. This gave a hostess a goal to work toward and a reason to invite the kind of people who were interested in buying products instead of just playing games. If I sold more than $110 worth of products at a party, I gave the hostess 10 percent of my sales in the form of 'Party Bucks' that could be used to buy other products. Additional Party Bucks or bonuses could be earned by showing my photo albums to friends, family or coworkers and by getting other people to have parties of their own."

Opal says she could have a profitable party with as few as eight people, but she often had at least twenty. "Once, though, one woman had a party and no one showed up," she recalls. "She was so upset she went into the bathroom and cried. I gave her a hostess gift anyway, and she later showed my craft albums to friends and generated several orders for me."

Opal stresses the importance of always being kind and considerate to people. A trusting soul, she never asked anyone for a deposit on a custom-designed order because everyone who came to her parties were friends of the hostess. "I thought it would be an insult to ask for money in advance," she says. "No one ever failed to pay me, and in taking thousands of checks over a five-year period, only two of them bounced, and both were later made good."

In her book, *The Apron Strings Lady Did It . . . So Can You!,* Opal describes home craft parties as a way to sell "handcrafted down-home goodness," noting that pioneer women traded and sold their handcrafts to each other, too. "They sewed, baked, and made dried floral arrangements. This was a wonderful down-to-earth part of history. The same knitting together of women happens at home craft parties today—a special bonding—as women brag about their children, explain a new craft idea, share low-fat recipes or tell why they need dried baby roses in the spray that graces the portrait of a beloved grandmother."

Opal stopped giving home parties in 1997 to pursue her lifelong dream of continuing her education and becoming a teacher. "People keep asking me when I'm going to give another party," she says, "but I enjoy having some time to myself now to once again explore my craft. Last year, after decorating the office at my children's parochial school without charge, people began to see me in a different light. Now I am often asked to decorate people's homes and offices. I'm fortunate that the preschool program I work for practices Creative Curriculum, because teaching craft techniques to children is the perfect job for a professional crafter like myself."

Once again we have a wonderful example of how life leads creative people to first one thing and then another. Opal is working on a new book now and converting her successful craft designs into patterns she can sell by mail along with her home party guide. "I love the thank-you letters I get from women who are using my book to build a successful party plan business," she says. "Life is good."

CHAPTER 6

Selling Through Shops, Galleries, Malls, and Other Outlets

When you find a product line that people like, is easy to make and inexpensive to buy, you'll have discovered the way to make a small business become larger quickly. It's then easier to sell your product line in more places because, by design, you choose to sell a lot, and a big seller is what every retailer wants.

PHILLIP COOMER, Owner, American Craft Malls

I F YOU DISLIKE person-to-person selling or are unable to travel to shows, selling through shops and other retail outlets may be more to your liking. The fact that this kind of selling can be done entirely by mail is a big plus for anyone who lives in a rural area.

Note that there is a difference between selling "through" retail shops and stores and selling "to" them. Selling "through" such outlets means that you will offer products at retail prices and collect that amount *less applicable sales commissions or rental fees* retained by a shop, gallery, craft mall, or store. When selling "to" shops, you will be offering products at wholesale prices, a topic discussed in the following chapter. Your primary "selling through" options include (1) craft consignment shops; (2) art galleries; (3)

craft malls and rent-a-space shops; and (4) local retailers, service providers, and institutions.

Craft Consignment Shops

L IKE FAIRS, CONSIGNMENT shops offer beginners a good way to find out what will sell and what won't. Many prefer this method of selling because there are no deadlines and no stress involved in producing goods. The main disadvantage of consignment selling is that a great deal of capital can be tied up in inventory, especially if you are working with several shops.

"I like working on consignment," says Kansas artist Ruby Tobey, who has worked with two or three consignment shops at a time for the past thirty years. "It fits my way of life. I need the money for supplies, but I don't have to have a regular income. I like to try new things, and shops are more willing to try new things if they don't have to pay for them first. I don't like to be obligated by orders for so many dozen of any item. To me, it is much easier to do the work as I like, send it out to my shops, and around the first of the month, several checks come in."

Ruby has worked with one shop in Wichita for over twenty-five years, but she says it's getting hard to find new consignment shops. "So many seem to be closing," she notes. After years of painting barns and windmill designs—which were profitable, but became boring in time—Ruby is now doing mostly florals. "I recently found an art gallery in New Mexico that is happy to have my china painting because it's so different from other merchandise in their shop."

DIFFERENT METHODS OF OPERATION

Years ago, consignment shops were all the same: sellers left merchandise on consignment, and when it sold the shop took a percentage of the sale and gave the rest to the seller. In the 1990s a new breed of consignment shop emerged, due in part to the popularity of (and competition from) craft malls and rent-a-space shops. Today, in addition to taking a higher percentage of sales, many consignment shops also charge small overhead or management fees or require sellers to work in the shop one day a week to lower the

amount of sales commission they must pay. Whereas it was once standard for craft consignment shops to take a sales commission of 25 to 30 percent of sales, most take between 40 and 50 percent now. Worse, I'm beginning to hear stories about consignment shops that are charging monthly rental fees of $20 or more on top of their regular sales commission. In my opinion, a shop must either be a *consignment shop* or a *rent-a-space shop.* Shop owners can't have it both ways, and crafters simply won't stay long in a shop that operates this way.

I do sympathize with retailers who are being faced with ever-increasing overhead costs, but craft sellers have too many marketing options today to give 50 percent of the retail price (or its equivalent in

sales commissions, management fees, or monthly rent) to a consignment shop without exploring other options first. A 50 percent commission makes sense if you create high-priced, one-of-a-kind items you can't easily sell elsewhere, but if you produce multiples of your products, you will make more profit selling them at fairs, holiday boutiques, open houses, craft malls, or rent-a-space shops. If you produce in even larger quantities, wholesaling may be the best way to go since a 50 percent discount and payment in thirty days is standard in this industry.

FINDING GOOD OUTLETS

All shops are different, each with a personality of its own. One shop can sell what another cannot, so your goal as a supplier is to give the right product to the right shop. Begin by checking out nearby shops and stores you can call on personally. When you're ready to market your work by mail, subscriptions to craft business magazines such as *The Crafts Report* will lead you to shops and galleries interested in art or craftwork on consignment or at wholesale prices. The book *Crafts Market Place—Where and How to Sell Your Crafts* (Betterway Books) may be a helpful resource. It includes listings of craft malls, retail stores, galleries, and other outlets across the country. Publisher Adele Patti also issues an annual *Directory of Craft Shops & Galleries* that lists the names, addresses, and merchandise needs of nearly 1,000 shops across the country that might welcome contact from you. (Most of these listings also include the date the shop opened, so you have some measure of its stability.)

A search for craft shops and art galleries on the Internet will also turn up outlets you may want to explore. A warning, however: Many information-based Web sites contain inaccurate information because the site owners are simply lifting information (illegally) from other sources without bothering to check its accuracy. One of Adele Patti's competitors, for example, is offering a list of shops online, many of which are out of business, according to her research. "I've also noticed that many people in chat rooms who are opening new shops are asking crafters to consign with them," she adds. "And in the same breath, they are asking others for advice on how to succeed in a craft shop business. This is not where I'd want to put my work."

Some craftspeople believe it unwise to consign work to any shop that isn't at least two years old. But, as you probably realize, many shops could not open at all if not for craftspeople willing to consign to them. Since many new consignment shop owners work especially hard to make their business a success, you should not automatically refuse to consign in a shop just because it's new. Check it out carefully and test it with a small consignment of merchandise to begin with. Given time, it could become an excellent outlet for you.

I recall a new shop owner who said she could not have opened if not for consignment, and her words echo those of many shop owners I have communicated with in the past. "We intend to try just as hard as all the others," she said, "and depend on getting trust from craftspeople. With this, our very good location, and a lot of hard work, we believe we will succeed. I love what I'm doing, and I love most of all the people who are taking a chance with me by consigning these first years while we find our market and get the experience we need to make the right buying decisions."

Notice that this shop owner said she loves "most of the people," not *all* of them. She and scores of other craft shop owners do not love consignors who make promises and don't come through; those who send shoddy merchandise after promising good things; or those who take their work from a shop shortly after consigning it because they need more merchandise for a crafts fair. "People like this are breaking their contract with me," the shop owner says, "but I let them do it because I know they'll be nothing but future trouble for me. I hate the sight of my 'blackball file' that holds the names of people who do marvelous work but can't be trusted."

Clearly, consignment selling is a two-way street and a cooperative form of marketing that cannot succeed unless both parties work together.

CONSIGNMENT AGREEMENT

Although it is an advantage to be able to sell to consignment shops by mail, it's a disadvantage, too, in that you cannot personally see what's happening to the merchandise you've entrusted to a shop. Having a good consignment agreement with the shop will eliminate many problems, however. (See the sidebar "Consignment Laws.") Make sure you

Consignment Laws

A standard consignment contract is not enough to protect one from loss in the event a shop goes out of business. If a consignment establishment goes bankrupt, consigned goods may be subject to the claims of creditors and be seized by such creditors unless certain protective steps have been taken by consignors. Several states have consignment laws, including California, Colorado, Connecticut, Illinois, Iowa, Kentucky, Massachusetts, New Hampshire, New Mexico, New York, Oregon, Texas, Washington, and Wisconsin. If your state isn't on this list, call your state capitol to learn if such a law exists. If so, note that each state's law offers varying degrees of protection, so be sure to learn exactly what is covered. Some state laws protect "art" only, excluding protection to items that fall outside the area of painting, sculpture, drawing, graphic arts, pottery, weaving, batik, macrame, quilting, "or other commonly recognized art forms."

know the following things before you place goods on consignment and spell out each of them in a written agreement (if one isn't offered, write your own):

1. Name and telephone number of owner (not just the manager, in case the shop closes owing you money or the return of merchandise)

2. Pricing (whether your suggested retail price can be changed)

3. Sales commission and other fees

4. When payments will be made

5. Type of sales reports you will receive

6. Who pays shipping costs (generally, the consignor must absorb both the cost of insuring and shipping merchandise)

7. How merchandise will be displayed (note any special requirements you have, such as "avoid putting in direct sunlight," or "keep in locked display case to avoid shoplifting," and so on)

8. What insurance coverage the shop owner offers consignors (generally none —refer back to "Insurance Tips" in chapter 3).

Art Galleries

IF YOUR WORK is more art than craft and carries a high price tag, you may find, as Charlene Anderson-Shea discovered, that you can get ten times the price for something in a gallery that you can at a fair. "I used to sell my handwoven jackets for $150 at fairs, until I learned I could get $1,200 for them when they were featured in the window of an art gallery," she says. (Because buyers have been conditioned to pay more for art than craft, sometimes you don't even need to change outlets to get higher prices. Merely calling a product by a different name will often justify higher prices in buyers' minds—for example, "jacket" vs. "wearable art.")

If you're trying to build a reputation as an artist (fine art or craft), selling through art galleries is clearly the best way to go. Although Barbara Otterson wholesales her Dreamweaver line of fine silver jewelry (you met her in chapter 2), she finds galleries a great outlet for her higher-priced, one-of-a-kind creations. "I'm looking for gallery outlets now for my new line of silver and glass goblets," she says. "I have a production line I can wholesale or take to art fairs, but my real interest is not in how many pieces I can turn out because this defeats the purpose of being an artist. Eventually, I want to move into one-of-a-kind work only."

I learned a great deal about how art galleries operate by speaking with Karen Boden, owner of Sable V Fine Art Gallery in Wimberley, Texas. "I opened my gallery

A. Bidwell

in 1992 because I wanted out of the corporate rat race," she told me. "Because I have many friends who are artists, I visited art galleries whenever I traveled, often placing their work in galleries by showing slides. I finally decided to open a gallery myself, settling in Wimberley because it's a beautiful area known for the arts." Pieces in Karen's gallery are priced anywhere from $5 to $40,000, her largest sale to date.

WHAT ARTISTS SHOULD EXPECT OF A GALLERY

In checking out a gallery, Karen says artists should find out what kind of advertising it does and ask for artist referrals.

"Ask if they place regular newspaper or magazine ads, do promotional mailings, and keep clients informed of what's new. Artists who consign with a gallery should expect promotions of their work, such as special exhibitions or shows. Because my gallery specializes in glass, we do an annual glass show as well as monthly themed shows. For example, in one show, we feature artists who create functional items with unique form; in our fun-and-games show, we feature kinetic sculptures, chess sets, kites, happy paintings, and so on. Our landscape show features outdoor sculptures, fountains, and landscape paintings. Our most popular event, however, is the annual children's art show. We accept all art submitted and give children a real contract so they'll learn something about selling and dealing with galleries."

A good gallery will also have salespeople who know the artists they represent, and understand the techniques of their work. As Karen puts it, "We show the work of over 200 artists from around the world and know everything about the artists we represent. When we sell their art, we're selling them."

WHAT A GALLERY EXPECTS FROM ARTISTS

Promotion works both ways. If a gallery is promoting your work, you must also promote the gallery. Don't try to make all sales yourself. Any time you exhibit at a fair, print flyers listing the names and addresses of shops and galleries that carry your work. *And make sure your retail prices on work at shows is the same as the prices on your work in a shop or gallery.* "Art has a certain value," says Karen. "It isn't worth less just because it's being offered at a fair. The worst thing an artist can do is put something in a shop or gallery at a certain price, then turn around and sell the same piece of art for half that amount at a show or directly from their studio."

There are several things an artist should *not* do when trying to get into a gallery. "Don't just drop in unannounced,"

Karen warns. "Always call or write first to make an appointment with the owner. When you bring in your work, don't bring anything that can't be left. When I look at an artist's work, I immediately think of people who might like to buy it. Often, however, artists say they can't leave anything because they need it for an upcoming art show. I don't want leftovers from a show. Also, an artist should not try to remove their art from the gallery to put it in an art show. I'm perfectly willing to send one of my clients to a show where I know one of my artists is exhibiting and let the artist take 100 percent of that sale. However, if the artist tries to arrange to sell future pieces to the client without referring them back to the gallery, I would consider that a breach of our professional relationship."

CONTRACT PITFALLS

Artists may be able to get 60 percent of the retail prices in some galleries, but most work on a 50/50 basis, and some have switched to a 40/60 basis, with the artist getting the short end of the stick—all the more reason to shop for new gallery outlets with care. "Make sure you have the opportunity to take special commissions, and to modify the gallery's standard contract if there is something in it you don't like," Karen advises. "The biggest pitfall relates to pricing and the amount an artist receives when a work has sold. If you consign work to a gallery and specify the wholesale price, that is what you will receive—even if the gallery has sold it for more than double. What this actually means is that the gallery can mark up your pieces as much as they want, pay you the amount you specified and keep the difference. Most artists will do better if they stipulate in their contract that they want a specific percentage of the retail price or the amount the piece sells for," Karen emphasizes. Example:

Wholesale Contract	Retail Contract
Gallery prices piece at $200	Gallery prices piece at $200
Artist wants $75	Artist receives $100
Gallery makes $125	Gallery receives $100

When you are ready to sell through art galleries, look for advertisements in art magazines. Some, like *Art in America* and *Southwest Art,* publish annual listings of galleries across the country and the kind of work they show.

Craft Malls and Rent-a-Space Shops

WHEN RUFUS COOMER opened America's first craft mall in Azle, Texas, in 1988 and continued to open additional malls over the next several years, he dramatically changed the way craftspeople sold at the retail level. It didn't take long for entrepreneurs across the country to copy this profitable

carol carlson

retailing idea; unfortunately, many did not adhere to the high standards Coomer set for the industry. Hundreds of independently-owned malls opened in the 1990s, similar to what happened in the 1970s when consignment craft shops were the rage and everyone was opening a new one thinking this was a great way to get rich quick. Countless consignment shops have since come and gone, and now we are seeing the closure of many independently owned craft malls as well. (Later in this chapter, you will find tips on how to limit your financial risk in such outlets.)

Although craft malls and rent-a-space shops are similar in the way they work with individual sellers, there are some interesting differences. First, rent-a-space shops tend to be smaller than malls. Second, merchandise is generally displayed not in individual booths, but areas within a shop, such as specific shelves, corner nooks, counter sections, wall space, and so on. Third, mall sellers decide how their wares will be displayed, whereas rent-a-space shops display goods to suit themselves. Finally, sellers in rent-a-space outlets may be able to lower the sales commission taken by the shop if they agree to work in the shop for a certain period of time. These differences aside, however, sellers should view craft malls and rent-a-space shops with the same financial eye.

RENTAL FEES AND LEASE ARRANGEMENTS

Sellers rent booth space in a mall, paying a monthly rental fee that varies considerably depending on the size of the display space, number of sellers, the town or city in which the mall is located, and the owner's "greed factor." Whereas you might be able to rent space in a small shop in a small town for as little as $20 a month, space of a similar size in a large mall in a major city or tourist area might command $350 or more a month. On average, however, expect to pay at least $85 to $150 a month. In addition to monthly rental fees, malls (and rent-a-space shops as well) also take a 4 to 8 percent (or more) sales commission, and sometimes tack on a service fee of 3 or 4 percent for handling credit card sales. (See the sidebar "Craft Mall Arithmetic," page 123.)

ADVANTAGES AND DISADVANTAGES OF MALL SELLING

When the craft mall craze hit the country, thousands of creative people saw only the advantages of selling in craft malls and their first cousins, rent-a-space shops. They could:

➤ sell in a shop atmosphere without the problems of consignment selling or the stress of wholesaling

➤ conduct market research on new products, test prices, and experiment with the best way to display and sell individual product lines

➤ have control over how their wares were priced and displayed

➤ enjoy year-round sales and regular monthly payments without the hard work involved in doing craft fairs and shows

➤ deal with craft mall owners and operators entirely by mail

➤ practice being a shop owner without the tremendous financial risk and responsibilities of store ownership

What many crafters didn't realize until after months of selling experience were the disadvantages of craft mall selling. This kind of merchandising is more costly than selling through fairs and consignment shops, and it is not recommended to amateur sellers who aren't savvy about pricing or the marketplace in general. Anyone who is having difficulty selling at craft fairs isn't likely to do any better in a craft mall or rent-a-space shop, where profits will be considerably less after all expenses have been deducted. On the other hand, products that "sell like hotcakes" at fairs or home boutiques may move quickly in malls as well.

Products in malls tend to be handled a lot, so you should expect to lose some merchandise not only to handling, but to shoplifting. (Note: The shoplifting problem can be solved by buying inexpensive security tags or labels that can be attached to merchandise. These are imbedded with a magnetic strip that sets off an alarm if people leave the store without paying for them.)

COOMERS MALLS

Coomers, Inc., is the nation's largest retailer of American handmade crafts, gifts, and decorations for home and offices, with sales in excess of $20 million a year through its thirty-two malls in nine states. "Our most successful sellers tend to sell in ten or more malls, some doing more than $100,000 a year in sales," says Dave Curran, President of Coomers. "Although some of our vendors enjoy a sales-to-rent ratio of 10, on average our crafters make 2.8 times their rent in sales. Some of our best sellers have tested their wares in several of our malls, enjoyed great sales success, and then decided they could do even better as wholesalers," Dave adds.

You can move a lot of merchandise through craft malls if your prices are

A Wholesaler's Secret

Rita O'Hara started selling dough art products at crafts fairs back in the mid-1970s. She sold with success for twelve years, until her husband died and she put everything on hold for a while. Later, when a friend who did ceramics brought Rita some terra cotta clay to play with, she got interested in selling again. "I found I could do the same designs and products I'd always made from dough art," she says, "only now I could get higher prices for them."

Rita has since remarried, and the way she operates her Stonewares business has also changed. Although she has been wholesaling her products since 1990, she also sells at retail through fourteen Coomers malls. She has good reasons for this, and readers who have locked themselves into wholesaling only should pay attention here.

"Selling through malls helps to even out our work load," Rita explains. "When we don't have a wholesale order to work on, we can ship to the malls, which are also the perfect place to sell things we *like* to make versus those we *have* to make for our established wholesale accounts. This gives me a chance to just play a bit and design and test new products. If we decide not to wholesale them, they will always sell in a mall."

All craft wholesalers tend to get orders of tremendous size that must be delivered within a specific time frame. Shops start to order in July for their big Christmas selling period and, by

right. Successful sellers confirm that the hottest-selling items are likely to be priced between $5 and $6, followed by items up to $15 or $20. Coomers says their average shopper spends $34, however, which means that higher-priced items in the $40 to $60 range will also sell in this market.

Can you successfully sell a single product through craft malls? You bet! Jim and Camille Miller, owners of Musical Treasures, sell 20,000 music boxes a year through all thirty-two Coomers malls, fifty-three other craft malls, and assorted fairs across the country. "We used to sell shadow boxes and miniatures at craft

October, craft wholesalers will have shipped most of their orders. Assuming terms of net thirty days, that means a craft wholesaler's income pretty much dwindles to nothing by November. Rita's craft mall strategy is a perfect solution to the cash flow problems that can develop at a time like this. "By selling through craft malls," she says, "we can make sales right up to Christmas, cranking out products as fast as we want. This also helps the lull we normally have in June before the new rush of Christmas orders comes in."

Rita's big sellers, both at wholesale and in the malls, are bisque hearts and other differently-shaped items scented with pure essence oil. "The clay holds the fragrance for a long time," she says, "but we also sell tiny vials of essence oil that can be used to freshen products and keep them delicately scented indefinitely. We mix our own terra cotta clay, cast, fire and decorate all products ourselves," she says. Items in her line are priced from $3 to $15, and one crafts mall booth may contain up to $10,000 worth of inventory. (Rita's sales-to-rent ratio is four or more. Anything less than this, she says, would be unprofitable for her.)

Notice how Rita keeps saying "we?" Her second husband, Jim, is a partner in her business. Although he had never done crafts before he married Rita, he now does all her casting work. "He was a quick learner," says Rita. "He retired recently from his job as a mechanical engineer and he's not concerned about being bored." (Sounds like another one of those "I need a little help here-honey" stories, doesn't it?)

fairs," says Jim, "but then I got this idea for a music box and found it just right for sale through craft malls."

Their product, a 3 by 3-inch music box that retails for $12.95, is beautifully wrapped in designer wall paper or gift wrap and ribbon, and is never meant to be unwrapped but simply given as a gift just as it is. Over a hundred tunes are available, and each box is labeled on the bottom with their business name and name of the tune. The boxes are displayed in small booths that cost between $35 to $85 a month, depending on where a mall is located. "We've been in only one of the eighty-five outlets we sell in," says

Jim. "We do everything by mail. Each of the malls sets up a display for us, and we get weekly reports of what has sold so we know when to ship in a new supply of products." Jim and Camille still like to do craft shows, but now they sell only their boxes. "We've found that anything priced under $20 will sell well at both fairs and in craft malls," they say.

Clearly, one key to success in craft mall selling is keeping your booth well stocked. If a mall isn't giving you weekly reports of what has sold, you won't know when it's time to restock your booth. Through its Internet site, Coomers has made it possible for their vendors to quickly access sales and inventory figures any time they wish. "About 3,000 of our vendors currently check sales daily, saving up to $100 a month on phone calls to each of their outlets," says Dave Curran. (To check out Coomers Internet site, go to www.coomers.com.)

AMERICAN CRAFT MALLS

Two of the first Coomers malls in Azle and Burleson, Texas, are now known as American Craft Malls and are owned and managed by Phillip Coomer. The success of these two malls has prompted Phillip to open three additional malls, one in Oklahoma City and two in San Antonio. "I plan to keep expanding my business," says Phillip, "but I have no intention of opening up stores all over the country. Instead, I am offering my services as a consultant to entrepreneurs who want to open a mall of their own in other areas."

Phillip was the first mall owner to promote his crafters with a site on the World Wide Web and, to my knowledge, he is the only mall owner who runs full-page color ads to attract buyers to his craft malls and online Web site. "The secret to success in running a craft mall," says Phillip, "is to make your crafters successful by delivering buyers for their products."

American Craft Malls' vendors have the capability of monitoring their sales and inventory figures online through the use of a vendor I.D. number and secure password. In addition to benefiting from Phillip's aggressive advertising program, crafters who sell through any of his malls can also get a free home page on his Professional Crafter Web site (www. craftmark.com). "You don't have to have a computer to sell through my online site," Phillip emphasizes, "and we take no commissions on online sales. All we need are photographs of products the crafter wants to advertise online. We scan them into the Web site and add the descriptive information provided. Depending on how a crafter wants to work, buyers can place orders by phone, fax, e-mail, or with an order form they can print out and mail with a check. If a crafter wants to accept credit cards as payment, but does not have merchant status, we can run credit card sales through our store but must charge 10 percent of the sale for this service."

REMOTE STOCKING PROGRAMS

Most craft malls offer a "remote stocking program" that enables crafters to work with them entirely by mail. This is a good alternative for sellers who live in rural areas where such sales outlets don't exist, and it also enables sellers to more easily match their type of products to the right buying audience. Working this way, however, does increase selling costs, and there are no guarantees that every mall will do a good job of displaying your products or keeping it properly stocked.

A couple of years ago, when Beverly Durant was working full time at her craft, she was selling thousands of her small angel dolls a year in 35 craft malls, most of them out-of-state. Initially, she loved the idea of working with malls by mail, and let them set up and maintain her display. In time, however, sales dropped in these remote malls, and Beverly began to focus on selling through malls within a hundred miles from home. "Most mall owners try to do a good job, but many lack design

sense and don't do a good job of reporting back when additional merchandise is needed," she says. "I've learned the importance of personally maintaining my booths with regular visits to a mall."

Avoiding Craft Mall Pitfalls

WITH NO GUIDEBOOKS on how to start and successfully operate a craft mall, everyone who has ventured into this field has been flying by the seat of their pants, making up their own rules as they go along. That's why mall owners today all have different operating methods, and why it's so important for sellers to ask certain questions before entering into a business arrangement with one of them. Prior to renting space, visit a mall several times to observe its method of operation and number of shoppers. Talk to as many vendors as possible about how sales are, whether there is a high-theft problem, and whether payments are being made on schedule.

A woman who was hired to run interference between the owners of a craft mall and its exhibitors during the last two weeks it was open told me to advise my readers to ask the following questions before signing a mall contract:

➤ What is the owner's full name, work and home addresses, and phone numbers?

➤ What other businesses does this individual own?

➤ How long has the mall been in business, and how many other malls are in this area?

➤ Do the cars parked outside belong to clerks or customers?

➤ Who has access to the products placed on display in the mall?

➤ Who can end the contract, and how much notice must be given?

➤ Is the notice period sufficient for me to retrieve my merchandise?

Most malls ask vendors to sign a lease for three to six months. In the event your sales are poor, be prepared to lose this money and chalk it up to experience. You might be able to limit your risk by entering a mall at the height of its selling season, namely Christmas. Jana Gallagher, who has a Web site through which many crafters network, says she is hearing the same thing from everyone. "Craft mall sales are good over the holidays, but for the rest of the year, it's hard to sell enough to make this kind of selling profitable. If I were trying a mall for the first time, I'd try to get in around October to cash in on the holiday seasons of Halloween, Thanksgiving, Christmas and Easter."

TIPS FOR MINIMIZING FINANCIAL RISK

Here are six other things you can do to minimize your financial risk when dealing with the type of outlets discussed in this chapter:

1. Select established malls with a good reputation—independent malls recommended by other crafters or one of the malls in the Coomers chain of stores. (Although some Coomers stores have closed for one reason or another, they've never left crafters holding the bag. They simply place a vendor's unsold merchandise in one of their other outlets.)

2. Carefully read any consignment or lease agreement you sign with a shop or mall owner. Know what you're getting, and what you're not. Pay particular attention to commissions and rental fees being charged, service fees, and security systems or other protection against shoplifting.

3. *Always* get the name, address and telephone number of owner of the shop or mall. If it should close with your merchandise locked up inside, you will need to report this person to the proper authorities.

4. Don't rent space in more than one craft mall or rent-a-space shop until you see if this kind of marketing works for your products and you are sure you can make enough sales to offset monthly rental fees.

5. When consigning to a new shop, limit the number of items until you have established a working relationship with the shop and see that payments are being made on time. Instead of putting all your work into one shop, spread it around in two or more outlets, and never put more merchandise in any one place than you can afford to lose.

6. Don't rely on shop owners or managers to keep track of what you send to

Craft Mall Arithmetic

Before signing a lease with a new mall, check to see how much traffic it has and then do a little arithmetic. Let's say a new mall opens in a small community, offering 200 spaces to local crafters at an average rental fee of $95 per month. At full capacity, the owners would figure to gross $19,000 a month or $228,000 a year. This may sound like a good way to get rich quick, but it doesn't work that way. If a mall can't attract enough buyers, its crafters won't stay. If everyone in a mall this size made even twice their rent in sales—and I'll bet a lot of sellers don't do this well—the mall would have to sell $38,000 worth of crafts every month. For sellers to make four times their rent (which is the minimum professionals say is needed for a good profit), the mall would have to sell $76,000 worth of product every month, or more than $2,500 a day. If a mall's average sale is $25, to sell $38,000 worth of crafts every month, it would need to pull in an average of fifty buyers every day.

Some sellers are realizing sales of ten times their booth cost, but I believe most sellers will be lucky to get three or four times their rent in sales. In other words, if you are paying $40 for space in a small craft mall, you would be doing well to have sales of $120 to $160 per month. If you were paying $150 for space in a larger mall, you would need sales of $375 to $500 per month. To sell at this volume, however, you might need to display three or four thousand dollars' worth of merchandise.

Barbara Brabec, *Handmade for Profit* (M. Evans & Co., 1996)

them on consignment or for placement in a craft mall exhibit. Keep your own records and carefully monitor the inventory in all your outlets so you'll know at a glance the value of your inventory in each place, which items have been paid for, and money you expect to receive in the future. If you don't do this, you'll never know if you're losing merchandise to shoplifters or what you're owed if a shop or mall suddenly closes.

Craft Mall Failures: A Sad Reality

ALTHOUGH I THINK craft malls are a great way for many artists and professional crafters to sell, I am disturbed by the number of malls that have come and gone in the recent past. Many crafters have lost hundreds or thousands of dollars' worth of merchandise when craft mall owners have stolen out of town in the dead of night. Although such closures probably make the local news (especially when there is evidence of fraud), few are publicized nationally, so crafters in one area may not be aware that similar things are happening in other parts of the country. Often, mall owners have taken not only the money owed to crafters for

the last month's sales plus their initial deposit, but sometimes their unsold merchandise as well.

In 1997, when I asked readers of my "Selling What You Make" column in *Crafts Magazine* to give me a report on mall closures in their area, I was astonished by what they told me. "The craft mall trend seems to be dying out in Southern California," Frances Driesbach reported. "In the last six years, my mother and I have sold our crafts through four different malls in the San Diego area that are now closed. Although we were given a week's notice to get our stuff out of the first one that closed, the owners filed bankruptcy and we never saw our last month's commission or rental deposit. A second mall in a busy shopping center closed after only two months when the manager reportedly lost her lease. We did well in another mall in a resort area until the owner decided to go to work full time for another company. In the last mall that closed, we had our best sales ever, but the owners decided to move out of state. We've concluded that either craft mall owners don't make much money running the malls, or else this business attracts a lot of flaky people. I can't think of another small business that has so little staying power."

Jeanne Walker of Des Moines, Washington, reported that half a dozen malls had closed in her area. "There are just too many shows and too many shops for the amount of buyers here," she says. You might think the best malls to consider would be in tourist areas, but a chat with Norma Jean Tosh in Alcoa, Tennessee, suggests otherwise. "Because so many tourists come through this area, a lot of people apparently thought it would be profitable to open a craft mall or shop," she says. "But in the past year, I can think of at least two dozen malls and shops that have quickly come and gone. There are a lot of tourists, but not enough to support this many stores." Discouraged by the losses she has suffered in malls that closed, Norma, like many other crafters, is moving back into consignment shop selling.

Joan Bleakly, a member of the Tucson Arts and Crafts Association, reported a similarly bleak picture in her area. "Six stores have come and gone, with five owners creeping away in the dark of night," she said. "The most recent closure was due to the owner's failure to pay rent and crafters had to hire an attorney to get their merchandise back."

It's too bad someone didn't start a national database of mall owners that have gone belly-up, because some of them have sneaked out of one town only to pop up in another to run the same scam a second time. For example, a reader in Franklin, Pennsylvania, sent a May 28, 1997, clipping from *The News-Herald*

about a former crafts mall owner who was placed on probation for five years, during which time he must pay back almost $34,000 stolen from crafters. Ironically, this man is reportedly facing similar charges in three other counties in the state, where he walked away from malls owing vendors there at least $75,000. That's chicken feed compared to the five mall closures in Tucson, however. Classified as embezzlement by the District Attorney's office, losses to these craft mall vendors reportedly totaled nearly a half-million dollars.

Although Beverly Durant is one of the most experienced craft mall sellers I've met, she hasn't been able to avoid losing money in malls. In January 1997, three Texas malls owned by the same individual suddenly closed without warning, leaving Beverly and hundreds of other crafters holding the bag. "The owner simply locked the stores and sneaked out of town," she reported, adding that she was out nearly $1,500. "Crafters not only lost their security deposit and December sales, but all the merchandise left in the malls as well."

In January of the following year, Beverly called again to report that another mall she had been selling through for five years had closed, filing bankruptcy. "Why do they always wait till December to close up and steal away?" she wonders. The answer is obvious: Christmas is the best selling season of the year, and any mall owner in trouble is going to milk the mall for every last Christmas dime it might yield. (If it's nearing Christmastime, and you're getting uncomfortable vibes about the financial condition of a mall you're in, it might be smart to remove the bulk of your merchandise—especially expensive items—just before it closes for the holiday. You can always restock after the first of the year if everything looks rosy.)

Although no one has kept track of the number of malls that have come and gone in the past few years, the annual *Directory of Craft Malls and Rent-a-Space Shops* first published by Adele Patti in 1995 offers an interesting perspective. Of the 138 shops and malls listed in the first edition, 25 percent of them were no longer in business a year later. Of the 234 listings in the second edition, 130 were new. Adele, who was gathering data for a new edition of her directory as I was writing this chapter, said people are still opening new malls and rent-a-space shops even as others are closing. "I think many small mom-and-pop craft shops and independently owned craft malls are struggling to survive," says Adele, "but I can't put my finger on what's causing this. Maybe there are simply more sellers today than there are buyers."

I hope most of the bad apples in this industry will soon be gone, but given the history of craft malls to date, you should stay alert to signs that a mall might be in trouble. Look for such things as (1) less than 75 percent occupancy; (2) crafters pulling out; (3) little or no advertising being done; (4) few shoppers in the store; and (5) late payments or poor accounting of sales.

"Paychecks arriving late is the foremost indicator of a mall in trouble," says Patricia Krauss, author and publisher of *Selling in Craft Malls.* "Other signs are an obvious lowering of standards in the type of merchandise being offered for sale. A lot of stores start being quality conscious, focusing strictly on handmade products; but as time goes by and they realize they have a lot of spaces to fill, they lower their standards. They promise in the beginning they're not going to be like the competition, but in most cases, within a year they are just like the competition because of the pressure to fill space."

Patricia has personally visited over 200 craft malls across the country as part of the research for her book. "I've walked the aisles, talked to anyone I could find in each store, and observed the different way malls operate. The most successful stores are located in tourist areas, in a busy shopping center, or on a well-traveled main street with good foot traffic. Crafters should look at other businesses near the craft mall and ask themselves if these stores are likely to draw the kind of people who are interested in buying crafts."

Other indications that a mall may be in financial trouble, Patricia says, are stores without a permanent storefront sign. "Signs are expensive in a shopping center, and if a store has only a temporary banner, it probably means they are undercapitalized. Pay attention, too, if there is a reduction in staff or the number of hours a store is open. This probably means fewer customers."

If you are caught unawares, and a mall closes owing you money or the return of your merchandise, immediately report the situation to the Better Business Bureau in the city where the shop is located. Also notify the Consumer Fraud Division of the District Attorney's office in the county where the shop is located.

Unfortunately, state laws that protect consignors do not cover craft mall sellers and, to my knowledge, no regulatory agents (aside from attorney generals' offices) are taking any note of craft mail failures. Thus your chances of recouping losses here are slim to none because unethical mall owners who skip town usually owe not only crafters, but tax authorities as well—and you can guess who's going to have first dibs on any money that is ultimately retrieved.

Local Outlets for Art and Crafts

I HAVE OFTEN been surprised by the innovative marketing methods some crafters have used to sell their work, not to mention the unusual outlets through which they sell. Here are examples of local outlets through which you may be able to make good sales.

MEDICAL OFFICES

A toymaker once told me how she sold toys of all kinds simply by approaching clinics in her area and asking if they would like a donation of toys for their waiting room. All they had to do was post a sign so patients could order duplicates of any toy a child liked. Sondra Lucente operates in a similar manner to sell her custom-made "Family Portraits" of wood dolls tastefully dressed to represent the family.

"My placement of appropriate samples in dental and medical offices, along with a stack of brochures, has generated several orders," she says. "A dentist's office may show a dentist holding the hand of a child having his or her first tooth pulled. In an OB-GYN reception area, the sample may be of a pregnant mom holding on to a sibling or cradling a newborn baby. My prices run from $35 to $160, depending on the size of the family depicted. Because I've been stung on a couple of custom orders, I now ask for a deposit of 50 percent from people I know and payment in advance from all others."

© Sondra Lucente

As the mother of adult twins, Sondra's business is aptly named Empty Nest Collectibles, and she especially enjoys doing twins and triplets. Many of her customers have come through word-of-mouth advertising as a result of networking with other families of twins and attending the conventions of organizations such as Mothers of Twins, and Triplets, Moms, and More. "I get a lot of unusual requests," she says. "Recently a woman in the military sent me a sample of her uniform, saying she wanted to be pictured as a pregnant mother in fatigues. And a psychologist I met at a twins convention wanted a replica of herself and her twin sister as children in pigtails for a gift for her mother."

SCHOOLS AND HOSPITALS

If you're involved with a school in your area and have a line of products that would be of interest to teachers, ask the principal if you may set up a display in the teacher's lounge to sell your products in return for donating a percentage of your sales to a special school fund.

One enterprising seller, upon learning there was no gift shop in a nearby hospital, was given permission to set up a display for a few days at a time to sell to employees and visitors in return for a donation of 15 percent to the auxiliary department. After raising $1,300 for the hospital after only five shows, she started looking for other hospitals in her region that might be interested in this idea.

RETIREMENT CENTERS

Here's a great market for anyone who has products of interest to seniors who need gift items but may have difficulty going shopping. "Selling here may be as easy as asking permission to set up a table of your wares, and you may not even have to pay a commission on your sales," says Joyce Roark, who sells in several facilities in her area between October and December. In addition to selling her jewelry line, she also offers to repair or modify jewelry pieces owned by the residents (adapting earrings, adding chains, changing clasps, and so on).

Joyce emphasizes that a presentation in this market needs to be benefit-oriented. "Explain why having your products in the center will be helpful to residents, saving time, money or stress," she says. "Because people with arthritic hands have a hard time wrapping gifts, I have increased sales by offering a gift-wrapping service."

RETAIL SHOPS AND SERVICE PROVIDERS

Although they can't be considered craft shops by any stretch of the imagination, many retail shops seem to be picking up on the rent-a-space concept and making a little space available to interested sellers. The key to success here is offering a product that complements other products in the shop. Garden or floral shops, for example, might be interested in any art or craft related to flowers.

Some sellers have discovered that any store with a big window is an open invitation to sell crafts. This idea works especially well in small towns where everyone knows everybody. You might place a terrific display of products on consignment that the store could sell for you in return for an agreed-upon sales commission. Or maybe you'd prefer to rent some window or counter space to exhibit certain custom-design items that could be ordered through the store in return for a sales commission to the owner. (See the sidebar "Equine Artist's Marketing Strategies.") Many crafters have worked up profitable arrangements with beauty shops, who may sell gift items through the shop for a 25 percent sales commission. Some have talked local hardware store owners into giving them a shelf to display hand-painted kitchenware and other home accessories. Restaurant owners might be interested in floral arrangements. Realtors and large businesses in the area might buy products for use as client or corporate gifts.

Clearly, your opportunities for sales at the local retail level are limited only by your imagination and aggressiveness in looking for new selling opportunities. As I was putting the finishing touches on this chapter, I received yet another example of innovative marketing from Susan Young. Recently, while working a temporary office job, she sold $100 worth of crafts to coworkers simply by handing them a flyer with illustrations of several of her new and inexpensive fall craft items. Indeed, opportunities to sell crafts are everywhere!

Equine Artist's Marketing Strategies

Leslie J. Miller has been painting in several mediums for fifteen years, often doing dogs, cats, people, and houses on commission. When she added horses to her line, she dubbed herself an "Equine Artist" and designed the charming logo shown here of a playful young horse painting a canvas.

Leslie has found feed stores and tack shops to be the perfect out-let for her equine artworks. "These stores attract only people interested in horses, and many of them sell sideline items such as art, jewelry, cards, and other gift items," she says. "If the shops I approach are local, I make an appointment and take along a framed sample of my art and photographs. If shops are outside my area, I send a special promotional package I've developed."

Either way, Leslie's selling method is the same. "I ask if they would be willing to display a piece of my artwork with a sign bearing my name and address so interested people can contact me for a commission job. Many of these stores are happy to do this kind of thing for nothing, but I always offer a 10 percent commission and pay more if necessary. I always place prices on the piece I leave so potential customers have an idea of the rates I charge (one price framed, another unframed). If someone buys the sample, I automatically pay a commission to the shop and replace the painting with a new one." (Leslie's prices start at $100 for a small black-and-white drawing and increase depending on the art medium, size of piece, and type of frame. Her highest-priced work to date was a $6,000 painting sold to a corporate client.)

If Leslie doesn't want to leave a piece of finished art for some reason, she uses a counter display card instead. "This is a colorful matboard with a mounted photograph of the subject type (dog, child, home) I am marketing. My sales statement with contact information is attached adjacent to the photo."

Leslie's focused marketing strategy has been highly successful. "If you can be businesslike while also being laid-back enough to be a friend of the shop's owners and representatives, the contacts you will make are astounding. Many of the clients I have gained this way become repeat customers. One woman commissioned me to do a head portrait of her dog. A few months later, her husband wanted a full-body portrait of his wife's childhood pony as a surprise birthday gift. Still others desire combinations of, for instance, a child and a dog, or the child and a pony. When I have successful examples such as this to show, they ultimately result in a lot of queries, and usually some wonderful commissions."

© Leslie J. Miller

Moving into Wholesaling

Our attitude has been to let the business grow as our expertise grows. In review, we feel that has saved us from making big expensive mistakes (we have made lots of little inexpensive mistakes). We have not overextended ourselves either financially or in our ability to produce. As soon as we are ready for each new expansion, the opportunity always appears.

LIZ FYE AND MARYN WYNNE, Flytes of Fancy

IF YOUR ORIGINALLY designed handcrafts are selling well at fairs, consignment shops, craft malls, or holiday boutiques, this is a good indication that wholesale buyers are likely to be interested in your products, too. There is much more to wholesaling than just being able to produce products in quantity, however. You must also have a keen understanding of the marketplace itself and a good knowledge of selling, promotion, packaging, and display. Above all, a successful wholesaler must be savvy about pricing, adept at han-

dling business and office management details, and good at organizing work to be done.

Since the topic of wholesaling crafts could fill a book by itself, this chapter can present only a brief introduction to the topic and a discussion of the barriers crafters must break through before they can do this kind of selling. By showing how others have gradually moved from selling at craft fairs into wholesaling to various markets, I hope to convince some of you that the profit potential of your art or craft is greater than you think.

Breaking Wholesale Barriers

T O BREAK INTO wholesaling, you must first break through three big barriers that commonly hold most crafters back from this type of selling: the attitude barrier, the pricing barrier, and the production barrier. Let's take a closer look at the first two now.

THE ATTITUDE BARRIER

Many crafters automatically pass on wholesaling because there is too much "artist" in their nature. "I would get bored making the same things over and over," says one crafter. "My enjoyment comes from making unique, one-of-a-kind items." Craft professionals who are trying to make a living from their work can't afford to think like this, however. Surprisingly, it is often possible for creative people to have it both ways. You may recall Barbara Otterson's remark in the last chapter about how she makes a living by wholesaling her production jewelry line, but satisfies her artistic desires by creating one-of-a-kind pieces that are sold at higher prices through art galleries.

Some professionals, whose first love is designing, may decide to focus on designing and marketing while leaving much of the actual production work to employees. This is the route Dodie Eisenhauer of Village Designs has taken. "After selling at craft fairs for a while," she says, "I broke into wholesaling by taking my line of screen wire products to a wholesale gift show in Dallas. I came home with $4,000 worth of orders for my angels, baskets, bows, flowers, and ornaments—a lot of business for someone who had previously sold only through craft fairs."

Dodie has since added a line of vine wire products to her line. I laughed when she told me she never goes anywhere without a pair of long-nose pliers and a spool of wire in her purse. "Whenever I'm stuck anywhere for more than five minutes, I start playing around with the wire to see if I can design something new my workers can produce for me," she says.

THE PRICING BARRIER

The topic of pricing is actually part of the crafter's "attitude barrier" because craft fair sellers always say, "Why should I sell my products at half the price when I can get full price for them at a show?" What most of these crafters don't understand, however, is that they are already selling at wholesale because their prices are too low to begin with.

Many crafters who sell only at craft fairs mistakenly believe the sales experiences they have here are indicative of buyers everywhere. But craft fair shoppers are a breed unto themselves, and they are not representative of the kind of buyers who traditionally buy in fine shops, stores, or mail-order catalogs. *Never assume that the retail prices you've placed on your crafts are the highest prices you can get.* Craftspeople who live in rural or depressed areas often underprice their products so local buyers can afford them. In many cases these same products offered to wholesale outlets in major cities would sell for two or three times as much. Urban sellers also tend to underprice their wares, mistakenly basing them on the size of their own purse and what they'd be willing to pay for such items.

If a craft fair product isn't underpriced to begin with, it can often be changed or redesigned in some way to permit increased production at a retail price that's high enough to allow for wholesaling. For example, a woodworker might make decorative shelves out of inexpensive pine wood for sale at fairs, knowing there is a limit to how much things will sell for in this market. But shelves of the same design made in a more expensive wood, such as walnut or oak, might easily wholesale for the same price the woodworker is now getting for the pine shelves and take less time to finish besides.

"You simply can't sell the same products at shows and in shops," says teddy bear maker Jan Bonner. "I don't try to wholesale low-priced bears at all but reserve these for the retail market. The lowest price I would put on a bear to be wholesaled is $45. Sometimes I produce bears in different sizes, selling a 9-inch bear at fairs and a 12-inch bear in stores. Or perhaps I'll dress them differently or use different furs. A lot of bear makers make a particular bear for a particular store at a particular price."

Just Change "Retail" to "Wholesale"

On closer inspection, you may find that your main problem in wholesaling lies not in pricing itself, but in your lopsided attitude about business and marketing. In fact, many crafters could break into wholesaling simply by changing one word on their price list: turning "retail" into "wholesale." That's exactly what Randall Barr did. In 1993, after having bypass surgery and deciding it was time to quit the oil business, Randall turned to crafts to have something to do in his spare time. He designed a line of "Time Flies" Birdhouse Clocks, started selling them at craft fairs, and suddenly found himself working around the clock (in more ways than one) to fill all the orders he was getting. Surprisingly, an ad in a consumer crafts magazine brought Randall more new wholesale accounts than retail buyers, and by 1995 he was selling 6,000 clocks a year, most of them at wholesale.

"I moved into wholesaling simply by doubling the prices I had been asking for clocks at fairs," he says. "I could have sold 10,000 clocks in 1995 if I could have figured out how to make that many," he says.

Cash Flow Problems

Cash flow problems are always a concern of craft wholesalers. First you need some money to advertise or support your wholesale promotions. Then you need money to buy supplies in advance. Then, depending on when customers want delivery (and the terms you are offering), you may have to wait weeks or months for payment. (See the sidebar "Five Questions Buyers Ask at Trade Shows.")

"You can put only so much money into a particular effort until you make more money," says Maryn Wynne, "so we're always limited by the reality of how much we can afford to put into a particular venture. This means not only being able to afford the costs of normal advertising and promotion but being able to buy all the raw materials needed when you get an exceptionally large volume of business."

While many crafters pay retail prices for all the supplies and materials they use to make products for sale at retail, the only way to break into wholesaling is to cut material costs by buying everything at wholesale. (Refer back to the discussion of this topic in chapter 2, which explained how to find needed supplies at wholesale prices.) One of the most important things you should do as soon as you start your business is establish credit with suppliers. Lacking supplier credit, hopefully you will have it with your banker, who may give you a short-term loan. (If the customer stalls payment, the unpaid invoice may serve as collateral for a loan.) Although the interest rate on credit card loans is high, having a card or two with several thousand dollars' worth of borrowing power could prove to be a lifesaver at a time like this. In fact, a surprising number of entrepreneurs have launched or expanded businesses on credit card power alone.

Since running a manufacturing company was never Randall's goal, he stopped making clocks in 1997 and is now licensing his designs instead.

Liz Fye and Maryn Wynne's approach to setting wholesale prices was similar to Randall's. While exhibiting at a dog grooming show, an interested sales rep asked them for their wholesale price list, which they didn't have and had never given any thought to. "We went home, played around with several different pricing formulas, and finally came up with what we thought were reasonable wholesale prices that would yield us a good profit," says Maryn. "The rep liked them and took on our Flytes of Fancy line. As it turned out, our wholesale prices were basically the same as the retail prices we'd been using at craft fairs. Today we wholesale mostly to pet shops through several reps."

If you need further proof that you're already selling your crafts at wholesale prices and don't know it, consider Jean and Steve Belknap's experience. After entering QVC's "Quest for America's Best" competition in 1995 and winning a spot on its Home Shopping Show, the Belknaps ended up with an initial order for 600 of Jean's "Tyler the Giraffe" dolls. Previously, this doll had been offered at craft fairs for $29, but the Belknaps decided they could wholesale it to QVC at $23. QVC offered it to 50 million viewers at $43.75—almost double (plus shipping and handling). Within minutes, they had orders for 600 dolls. "I had no idea I could get this kind of money for this product," says Jean. "To see 600 dolls sell in minutes on national TV blew my mind. It would have taken us an entire year to sell that many at craft fairs."

The Production Barrier

THE FEAR OF being unable to produce in quantity is the third big barrier crafters have to get past before entering the wholesale arena. The thing to remember here is that you can always control quantity either by limiting the number of products offered at wholesale or selling selectively to a limited number of outlets. As doll maker Maria Nerius puts it, "I only wholesaled what I knew I could produce and make money at. I sold designs for items I knew I couldn't make much money from. You have to be very logical."

Although you may worry that some-one will want several hundreds items, most shops and stores will probably order in quantities of one to three dozen at a time. By getting your feet wet in whole-saling first to small shops and stores, you will learn whether you are capable of fill-ing larger orders or not. (The only time you are likely to get a huge rush of orders is when you go to a major trade show or promote to a huge national market, such as that served by a mail-order catalog house or home shopping network.)

"Ours is a labor-intensive business, but we don't worry about being able to fill orders because we can control the volume of business we get by controlling the amount of advertising we do and the number of sales reps we use," says Maryn Wynne. "Being in control is what business is all about. If you market more, you have to produce more. The only difficult time is when you get a big order unexpectedly. As micro business owners, we naturally feel compelled to fill orders no matter what, unlike big businesses who have no qualm about not doing this."

MOVING FROM CRAFT FAIRS TO TRADE SHOWS

Former craft fair seller Deb Otto urges professional crafters to give serious con-sideration to wholesaling for two reasons. "First, because stores buy six months in advance, trade shows are heavy in Janu-ary/February and June/July, which are normally slow periods for crafters. This is a good way to recoup after retail Christ-mas sales have died down, and do some good selling before it's time to start all over again. Second, when you do a trade show, you get advance information on what's going to be hot at craft fairs two or three years later, so you can be the first to bring a new idea to your neck of the woods. Anytime you do a big show, be sure to take a qualified adult representa-tive with you so you can have time to walk the show and just see what's out there. I've learned a lot from trade show exhibitors, who are very open-mouthed about their success so long as your prod-ucts do not compete with theirs. Often they will take new wholesalers under their wings and teach them the ropes, sharing information you won't be able to get any other way."

Deb has been wholesaling her prod-ucts since 1984 and also selling them at retail in her own shop since 1994. She accidentally stumbled into wholesaling when she was a new mom looking for something to occupy her mind. "I made a stiffened burlap basket with a rope han-dle for my husband's aunt," she said. "Upon taking it to the local florist to fill with flowers, she asked me to make eight baskets for her, then twenty, then forty, then more. A couple of years later, after selling the baskets and other items in local craft shows, I met a friend who suggested I read *Creative Cash.* That gave me the idea of selling my basket as a pattern and kit. Then a sales rep who saw me at a crafts fair asked me to make baskets she could sell to her wholesale clients. Suddenly, I found myself doing cash-flow forecasts and net worth statements so I could get a bank loan for supplies. Then I began to train half a dozen women to make baskets for me."

An image from Deb Otto's "From the Hand of Hannah" framed print and notepad line. She signs "Hannah" in memory of her grandmother R. Hannah Bantel, who encouraged her business endeavors from the beginning.

See what I mean about one thing leading to another when you least expect it? Today Deb wholesales a line of sweatshirts, T-shirts, and framed prints, and owns her own retail outlet, Henri's. Opened in mid-1993, the shop was first housed in half of an old hardware store in a nearby town and later moved to a strip mall in Storm Lake, Iowa. In mid-1995 Deb leased a 4,000-square-foot building on main street, turning half the upstairs into a retail store with a stock room and two dressing rooms. The rest of the building was turned into Deb's art studio, storage space for inventory, and a shipping room.

After selling to a few wholesale accounts in earlier years, Deb entered the big-time wholesale arena in 1994 by exhibiting at gift shows in Kansas City and Chicago. At these two markets, eighty stores gave Deb $20,000 in business, and she also found a permanent showroom in both Kansas City and Chicago that would carry her line. (See also Deb's special tips in the sidebar "Five Questions Buyers Ask at Trade Shows" on page 145.)

Time and Family Concerns

IF YOU ARE a dyed-in-the-wool craft fair seller, you probably feel as though all you do is make products for sale and there is no way you could increase your production because you have no more time. What I want you to think about, however, is the amount of time and *physical effort* (no small thing, the latter) you are now expending by selling through craft fairs. Have you ever figured out exactly how many hours a year you spend packing for fairs, traveling there, unloading, setting up, sitting around waiting for sales, tearing down, reloading, and traveling back home again? What you need to ask yourself is how much more product you could make for sale if you didn't have to spend so much time selling it. Or maybe you're selling through a dozen craft malls and running back and forth constantly to replenish stock or set up new displays. If so, maybe it's time to do a study of just how much time all this work is taking, and whether it could be better spent making products that could be wholesaled.

MANAGING TIME AND STRESS

Professional crafters—all home-business owners, in fact—tend to push themselves relentlessly as their business begins to grow, so everyone who starts a crafts business at home must be concerned about time and stress. Sixty- to eighty-hour weeks are common here, and if you've ever found yourself working this long and hard, you know there is a limit to how long you can do this before you collapse. When a business reaches this point, it's time to step back and look at the big picture and decide whether you're going to

limit your output or expand by hiring help.

If you plan to work alone and do all the work related to making and selling your products, think now about the limits to which you'll push yourself. It's amazing how we can see the effects of overwork on other people yet not see the same thing happening to us. I know what I'm talking about here, folks, because I've been self-employed for nearly thirty years, and for most of that time I pushed myself to the bloody limit time and time again, often suffering periods of mental burnout or physical exhaustion as a result. I've finally learned to pace myself and life is much sweeter as a result.

© Jan Bonner

Often, when trying to fill her wholesale orders in the past, teddy bear maker Jan Bonner has worked herself to a state of exhaustion. "If I were doing it over again, I would take more time to enjoy life," she says. "I was so intent on making sales in the beginning that I often worked long and late. A certain amount of drive is good, but a balance is best. If I were doing it over, I would also look differently at my wholesale business. Instead of trying to emulate major manufacturers who do thousands exactly the same, I would have realized I'm a small personal business whose customers like variety and short runs personalized for them."

Today, Jan is wholesaling less and focusing more on selling designer bears, such as the one shown on page 139, to individual collectors. Every time she does a bear show, however, she automatically attracts shop owners who may want to order from what's on the table or take what they want. "Bear shows are expensive," she says. "When I go to a show I spend around $500 on booth fee, plus hotel, travel expenses, and labor. Expenses may run $1,000 a show, so if the weather's bad and you only make $3,000 that weekend, your profit margin is mighty slim."

Finding Your First Wholesale Buyers

I F YOU PLAN to advertise your hand-crafts, patterns, or kits in a consumer magazine, be prepared to get a few wholesale inquiries along with orders from individual buyers. While writing *Handmade for Profit* (Evans, 1996), I interviewed eight sellers who had placed an ad in an issue of Better Homes and Gardens' *Crafts Showcase,* selecting them at random. In discussing the kind of response each advertiser got from his or her ad, I was surprised to learn that most had received wholesale inquiries from shop owners. Like Randall Barr, jewelry maker Carolyn Choate was also surprised by the response to her ad. "It opened important wholesale doors for me," she says, "leading directly to other people who are now showing my line in wholesale markets in five major cities." (Interestingly, Carolyn received barely enough consumer orders to pay for the cost of her ad, proving that wholesale buyers often want what crafters can't sell to individuals.)

Just as independent sales reps browse trade shows looking for professional crafters who can produce items in quantity, so too do retail shop owners and other buyers browse art and craft fairs in search of new products. A while back when Jean and Steve Belknap were selling at a retail crafts fair, they accidentally found a wonderful niche market when a zoo purchased $500 worth of Jean's "Noah and Friends" products for sale in its gift shop. "All of a sudden, a new wholesale market opened up for Jean's dolls through the Zookeeper's Association," says Steve, "and one we can easily supply."

Selling to Tourist Shops

When wholesaling to shops in a tourist area, try these ideas to boost your sales:

1. Give the shop owner greater incentive to buy from you by offering volume discounts, exclusivity on certain items and exchange privileges.

2. Give shop owners more information about yourself and your product.

3. Sign your work and consider producing limited editions.

4. Ask shop owners if they would like to have you come in for a day to demonstrate your craft and chat with customers (called "doing a trunk show").

5. Offer suggestions on the best way to display your crafts in the shop.

When you're ready for a few wholesale shop accounts, either prepare a nice package of information to send by mail, or spend a couple days in the nearest large city scouting for shops and stores that seem right for your products. (Always call first to set up an appointment with the buyer.) Display products attractively to buyers and have a professionally printed price list and order form. For ordering purposes, product samples should be tagged with a code number, wholesale price, minimum quantity requirements, and availability of different colors or sizes. If your work is too large or too heavy to carry around with you, prepare a portfolio of information that includes photographs (done by a professional photographer) of your product line.

Wholesaling to a Niche Market

As CONNIE COLTEN learned, it is possible to build a successful wholesale business around a single product, especially when that product fills a special need in the marketplace. A home sewer and mother of five who always breast-fed her babies, Connie got started in business by designing sewing patterns for breast-feeding mothers, things she herself had used. Although these products had limited success ("the market was small and made even smaller by the fact that mothers had to sew to use my patterns," says Connie), they ultimately led her into the wholesaling of a simple product that will sell as long as mothers anywhere continue to breast-feed babies: a reusable cloth nursing pad. "There are commercial, disposable paper nursing pads on the market, but the benefits of my product are that they are gentler to the skin, reusable, and appealing to anyone who is concerned about ecological issues."

Initially, Connie selected ten companies she thought might be interested in this product, sent samples, and found Motherwear, which was then looking for a more dependable supplier than the one they had. "The company was small when I first connected with them," Connie says, "but we've grown together. I used to supply from 200 to 400 pairs of pads a month; now my orders are ten times that size. You want to have gradual growth, but there's no assurance of that. A big order can put you under almost as quickly as lack of orders."

Connie was fortunate in that she had a couple of years' experience under her belt when she accidentally lucked into her first huge order for a different product she no longer makes. "I learned that a particular company was looking for someone who could sew 60,000 goggle bags for racquetball players, made a bid, and got the job," she recalls. "It was quite a challenge to switch my thinking from 2,000 units to 60,000 units. In figuring the price on 60,000 goggle bags, I first calculated the cost of materials and did a few bags to learn time, then figured how much I'd pay my kids to help with the order. All of them helped me on this order. My oldest son had always worked on the business with me, but for this particular order another son did some sewing and cutting of the cords for the drawstring top. After I'd serge a batch of 400 bags, my daughter would turn all of them and my youngest son would carry trays of bags from one production center to another."

Connie set a wholesale price of 52 cents on this order. Later, when she got a repeat order from a different goggle supplier, she raised the price to 61 cents. That may not sound like much, but when you multiply the difference of nine cents times 60,000 units, the resulting profit is $5,400.

FIND A NEED AND FILL IT

Like Connie, Betty Marx also produces for a niche market, reaching it through a special-interest catalog. After enduring a total laryngectomy and radical neck dissection in 1987, Betty spent a lot of time trying to find jewelry that would cover the patch that covers the hole in her neck.

Scarves weren't practical, she found, because they slipped or impeded breathing. Her solution to this problem was to expand her Ultrasuede accessories business to include custom-designed jewelry for herself and other laryngectomees. When men started asking for something attractive, she designed an ascot line for them. Her products have been selling in the *Luminaud* catalog (one the largest suppliers of stoma covers in the United States) since 1994. In trying to sell to this catalog house, Betty first sent a letter. When it received no reply, she made telephone calls until she connected with someone who would look at samples. Since Betty uses a prosthesis for speaking, this was not easy to do—something clearly outside her comfort zone. She says her success in selling to this niche market was a simple matter of finding a need, trying to fill it, and then plugging away. "You must be persistent!" she advises.

Doing Trade Shows

TREMENDOUS SALES POSSIBILI-TIES await sellers who can meet the challenge of a big trade show, but this kind of selling isn't for everyone. Professional crafters generally avoid the big gift shows until they've been wholesaling for some time, sticking instead to doing wholesale craft fairs only. Sales at such events are impressive, too, with exhibitors often bringing in $15,000 to $20,000 or more in sales from a single event.

FINDING/SELECTING TRADE SHOWS

Information about upcoming wholesale craft shows will be found in trade magazines, which are not on newsstands but available in libraries or by subscription. In particular, you should sample issues of *The Crafts Report* and *Craft Supply Magazine*. Another vital publication for craft wholesalers is *Craftrends/SewBusiness*, not because of its show information (which is geared to craft suppliers), but for its industry information. "Although this is a trade magazine for retailers, it's also the most important trade journal for professional crafters because it gives trends, colors—all the advice retailers need and rely on," says Maria Nerius. "Since crafters are actually moving mini shops, the info presented to retailers affects us, too." (Several trade publications and selected show promoters are listed in Resources.)

Many craftspeople have exhibited at trade shows not really expecting to sell much, only to be bombarded with orders and placed in a panic situation when they suddenly realize they have taken more orders than they can possibly fill. On the other hand, an exhibitor might not receive many orders at all. Either way, doing a trade show can be something of a shock. After exhibiting in his first commercial gift show, a Wisconsin toymaker reported, "I tried my first trade show in Kansas City and it will be the last, as I lost my shirt on the deal. I can't compete with plastic imports." Later, this craftsman tried one of the larger craft trade fairs and reported on what he learned this time around. "I see that I have to clean up my act," he said. "For this to work, I must have a totally professional image and look as if I know what I'm doing—brochures, invoices, letterhead, price lists, and so on." As you can see, even a professional craftsman can find a trade show intimidating.

THE ROSEN SHOWS

The same methods used to select good craft fairs must also be used to select the right trade shows. Each has its own personality and tends to draw a certain kind of buyer. Jeweler Barbara Otterson first started wholesaling through the Beckman shows (produced by Industry Productions of America Inc.), but found them too country-oriented for the high-end art products she was offering. "I've switched to doing the Philadelphia Buyers Market now (produced by The Rosen Group) be-

cause their buyers are more interested in unique one-of-a-kind work," she says.

It appears that many crafters like the Rosen shows because they deliver a big variety of buyers, yet aren't so large that sellers are swamped with a volume of orders they can't fill. These shows are juried, of course, and you can't even get into them until you have three wholesale accounts who will give you a reference.

Remember Rita and Gary Villa of Smidgens, Inc., the company that offers laser-cutting services and wholesales Rita's dollhouse miniatures? When sales of miniatures began to drop, Rita decided it was time to design a new line of products that Gary could laser-cut for her (see the sidebar "Cut It By Laser!"). Under the name Turkey Bird Studio, she now designs and wholesales picture frames, clocks, and CD racks in the form of animal shapes like the sample shown here. "I airbrush them in wild colors for the kids," she says, "and sales have been fantastic. The first time I displayed the line at the Rosen Philadelphia Market, I sold $12,000 worth of products to sixty stores."

© Rita Villa

Five Questions Buyers Ask at Trade Shows

Deb Otto, of Henri's, offers the following: In addition to knowing the selling points of your line—its uniqueness, your best sellers, and so on—here are the five questions buyers will ask at every trade show:

1. What is your minimum order? Are there minimums on reorders? This can be piece minimum or dollar minimum—usually never less than $100.

2. What is your shipping date? Some want only immediate delivery; some will want to delay shipment up to six months. Know your time frame on handmade items. Telling the truth on delivery dates is better than promising soon and delivering later.

3. Do you have a market special? What would make them place an order now—at the show—versus taking your material home to consider with other lines in competition with yours?

4. May I have your brochure? Never, never, *never* attend a market without ordering information *with pictures* they can take for future reference. Keep it easy . . . code number, prices, color choices, and so on. Many shows are doubled with phone-in orders following the show. Of course, don't forget your business cards and customized purchase orders, too.

5. What are your terms? Will orders be shipped COD, credit card, pro forma (you call for a check when order is packed and ready), or Net 30 (they have thirty days to pay after shipment is received)? Avoid Net 30 unless you want to check their references thoroughly (allow two or three weeks to do this before shipping). On large orders, you can often ask other wholesalers at the show if a particular company pays on time or at all. Bad-paying accounts *always* try to target new exhibitors with larger orders, but there are good-paying accounts that place large orders, too. Just be careful here.

Make sure you can confidently answer the above questions so there is no doubt in a buyer's mind that you know your business. Remember that any worker in your booth will need to know these answers, too, so jot them down, even if you just give the list to a neighboring exhibitor so you can take a bathroom break.

Rita broke into this show by first placing a small display ad in *Niche,* The Rosen Group's trade publication. "This brought me several new wholesale accounts, convinced me that I had the kind of products that would sell at a Rosen show, and enabled me to gain entry," she says.

Selling Through Gift Marts and Sales Reps

WHEN YOU HAVE streamlined your production capabilities, fine-tuned your product lines, figured out prices that will yield a profit, worked out packaging kinks, and designed effective printed materials, you may be ready to explore selling through a gift mart or sales representative. Many gift marts and showrooms have temporary space available at reasonable monthly fees, just right for the crafts seller who wants to test the wholesale market before signing with a sales rep. This allows for direct sales to individual shop owners who come to the mart to browse.

If you decide to work with sales reps, make sure your pricing allows for the rep's sales commission. Depending on the rep, this will generally be from 15 to 20 percent of the wholesale price. As the link

between manufacturer and retailer, it is the sales rep's job to get orders for the manufacturer, who must then ship and bill the customer. Normally, sales reps receive their commission only after the manufacturer has been paid. Not all reps will accept this arrangement, however—some will expect commission payments monthly, whether the manufacturer has been paid or not. Since few reps are concerned about the credit worthiness of the accounts they sell to, a craft seller can easily get stuck for the commission on accounts that do not pay. (I'll never forget what one rep told me years ago: "I just take orders. It's not my job to be a bill collector.")

"Working with sales reps can be a good situation or a disaster," says one wholesaler. "My best experiences have been with reps who had a permanent showroom in a market. They did not charge a fee for showroom space, and only expected a commission after I received payment for the order."

Dodie Eisenhauser seems to have found a good balance. She does several trade shows a year and works with a sales rep who has a permanent showroom in Atlanta. As she has learned, however, working with sales reps can be very expensive in terms of samples needed. "A rep group may need an entire set of samples for its showroom, plus four or five pieces for each of its road reps," she says.

Cut It By Laser!

I know many creative people have a "thing" about everything having to be painstakingly crafted by hand, but I think this idea can be pushed too far. For example, do you really think it matters to a buyer whether you, personally, have sawed the wood shapes you paint and sell? If you've been doing intricate, time-consuming paper cuttings, consider that hundreds of the same design could easily be cut by laser and sold for the same price as one cut by hand. Ornaments, clock parts, picture frames, mat boards (with special shaped cuts to frame a picture), miniatures, and shapes such as the samples shown here are just some of the designs that can be cut by laser.

Just imagine how many more products you could sell if you didn't have to do all that sawing or cutting yourself. Thanks to laser technology, small pieces can now be cut for pennies apiece from a variety of materials including wood, masonite, acrylic, fiberboard, illustration board, and various papers. (Price is based both on size and type of material.) What you would spend for laser cutting could easily be offset by profits from other products you would now have time to make. In short, taking this simple step in manufacturing your product could enable you to move from retailing to wholesaling overnight. (See Resources for the address of Smidgens, Inc., which offers affordable laser-cutting/engraving services to crafters.)

"A year ago, I signed with a rep agency in Hawaii who needed $700 worth of samples, but to date I have received only two orders and I doubt this investment will ever pay off."

A while back Dodie tried a new market by exhibiting in the Vegas Floral Show. "I think we all have to think about trying new markets," she says, "because if one goes down, another will be there to tide us over."

Sometimes, the only problem with sales reps is that they generate more business than a crafter is prepared to handle. Six years before she began to sell through Coomers craft malls, Rita

O'Hara marketed her products at the wholesale level, through gift markets and five sales reps. "We finally dropped the reps because they kept us so busy it just wasn't fun any more. Reps are good for a business, and they brought in a lot of new accounts, but we've learned that just because you build your business this way doesn't mean you have to continue. Probably half of all the wholesale customers the reps initiated for us are still buying from us now. If you have a good product they want, they will continue to call."

© Rita O'Hara

The Importance of Planning

A HOUSE IS JUST a home . . . except when it's suddenly turned into a combination factory and warehouse. Nothing can throw a family into overdrive quicker than a $10,000 order that must be delivered in three weeks. If no planning has been done beforehand, it's going to take a lot more than patience and a good sense of humor to survive the experience.

As I was writing this book, Marie Slovek wrote to tell me her Prairie Moon Originals business was out of control. "Last spring, after putting many of your suggestions to use, business was brisk. Then I decided to return to my first love—teaching school. I was offered a job in a one-room schoolhouse on the prairie, which was something I'd always wanted to try. So crafting went on the back burner. However, much to my surprise, a mail-order catalog on the East Coast picked up on one of my products and asked permission to feature it. It has been a runaway success. My once tidy and organized house has turned into a total manufacturing and drop-shipping hub, with relatives and friends helping to fill the never-ending arrival of purchase orders. I've learned you have to be ready if the big break hits, which I obviously wasn't. I also see that doing this seriously full time is lots of work. This was sort of a dream-come-true-turned-into-a-nightmare. I am obligated to continue teaching this year, and my little girls, aged three and four, are getting used to Mom saying, 'I'm sorry, Sweetie, I have to finish these boards.' Now I am struggling to decide whether to continue teaching or to go with this crafting and designing career. Decisions, decisions!"

© Marie Slovek

PRAIRIE MOON ORIGINALS

Prior to jumping into the wholesale ring, you need to do some serious planning. First you need access to cash to cover the cost of supplies and materials and space to store them on delivery. Because the production line of any big order will naturally overflow into the house, the next big consideration is figuring out where work centers will be set up and who's going to be working at each of them. (Unless a business already uses outside help, most crafters simply enlist the aid of family members and friends.)

The year Randall Barr was trying to keep up with orders for 10,000 of his hand-crafted clocks, he sent a quick note saying, "We're going crazy trying to keep up with production. Everyone in the family is helping out and we're all working very long hours." (Later Randall farmed out some of his production work to Veterans Industries, a program of the Veterans Administration.) When Dodie Eisenhauer came home from her first wholesale show with $4,000 worth of orders, the first thing she did was hire help. "I had done my homework on employees before I went to the show, however," she says. "I knew the tax and legal implications of hiring part-time workers and I had a list of people all lined up ready to go to work if I needed them." (See the sidebar "Hiring Outside Help," page 152.)

Jean and Steve Belknap weren't so well prepared to handle the biggest order of their life—the QVC order I mentioned in an earlier chapter. "Our biggest concern was whether we could produce that much merchandise if we got the order," says Jean, "but we never imagined the order would be as large as it was. Realizing we had just committed ourselves to producing 600 dolls within two months, we drove home in a state of shock," Jean recalls. "The first thing we did was get a loan to cover the cost of all the needed materials and a second sewing machine."

You can imagine how the Belknaps felt, then, when QVC placed a second order for 468 dolls. "We had been given two months to deliver the first 600 dolls," Jean says, "but QVC wanted the second order delivered three weeks after that. So the problem was how to make 468 dolls in three weeks (about twenty-two dolls a day) when we were currently turning out only ten per day. With incredible effort on the part of family and friends, we managed to do it, but Steve and I worked from three in the morning to nine or ten at night the whole time."

TEA-DYING IN THE KITCHEN

The Belknap's story, first shared with readers of my "Selling What You Make" column in *Crafts Magazine*, is a perfect example of what goes on behind closed craft doors when a crafter gets that first big wholesale order and isn't prepared to handle it. While making you chuckle, it will also give you a better understanding of the importance of planning before you invite orders in a "big time" wholesale market. Clearly, it is one thing to enter a small wholesale craft show and quite another to offer your product on a home shopping show.

© Jean Belknap

With an order for 600 dolls in hand and a bank loan to pay for all the necessary supplies, Jean's next job was to make a production plan. "I literally dissected my product to figure out all the individual pieces and steps necessary to produce a Tyler doll," she says. "I figured I would need 600 yards of muslin, several bolts of fabric for the doll clothes, fiberfill, burlap, jute, paint, thread, tags, and over a thousand buttons. I also had to find packing boxes, tissue, and shipping cartons that would satisfy QVC's specific shipping instructions."

The first big production step involved preparation of the material. Being the artist she is, Jean wasn't satisfied with using fabric for the doll's body right off the bolt. Instead, to get just the right color for Tyler's face, she used tea-dyed muslin. While it had never been a problem to dye a few yards at a time, doing all the yardage for this order proved to be a real challenge. While Jean was cutting fabric into manageable six-foot lengths, Steve (the only one who knew the secret tea-dying formula) was making a list and checking it twice. He figured he needed eight pounds of coffee, 400 giant commercial tea bags, two 30-gallon dye vats (trash containers, actually) and every coffee and tea pot he could get his hands on.

Picture this: It's 5 o'clock on a cool October morning when work begins, but the kitchen soon heats up to 95 degrees because there are two electric coffeepots going, two regular percolators on the stove, a giant cauldron of boiling water for the tea bags, and another pot for more tea. As soon as the first batch of tea and coffee is done and poured into one of the trash containers waiting in the dining room, Steve repeats the process—ten times in all. Before long, the kitchen is a disaster area. "By the time both containers were filled, the kitchen was so hot I thought the wallpaper was going to roll off the ceiling," says Jean. "Steve was tea-dyed, his hair matted to his face, the floor was tea-dyed, and the dog was damp from all the humidity in the house."

Because only 100 yards of fabric could be dyed at a time in each container, and the fabric had to sit for a day or more before it reached the right color, this whole tea/coffee-making process had to be repeated twice more to dye a total of 600 yards. Once dyed and dried, the fabric then had to be ironed before pattern pieces could be cut. This was a week the Belknaps will never forget, I'm sure, but it was only the beginning of the actual production process.

SETTING UP PRODUCTION CENTERS

The next thing Jean did was divide the house into production centers, based on the individual steps involved in constructing her doll. (This is a totally foreign concept to the creative person who has been used to making one product at a time, but absolutely essential if one plans to wholesale.) "The whole house was in turmoil for three weeks, with something different going on in each room," Jean recalls. "Bolts of fabric were stacked everywhere in our upstairs sewing room. "The living room housed more than a dozen 25-pound boxes of fiberfill stuffing and other materials. The den had dozens of boxes and shipping cartons stacked floor to ceiling. After using one room to first cut all the muslin body pieces, we would turn it into a sewing room. After all the body pieces were sewn, the room would become a painting room. When all the body pieces were done, we repeated the process for the clothes, horns, hooves and hair, first cutting, then sewing."

At one time or another, nine people worked on this order. Although Jean and Steve had met the biggest challenge of their lives, they were literally exhausted and numb from lack of sleep. "It took a month for us to feel normal again," Jean told me. "Although we would never want to repeat this particular experience, it taught us a lot. By having the courage to step out on faith, we have been able to learn and grow."

DESIGNING OUT THE DETAILS

If Tyler the Giraffe had been made of regular fabric and not tea-dyed muslin, the Belknaps would have saved themselves a week's worth of hard physical labor. The moral of their story, then, is never to wholesale any product that has this kind of tedious detail to it. To profit from wholesaling, you have to "design out" the little details, streamline the design, and simplify the production steps.

Hiring Outside Help

Because of the tax and legal dangers of using independent contractors or home workers today, many small manufacturers are hiring "statutory employees" instead. Such workers do cost an employer more than independent contractors (one must pay Social Security and Medicare taxes on their wages), but less than regular employees, for which unemployment taxes must also be withheld.

The current danger of hiring independent contractors these days is that the IRS is aggressively working to change the status of all independent contractors to employees. When this happens, an employer has to cough up all the back taxes that weren't paid in earlier years—an expense that often runs into thousands of dollars and puts a small business out of business overnight.

I cannot overstress the importance of doing your homework on this topic. If you are currently hiring people who work *only for you and no other employer,* discuss your situation with a trusted accountant or attorney versed in labor law to learn what you must do to operate your business legally.

Dodie Eisenhauer has the right idea. "Production begins with the design itself," she says. "While designing a new product, I am always thinking about how the product will be constructed, how it can be broken down, and what individual activities can be produced by one of my employees. I design all my new products around basic components. For example one person may make curly wire for me that can be used in several different products. Another may cut lengths of vine wire, from which I might make Christmas trees or cats in different sizes, depending on the lengths of wire that have been cut. That way, I don't have to train my employees to make an entire product. Always, my goal is to keep my products complicated enough that others won't try to copy them, yet simple enough that I can easily teach other people how to make them."

As an artist, Dodie understands that one of the hardest things the creative person has to do when moving into wholesaling is remove themselves from their products. "Many creative people don't

© Dodie Eisenhauer

like to let go of their products; they want to be in control, do it all, feel they're the only ones who can do what they do. But you can't succeed in wholesaling with this attitude. In the end, it boils down to whether someone wants to make extra money or earn a living."

In Summary

CLEARLY, WHOLESALING REQUIRES a more professional attitude, a greater appreciation for the worth of your products, and a businesslike approach to marketing. You may have to hire employees, take workshops to learn more about how to manage and market your business, make out-of-town sales trips, exhibit at trade shows and so on. It is at this point that hobby sellers are separated from the professionals, where many either back away or go forward in a totally new direction.

Americans are spending millions of dollars each year on hand-crafted merchandise, but most of their purchases are being made in places other than where most of today's crafters sell. Thus, if you want to make more money, it follows that you must (1) produce more goods of higher quality; (2) be brave enough to charge what they are really worth; and (3) place them in the trade outlets used by professionals.

CHAPTER 8

Turning Designs into Dollars

Since I knew the day was soon coming where mass producing finished handcrafts would either burn me out or I would have to bring in hired help to fill orders, designing seemed to be my best bet.

ANNIE LANG, Annie Things Possible

FEW DESIGNERS CAN earn a living by designing only, but if you have "designability," there are a number of ways you can combine it with other talents, skills, and know-how to make money—sometimes a little, sometimes a lot. You might:

➤ Sell how-to projects to magazines

➤ Create craft or needlework design books or leaflets

➤ Develop and market patterns

➤ Develop and sell kits

➤ Design for manufacturers

➤ License designs to manufacturers

This is the longest chapter in the book, but it may also be the most valuable because the kind of information it contains is so difficult to obtain. By introducing you to several designers who have done the things mentioned above, I hope to make you fully aware of just how far your designing abilities might take you.

Selling How-To Articles to Magazines

Your DESIGNS MAY be good . . . but are they *original?* Editors generally ask designers to sign a release certifying that the material being submitted is original in design—not previously published nor utilizing any part of previously published material.

"There are subtle distinctions between that which is original and that which is adapted from, inspired by, or just plain stolen from something else," an editor comments. "We have to be very careful when we work with beginners. Crafters often start with a commercial pattern and modify it or improve it each time they make it until they feel the resulting product is truly their own creation. To avoid legal problems, we need to know if a crafter has borrowed ideas from another source."

WHAT EDITORS WANT

Generally, craft magazine editors want projects with mass consumer appeal—things that are easy to make from supplies that are easy to find. Most of all, they want detailed how-to instructions.

"Never assume knowledge on the part of a reader," says one editor. "People use how-to-do-it instructions because they want to make the item described. If they already knew how to do your craft project, they wouldn't need you to tell them how. So don't let them down by omitting any step in the process, no matter how simple it seems to you. Craft beginners can become confused very easily, and they need to be led step-by-step through the complete process."

How much money can you expect to make from the sale of a how-to article? This can vary from $50 to $250 or more, depending on the design, your reputation, and the magazine's articles budget.

MAKING SUBMISSIONS

Buy sample issues of magazines on the newsstand, then write to each one requesting their Writer's Guidelines Sheet. Prior to submitting an article idea to any magazine, study the content of a recent issue to see if your idea is comparable in type and quality to what is currently being published. Include a self-addressed stamped envelope with any inquiry to an editor, and do not send samples unless they are requested.

Don't be afraid to submit an idea, but be prepared for rejection. Craft editors do buy from beginners, but there are many reasons why an idea might be rejected.

First Rights/All Rights Sales

In offering your work for publication—and this might be an article, a poem, a design, pattern, or how-to instructions for some project—you must consider whether you are going to sell only first rights or all rights to that publisher. If you elect the latter, which some beginners have to do just to get published, you will automatically lose ownership of the copyright to your material. Selling all rights means you have conveyed your copyright to the publisher, and you cannot use that material again without the publisher's written permission.

Selling first rights, on the other hand, means you have given the magazine permission to print your article once, for a specified sum of money, after which time you alone have the right to re-sell that article to someone else, reprint it in a publication of your own, include it in a book you are writing, incorporate it into kit instructions, and so on.

Barbara Brabec, *The Crafts Business Answer Book & Resource Guide* (M. Evans, 1996)

"The biggest mistake beginners make is omitting crucial information in their written instructions for a project," says Nona Piorkowski, editor of *Crafts 'n Things* magazine. "Usually, they're so familiar with the project they don't realize they haven't explained the most important step in putting it together or the most important material to use. Sometimes we ask people to redo a project, or we may redo it ourselves. But if this happens frequently, we won't work with the designer again as we don't have time to redo everyone's projects."

Some ideas are rejected because they haven't been submitted in a timely manner. Most magazines want projects about eight months in advance of publication, which means you should submit project ideas for a Christmas issue in March or April at the latest. Sometimes a project is rejected not because there's anything wrong with it, but merely because it doesn't fit a magazine's particular needs at that time.

"Don't take rejection personally," Susan Young emphasizes. "Just offer it somewhere else. It may take four or five years to become even slightly known as far as magazines are concerned, depending on how hard you work at getting their attention. For every small item I've had accepted, twenty or thirty have come back with a note saying, 'We can't use this but please try again.' In the beginning I tended to let that discourage me, and sometimes I even took it personally. You can't allow those feelings to surface, however. You have to remember that there are literally thousands of people trying to break into this business, so the competition is tremendous compared to even a few years ago. Those who don't give up and who can deliver what they promise, on time and with courtesy, will be able to hang on for the long haul."

Writing Craft and Needlework Design Books

UNLIKE TRADE BOOK publishers who sell to bookstores, book clubs, and libraries (see next chapter), craft publishers produce design and pattern books or needlework charts that are sold through craft supply shops or fabric, needlework, and yarn shops.

BOOKS

The 8 1/2 by 11-inch four-color design and project books you find in your favorite craft or needlework supply shop are called "floppy books" in the trade. Craft publishers generally offer a flat fee for a collection of designs or projects to be published in a book, paying from $1,000 to $2,000 for all rights, according to reports I have received from several designers. (Selling "all rights" means the designer can never use those projects or designs again, but the publisher can reuse them without further payment to the designer. See the sidebar "First Rights/All Rights Sales.")

Professional designers should always think twice before selling all rights to their designs, but beginning designers benefit greatly from this kind of publishing because it helps them gain recognition in the industry and often leads to more profitable writing and designing ventures. Having a beautiful color book of your own is profitable in other ways, too, particularly if you plan to sell the book yourself. (Make sure your publishing contract includes a clause that allows you to buy copies at wholesale.)

Nancy Bell Anderson has found this kind of publishing both profitable and satisfying. Her specialty is clothespin dolls, and she and her daughter, Heather Bell Henry, have written *Tribal Playmates* and *Clothespin Kachina Dolls* for Design Originals. "Because I teach and run a small Clothespin Museum, I have a ready market for these books," Nancy says.

Carol Krob has been a designer for the craft and needlework industry since

1980 when she founded Carol's Creations. To date, Carol has sold nearly 300 design projects to magazines and done eighteen books, most of them for Annie's Attic and Design Originals. Each of her books includes a selection of designs for a particular type of item, from angels or hearts to beaded ornaments, jewelry, or accessories. "I buy quantities of each title for sale through my mail-order catalog," she says, "but mail order is just a part of my overall business. Mostly I am involved in selling my designs to magazine and book publishers."

© Carol Krob

Carol's foremost professional and personal goal and new motto is to "Stay in Step With Today's Creative Spirit," as suggested by her logo, shown here. She advises beginning designers to pay attention to what's happening in the industry. "Many things are changing. To be professional means keeping up to date with what's going on in the industry and with individual publishers. Keep your writer's guidelines up to date by calling publishers

to get their most recent information," she urges, adding that membership in the Society of Craft Designers (SCD) is "a must" for all craft designers and writers (discussed further at the end of this chapter.)

NEEDLEWORK CHARTS AND LEAFLETS

Needlework charts and design leaflets usually present a single project, and publishers in this field also buy designs outright. To learn what they want from designers, find addresses on the back of needlework charts and write to each one for their Writer's Guideline Sheet.

Carol Krob has also done several needlework leaflets for Annie's Attic. "All of these projects have been accessory items for eight-inch fashion dolls that are worked on plastic canvas. I've done office furniture, dinner party accessories, miniature ornaments for a Christmas tree, and so on." Leaflets like the ones Carol Krob has done are also called project sheets, and they are more often published by manufacturers than craft publishers. For more information on this topic, see the section "Working with Manufacturers."

Darla Sims has had over fifty of her design books published by Leisure Arts, one of the oldest craft publishers in the country. Darla's love of knitting sweaters and creating original designs for her

Cooperative Publishing

If you happen to be a decorative painter, you will be interested in how artist Annie Lang has published eleven books to date without laying out any cash up front or having to sell them herself. She is published by Eas'l Publications, which specializes in decorative painting books and works cooperatively with its authors.

"After I joined SCD, I received information that guided me through every phase of the designing industry," she says. "I mailed out a stack of queries hoping to get my designs published in a book, and several weeks later I signed a contract with Eas'l Publications. What's nice about this kind of publishing arrangement is that I hold all copyrights to the designs in my books and can license them or use them in any other way desired."

Unlike regular self-publishing, where the author must pay for all production costs up front and then figure out how to sell the book besides, Eas'l handles all production, warehousing, and marketing of books for a fee. Promotion is done through mailings to a network of distributors in the United States and worldwide, through press releases and trade show exhibits. Advertising is done in various trade magazines, with the cost shared by authors. Once production costs are recovered, the author gets remaining earnings, receiving a check each month for the previous month's sales.

daughters became an exciting career in the late 1970s, when she began to design sweaters for national magazines. Two of her Leisure Arts crochet and knitting leaflets have sold millions of copies. Years of designing for magazines and book publishers eventually led Darla to write *Making $$$ at Home—Over 1,000 Editors Who Want Your Ideas, Know-How & Experience* (Sunstar Publications).

Developing and Selling Patterns by Mail

PERHAPS THE MOST profitable way to use original designs—and one of the easiest things a beginner can do—is develop and sell patterns by mail. You can start out small, selling just to people on your own mailing list, but I urge you to think in bigger terms right from the beginning—much greater profits can be realized when you move into wholesaling and can sell in volume to buyers all over the world. One key to success here seems to be in offering patterns for things consumers aren't likely to see in a crafts magazine, and they don't need to be as quick and easy as the projects found in magazines, either. Here are some examples to get your creative juices flowing.

STICK ANIMALS

Kimberly Stroman Doffin, the owner of K & R . . . in the Country, has been promoting craft shows for sixteen years and selling her own products since 1984, both in finished form and as kits and patterns. "I began by selling designs to crochet magazines," she says. "Now I design my own sewing and wood patterns, design in various mediums for magazines, and have two design lines I plan to license."

© 1982–1996
Kimberly Stroman Doffin

Kimberly's newest patterns are stick animals (hobby-horses) that so far include a horse, a giraffe, and the cow shown here. She sells by mail to individuals, using full-color flyers with ordering information on the back of each.

CLOTHES FOR CEMENT GEESE AND BEARS

"My Personal Designs goose clothes pattern business started as a way to make some extra money but it's a serious business now," says Vicki Stozich. "I began by designing six patterns and putting an ad in the local paper. Now I now have sixty-six patterns and I've diversified into selling cement bears and clothing for them. I used to offer a free brochure, but following advice I found in *Homemade Money*, I now charge $1 for a brochure. When people send the dollar, I send a coupon for $2 off their first order. This covers my cost, and most people will use the coupon to try a pattern. Once they see the quality, they usually order more."

SYRUP DOLL PATTERNS

Myra Hopkins designs "Cloaks of Elegance" patterns for syrup bottle dolls, selling them by mail to individual customers in the United States, Canada, and other countries. Myra is good at getting publicity for her business. After being dubbed the "Syrup Bottle Queen" by her local paper, she was interviewed on a Baltimore TV station and invited to speak for the Maryland Chapter of the International Doll Makers Association. In 1997 Myra's patterns were selected by the National Mail Order Association as one of the Top 50 in their search for the most interesting products sold by mail. By sending a press release about this award to newspapers and radio stations, Myra got several additional interviews and a big spread in the *Baltimore Business Journal*.

© Myra Hopkins

Myra surprised and delighted me by sending a clipping of this color article in which she was holding a copy of my *Homemade Money* book. She told the reporter how helpful this book had been to her business, and later told me my advice to get some publicity was the most profitable bit of business advice anyone had ever given her. "I have found that press I receive does as good as any advertising, especially since my project is particularly aimed at crafters who create for fund-raising bazaars and fairs."

Many groups have used Myra's patterns for fund-raising purposes, and Myra has raised $10,000 for her church over the past ten years by donating several of her dolls for sale at each year's annual holiday bazaar.

WOOD CUTOUT PATTERNS

In addition to selling how-to articles, Susan Young has started a pattern line she markets through a catalog sent to individuals on her mailing list. Her Peach Kitty packages include a pattern for an ornament or other design to be cut out of wood, with instructions on how to paint it. Some packages include the wood cutout itself, or an accessory item. Packages sell for $4.95 to $6.95, depending on contents.

© Susan Young

Incidentally, Susan is a cat lover who recently formed a business alliance with Susan Nelson, a crafter who makes a line of products for cat lovers, including tote bags. Susan Young is now doing exclusive wood cutouts for Susan Nelson (like those shown here), who is attaching them to her tote bags as a little "cat bonus" for buyers.

I am delighted by this because I was the one who brought these two Susans together the day letters from both of them crossed my desk at the same time. The mutually profitable arrangement they have made with one another suggests that other crafters might profit from similar cooperative ventures.

A Shop Owner's Tips for Pattern Sellers

I HAD AN INTERESTING conversation with a local shop owner in my area who prefers to remain anonymous—I'll call her Anna. She told me that most of the pattern sellers she deals with are very unprofessional, and she wishes all of them would make her life easier by doing the following things.

BE PROFESSIONAL

"Ninety percent of the people who are trying to sell us patterns don't have a clue as to how to run a business," says Anna. "They don't understand packaging, shipping, or invoicing. I've had people send me their invoice on the flap of an envelope and try to charge me extra for the box they used to ship patterns to me. People go off on vacation and never check the messages on their answering machines. Sometimes they just go out of business, leaving us wondering what happened. Pattern sellers who are serious about making money must run their businesses professionally. They need printed stationery, business cards, and invoices with their name and address printed (or at least rubber-stamped) on them.

"Many pattern sellers are also careless, often leaving out important sentences and instructions," Anna adds. "So many people who buy patterns from us bring them back, asking us to explain how to do a certain part of the instructions they can't figure out. When you're writing instructions for the mass consumer market, you can't take anything for granted. Instructions must be clear and complete. Include all the little how-to details, such as what the seam allowance is, maximum thickness of fur that can be used, whether the nap of fabric is important to the design, and so on. When you think your pattern instructions are perfect, give them to someone who will honestly critique them for you—preferably a beginner."

PRICE FOR THE MARKET

You must build in all costs, but don't overprice the package, Anna emphasizes.

"Most patterns today are selling for around $6 retail, but some are priced as high as $9. That's too much to charge. Don't try to make so much on one package, but think in terms of volume. Whereas you might sell ten packages priced at $9, you might sell a hundred priced at $6."

PAY ATTENTION TO PACKAGING

Cardboard headers may look great on a pattern, but Anna says shop owners don't like them because they take up too much room and customers only tear them off the hangers. "Patterns should be packaged in a standard zipped plastic bag with a hole punched in the center," she advises. "The most important thing of all is the color photo. Pattern packages with a photo sell two-to-one over those without. Keep the photo simple—don't put cutesy stuff in the background that detracts from what you're selling."

Above all, avoid the "cardinal sin," which is to include in the package a list of all the other patterns and designs you sell by mail. Shop owners won't sell the pattern packages of designers who try to steal business out from under their noses. If such advertising literature is found in a package, it will be removed and the designer will not get reorders.

Finally, double-check the packaging of all your pattern packages to make sure everything is included. "Many of the pattern packages we get are missing a sheet," says Anna, "probably because the designer lets her kids put the packets together and she doesn't bother to double-check them."

COPYRIGHT PROBLEMS

My conversation with Anna took an interesting turn when she commented on how blatant shoppers are about stealing patterns and copying designs from books for sale in the shop—one reason why she requested anonymity in this book.

"Many people who browse through the pattern section remove photos or actual pattern sheets from individual pattern packages, and we're out the money for them," says Anna. "The other day, a woman blatantly asked us if she could copy a page out of one of the books. When I said no, she got angry and left. We have to sell all our books and patterns on a no-return basis; otherwise people would buy them, copy what they want, and return them. We used to have chairs and a table in our book department, but we had to remove them because this made it too easy for customers to sit and copy designs. Now they sit on the floor and we try to stop them whenever we see them, but sometimes we're too busy to do this."

Anna shudders at the thought of all the copying going on in the crafts industry today. She knows for a fact that one woman comes into her shop regularly and buys all the new patterns, then turns around and changes them a bit here and there and sells them to one of the major pattern companies. "Big companies don't care where the designs come from," says Anna, "but designers who work this way are setting themselves up for a lawsuit if the original designer ever catches their rip-offs."

Anna suggests that professional pattern designers make a point of buying copies of every new pattern that in any way resembles their designs, just to make sure their copyrights aren't being violated.

Wholesaling a Pattern Line

E LEENA DANIELSON FIRST sold her country primitive dolls at craft fairs, then turned her creations into Cranberry Junction patterns that are now wholesaled through a trade show twice a year. The fifty-one patterns in her line are often accentuated with twigs, vines, berries, clove-spiced buttons, primitive

Brantley Bear   Fendley Frost

stitches, and old lace. (Many of the shops that sell her patterns also carry some of these accessories.)

Eleena might still be selling her dolls at fairs if not for a chance meeting with another designer at a show. "She was just a friendly stranger who encouraged me to sell my patterns as she was doing," says Eleena. "I jumped at this idea, but I had no one to talk to about it, so I began by studying all the pattern offerings at stores, buying them to learn how various designers wrote their instructions. I first wrote in detail how to make a particular doll, then kept simplifying the instructions into steps, then categorizing them by sections. To make sure people who weren't crafty could make my dolls, I supplied materials and patterns to several friends and let them keep what they made in return for giving me their input. It's amazing how your instructions will always seem clear to you, but others will see things you can't."

BEST TRADE SHOW FOR DESIGNERS

"The idea of wholesaling my patterns at a trade show was one of the scariest things I had ever contemplated," Eleena recalls, "but I knew this was a necessary first step in breaking into the market." She and others have told me that the only show a pattern seller needs to do is the international Quilt Market, which is the nation's only wholesale trade show for the quilt industry. Fall shows are always in Houston, but spring shows are presented in cites in other parts of the country. To gain admittance to this show, exhibitors must have been in business for at least a year and be wholesale suppliers to the quilting, soft craft, or needlework industry. In addition, their products must be approved by the show's Market Screening Committee.

TRADE SHOW DISPLAY TIPS

Eleena recommends that beginners reserve the smallest booth space possible. "Doing this show means connecting with new and repeat wholesale buyers all over the world," she emphasizes. "For the first show, you should display a minimum of ten to twelve products. For each show thereafter, you should offer at least five to ten new designs. Always take to a show a couple of items for that particular season, but remember that most buyers will be buying for the next season. Thus you should offer fall and winter designs at the spring show and spring designs at the fall show.

"For each pattern being offered, make up a model and display it and the pattern on a display board, perhaps pinning the pattern to the doll itself. I also use a card that includes the product's stock number and name of pattern in large letters tacked on to the product somewhere so buyers don't have to strain their eyes to get the number off the pattern."

Eleena's patterns retail at $6 and wholesale for half that amount. She says her buyers usually buy three to six copies of a pattern. She recommends a minimum order of between $36 and $50. "If a buyer wants only one pattern, they must pay the full retail price," she says.

In addition to her pattern business, Eleena owns E&S Creations, which offers a line of her originally designed hangtags for crafters. She still sells her originally designed dolls at one craft show a year in Idaho Falls. "I've been doing this show for eight years and I just can't give it up because I love it so and I've made so many friends there," she says with a grin. "People come and look for me each year because they see my patterns in stores and want me to sign their dolls."

Ah . . . the sweet bonus of designer fame!

Developing and Selling Kits

M ANY ARTISTS AND crafters have expanded their businesses by developing kits, often in response to craft fair shoppers who say, "I could make that myself." Others simply see kits as a natural way to diversify or change the direction of their business. The following examples will suggest ideas for kits you might develop.

DESIGNER EGG KITS

Linda Markuly Szilvasy is an artist who specializes in decorating eggs in sizes ranging from the tiny finch to those of the ostrich and emu. Through the years, her Exclusive Designs business has involved teaching, the manufacturing of a special hardener for her eggs, and the writing of a book, *The Jeweled Egg* (no longer in print). Linda has always signed and dated her work, producing one-of-a-kind or limited editions for sale in art galleries or to private collectors at prices in the $500 range. Because her work is so expensive, and because there are so many "eggers" who like her work, she has been selling kits for some time.

"These are quite profitable," she says, "and very popular with my customers.

There are a lot of serious egg artists out there—more than anyone would imagine. I have a regular list of people just waiting for my next original kit design. I usually issue two to four new kits a year, make up a maximum of fifty or sixty kits of each design, and sell them for $50 or more as limited editions that will never be reissued."

DOLL KITS

Eileen Heifner started making porcelain dolls in 1984, which she sold for a while at fairs and through a local artisan's cooperative. When people started asking her to tell them how to make the dolls, she began to teach four to six people at a time in her home-based studio twice a week. "Basically, they were putting together kits I provided," she says, "and this eventually led me to open a doll shop in my home, which is on a farm in the New England countryside."

Today, Eileen sells only fine porcelain doll kits and accessories through her mail-order catalog, which she advertises for $1. "Over the years, my business has grown far beyond anything I could have imagined," she says. "At one time only collectors were interested in dolls, and it was considered a rich person's hobby. Now, with less expensive reproductions available, people everywhere are using dolls as decorative accessories. To meet the growing demand for our product, we finally decided to stop manufacturing dolls ourselves and have them made in China. Although the quality of the imported dolls isn't as good as the ones we so meticulously poured, finished, and painted ourselves, importing has enabled us to drastically lower our prices and also offer our products at quantity discounts to crafters who want to make them for sale at fairs or teach doll making in their home."

If you're thinking about having a product manufactured overseas, Eileen suggests you get help from your local small business development center. Networking with other business owners or attending toy fairs will also lead you to overseas manufacturers. "This is a very complicated topic that requires intense study," Eileen emphasizes.

STITCHERY KITS

Carol Krob is recognized for the elegant heirloom quality of her designs, which typically combine elements of cross-stitch, needlepoint, crewel, and beading, along with metallics, jewels, and specialty threads and trims. In addition to creating projects for magazines and book publishers, she sells a line of original charted designs and kits through her mail-order catalog, along with a selected stock of needlework supplies and all her design books. Her customers have the option to buy only the needlework graphs or all supplies, including Aida fabric, embroidery floss, beads (if part of the design), needles, graphs, and instructions. Products include ornaments, jewelry, bookmarks, Christmas cards, gift tags, and beaded pictures. The catalog is advertised at $1, which is refundable with a customer's first order of $5 or more.

CLOTHESPIN DOLL KITS

Nancy Bell Anderson is a former teacher and 4-H leader who has turned her understanding of children into a diversified business called Northwest Craft Adventures. She owns and operates a small Clothespin Museum, presents workshops and classes on a variety of topics, writes design books, and makes up clothespin doll kits like those shown here.

Depending on the design, a typical kit package includes a pattern, directions, clothespin, craft picks (arms), leather or fabric, lace or ribbon, floss, and other

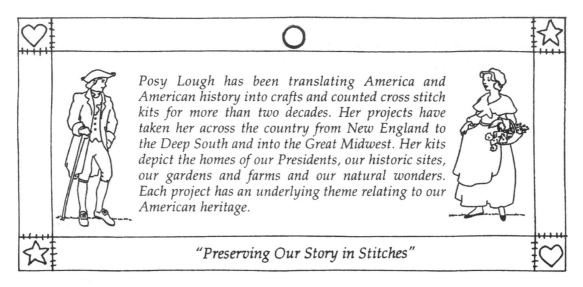

Posy Lough has been translating America and American history into crafts and counted cross stitch kits for more than two decades. Her projects have taken her across the country from New England to the Deep South and into the Great Midwest. Her kits depict the homes of our Presidents, our historic sites, our gardens and farms and our natural wonders. Each project has an underlying theme relating to our American heritage.

"Preserving Our Story in Stitches"

Above, the back side of the header Posy uses on her needlework kit packages.

decorative items, such as feathers or beads.

HISTORIC NEEDLEWORK KITS

Posy Lough has been translating American history into crafts and counted cross-stitch kits for more than two decades, marketing her line as The Posy Collection. She originally sold her crafts to gift shops, department stores, and museums, but through the years has found it most profitable to do custom design counted cross-stitch kits for specific museums, historic sites, and other organizations that emphasize the heritage of America.

"All of these places have a gift shop, and they're always looking for things to sell in their shop (or on their Web site) that people can't find anywhere else, so I design and manufacture kits exclusively for them," Posy explains. "Needlework kits are popular because they enable people to create their own souvenir of a particular place."

Some of the places for which Posy has created custom kits include the Biltmore Estate, Norman Rockwell Museum, Henry Ford Museum, Monticello, Mount Vernon, and the George Bush Presidential Library. For the latter, Posy did five projects for its opening, including the White House Prayer, a Christmas ornament indicative of the patriotic boy/girl rag doll ornaments Mrs. Bush always put on the Christmas tree, and a design motif from a rug she needlepointed when she was in the White House.

"I love history and I love our country. It's a labor of love, telling America's story through cross-stitch embroidery," says Posy, who works with expert designers and stitchers to develop new products. "My greatest strength lies in bringing everything together. I make contact with museum staffs and work closely with them for historical and architectural accuracy, come up with ideas for symbols and motifs that could be depicted in a needlework sampler, and handle all the related business details."

A former teacher with a degree in education, Posy has gained her business training from on-the-job experience and reading many magazines, journals, and books on craft designing, running a small business, and marketing products. She is quick to say she couldn't do all the work involved in her business without the help of her husband, Tom, who writes the kits' historical sketches and handles the photography and computer work related to the business. Their son, Kyser, now fifteen, has been helping with the business since he was seven, doing age-appropriate work. Posy hopes her success story will motivate other designers to explore similar opportunities.

"If you have a museum or historic house in your area, you may find it ready and waiting for the special kits only you can design," she encourages.

Designing for Manufacturers

A NNIE LANG, THE inspiring designer you first met in chapter 1, works with manufacturers, something few beginners can hope to do without some experience under their belt. "Designing isn't for everyone," she says. "It's a lot of work—long hours, sometimes unreasonable deadlines—and your reputation as a professional is on the line with each phone call and project submission. Paychecks don't arrive a week later, they often take months. Still, it's really fun to have a shipment of felt arrive on my doorstep with a request to come up with twelve to fifteen projects for kids aged seven to twelve, which will fit on x-amount of space, using three colors and two basic related craft supplies—finished designs needed in ten days. This is not a business for those who procrastinate."

As members of the SCD, professional designers rarely have to seek this kind of work. Manufacturers belong to this organization too, and everyone has access to information about other members through a directory. Manufacturers use the directory to find designers who might create craft projects using their materials. Susan Young confirms: "Because I am included in the SCD directory, several times a year I receive complimentary samples from various product manufacturers, everything from bolts of ribbon to felt fabrics to acrylic paints."

PROJECT SHEETS

A good way for beginners to start working with manufacturers is to design project sheets. Perhaps you've gone into a shop to buy something and received one of these project sheets yourself. They are either offered free to shop owners, or provided at low cost. After you've used a particular supply item for a while (ribbon, glue, beads, yarn, and so on), you tend to stumble onto interesting new uses for the material. Or, perhaps you've simply created an original project that uses a particular supply item. Designers with good ideas on how to use certain supplies and materials should contact the manufacturers of those products and ask if they purchase project sheets for their dealers. Ask for samples to serve as a guideline for the sheet you want to send.

Depending on what a manufacturer wants, a project sheet might be a simple 8½ by 11-inch black-and-white design sheet or a four-color pamphlet. Both are distributed to shops and stores to promote the sale of a certain product and are usually hung by a display of that product

in the store. The amount a manufacturer will pay for such designs varies, just as it does with magazine editors. Designers I have interviewed say the price can range from $50 to $150 per design for a simple black-and-white project sheet, and $450 to $750 or more for a color leaflet, depending on the number of projects it features. One designer said she had received $1,800 for a particularly complex project published as a color leaflet.

Please understand that all prices in this chapter are offered as guidelines. It is very difficult for designers to get this kind of information because no one wants to speak about what they have received in case it is more or less than what others are receiving. By comparing what some designers have received for various types of work, however, I have come up with figures that at least offer a starting point for beginners. Professional designers can always negotiate prices, of course.

FREE SUPPLIES

Nancy Bell Anderson has designed five project sheets for DMC, a thread manufacturer. Each of these colorful pamphlets include four of Nancy's clothespin doll designs that use DMC threads. She was well paid for these designs and received a substantial supply of leaflets for her own promotional purposes. "This kind of designing is doubly profitable to me," Nancy says, "because it is helping me to build up my IRA account."

An added benefit of designing either for manufacturers or for magazines is that you'll never have to buy supplies again. "Once you have credibility as a designer," Nancy says, "you can pick up the phone and call any craft manufacturer in the country and tell them you'd like to design some projects using their materials. They will immediately send you a box of supplies. All my clothespins, for example, are supplied by Forster Mfg. Co., Inc., and DMC keeps me well supplied with their threads."

Note that most manufacturers also pay designers a small fee (from $25 to $70) whenever they sell a design project to a magazine and mention the manufacturer's product by its brand (trade) name. This, of course, is the kind of valuable publicity that sends consumers into stores to buy the material.

Other designers have also told me how generous manufacturers are about sending supplies, and I've even discovered this for myself. When I was invited to appear on *The Carol Duvall Show* (HGTV), I wanted to make something special to wear. Remembering a beautiful ribbon vest I'd seen in a craft magazine, I decided to design a vest of my own. I called Wrights® to ask if they might send

me a supply of their designer ribbons for this purpose and they immediately sent me a fabulous selection, enough for two vests, in fact. Although my colorful vest brought many compliments, I wasn't able to mention on Carol's show that I had made it of Wrights® ribbons, and I've always felt bad about this. Still, that particular show has been rerun countless times and I like to think that my vest has at least prompted some viewers to think about being more creative with ribbons.

HOW TO PROTECT YOUR IDEAS

If you are thinking about offering your great idea to a manufacturer—particularly one outside the crafts industry—be careful. When I first researched this topic twenty years ago, an authority in the crafts industry told me that individuals who try to sell to manufacturers are more likely to have their designs and ideas pirated than purchased—and, often, the larger the company, the greater the chance of this happening. A manufacturer may say, "Yes, I'm interested" when a brief explanation of an idea is submitted, and "Sorry, not interested" once all details have been provided. A year later that same idea may be on the market, only the designer won't get anything for it. It will have been cleverly adapted or subtly changed or, in other words, stolen. So, for the benefit of unsuspecting beginners everywhere who are treading into manufacturing waters and don't know what they're doing or who they're dealing with, the following guidelines will help you protect your rights:

1. Do some research to get an idea of whether the people you are interested in offering your idea to are reputable and currently showing an interest in the type of product you offer.

2. Do not send an unsolicited idea to even the most reputable company, since this constitutes "public exposure" of the idea, according to both the patent and copyright laws, and automatically gives a company the right to steal it from you.

3. Your initial letter to a manufacturer should describe your idea in general

Designing Animatronic Figures

When I first connected with Karen Lyons back in the 1980s, she was designing teddy bears and other toys for sale at fairs and shops. When she moved into wholesaling and the publishing of toy patterns, she was noticed by large toy companies for whom she began to do freelance designing. "It was my designs that were used by the Matchbox Toy Company for the Pee Wee Herman shows," she says. "Most of what I do now is for toy manufacturers who have an idea that I make come alive. I get most of my business through word-of-mouth advertising, and do 80 percent of my business over the phone, by e-mail or fax. When a proposal is accepted, I create prototypes for the client to review. When approved, the production pattern is sent for manufacture."

Karen also does large displays for trademarked characters and animatronic robot characters as seen in Disneyland. How did she learn *this,* I wondered? "A company, Astrosystems, was building animatronics, but were having trouble with durability," she says. "They worked closely with Disney, but wanted to branch out into building characters for trade shows. It turns out that the moving/talking characters we see in amusement parks are all made of latex foam. Even the fur is applied to a latex base. Latex wears out fairly quickly, so characters are frequently replaced. Someone who knew I did wacky things (à la Pee Wee Herman) mentioned my name and called me for an interview. Boy! It was a challenge!

terms only and should include some information about your background and experience. In this letter you should predetermine the company's interest in the possibility of looking at your idea, and ask it to sign an agreement that says, in essence, that it will receive your idea in confidence, and will protect your rights to it. (Use impressive originally designed stationery to signal you are a professional businessperson.)

4. If you approach a manufacturer and receive a special submission agreement or waiver to be signed, *read it carefully.* All rights should remain your property unless otherwise agreed on by all parties concerned. Think twice if a company offers you a small flat fee and asks you to relinquish all rights: It is not always wise to trust a company about the worth of your design. In truth, they may believe your idea to be quite valuable, but

"The latex characters are made from molds taken off sculptures, no seams involved. All I had to work with was a basic steel skull with a metal jaw. Fur doesn't stretch like latex, so I had to build in all kinds of tricky folds and darts. Then I had to design a complicated Velcro system because they had to be able to remove the character from the head skeleton. It's a long story, but in my early years I did splice together a video (still available), and I gave lectures about how I designed and built the animatronic skins. I don't do a lot of these characters nowadays because budgets are too slim in most companies, but I have used the experience to build fully armatured display characters. These sell for between $500 and $1,000, whereas animatronics run about $10,000."

What an interesting business Karen has developed from what was once just a little teddy bear business! Her advice to designers interested in working with toy companies? "Watch out for 'flash.' I've had many dealings with very slick toy company executives who promised much more than they could deliver. Some of the most unassuming people have the best offers."

The drawing shown here is of a six-foot animatronic rat Karen designed for an environmental company. "At trade shows, it would come out of a trash can and threaten people," she says. "One time when the vice president of the company was giving a talk, he was totally upstaged by the rat, who got out of sync and started bobbing up in the middle of his talk."

if you've given them any reason to believe you're just a beginner, they may think you'll be thrilled to receive a small check.

5. Never send samples of anything until you have a satisfactory contract, and never send original copies of designs or informational materials since they might be lost in the mail.

6. Don't sign *anything* without advice from an attorney.

7. Copyright all designs and written instructions before submitting them to a manufacturer. Safeguard other ideas by keeping records of how and when they were conceived. Include sketches and notes that give a full understanding of the subject matter. Sign and date everything. Show this material to a trusted witness and ask him or her to also sign and date the papers. This will help prove (should it ever be necessary) that the idea originated with you on a particular date. Some people put such information in a registered letter to themselves, then retain the unopened letter in a safe place until such time as it might be needed.

Licensing Designs to Manufacturers

A NATURAL WAY for designers to increase profits is to license their de-

signs to manufacturers. Some designers get up the courage to approach manufacturers while others are approached by manufacturers who have seen their products or designs somewhere. After exhibiting in a show, Randall Barr was approached by a sales rep who said he knew a company who might like to license his clock designs. At that time, Randall knew absolutely nothing about licensing and he says the deal he made with the manufacturing company wasn't the best. "When they made their run at me, it was like taking candy from a baby."

In talking with Randall and other designers about the ins and outs of licensing, I quickly learned this is far too complex and specialized a topic to be discussed at length in this book. I do, however, want to provide some perspective on how a designer's ideas end up on other products, or become whole new products themselves, like Maureen Carlson's Pippsywoggins.®

LICENSING HAND-CRAFTED SCULPTURES

Pippsywoggins® are "Little Friends From the Edge of Imagination,® born from the dreamsongs of butterflies," says Maureen, who is as gifted a writer and storyteller as she is a designer. She recently entered into a licensing arrangement with a company that is now reproducing her five-inch original clay sculptures. Each hand-crafted resin piece is hand painted by skilled artisans to capture Maureen's whimsical style. Marketed as collectibles, each piece is numbered and sold in a special gift box.

Like so many other creative individuals profiled in this book, Maureen had no idea where her ten-year-old hobby of making clay mushrooms and whimsical little people was going to take her when she started Wee Folk Creations in 1984. Five years later, when her husband, Dan, was laid off from his job with a computer company, he decided to join Maureen in her business. "In the beginning I sold my original one-of-a-kind polymer clay pieces, primarily at the Minnesota Renaissance Festival," says Maureen. "In fact, I had become something of an expert in that relatively new material, and in my eleven years at the festival had developed a local following. I started teaching because people just kept asking for classes, and their need for supplies made it easy for us to move into the sale of supplies. Today, I continue to write, teach, demonstrate, and design, while Dan manages the business and handles the wholesale and retail sales of our clay supplies and videotapes."

An interesting thing I'm seeing more and more in the crafts industry is how people who were once hobby crafters have not only developed successful businesses of their own but have gone on to form business alliances with others who were once hobbyists themselves. Maria Nerius's story in chapter 12 is one example. Maureen's story is another. Her Pippsywoggins® are being produced by Gift Connections, Inc., a sister company of Craft Marketing Connections, Inc., which is owned in part by Cindy Groom Harry®, once a hobby crafter herself who has trademarked her own name because of the design and consulting work she does. Here's how Cindy worked with Maureen to get this product on the market.

"At a 1991 SCD seminar where Maureen's clay sculptures were showcased, I bought one of her creations," says Cindy. "We didn't know one another well at that time, but it was fortuitous that we ended up sitting together on the airplane coming back home. Maureen talked about her interest in finding a way to mass produce her work because she couldn't begin to keep up with the demand for her one-of-a-kind creations. I naturally began to ponder her problem and think of ways our company might help her."

CRAFT MARKETING CONNECTIONS

This corporation is owned by Cindy, her husband, Lee Harry, and Dean Fitch. Until recently, the corporation was involved mostly in consulting and project-based activities for craft manufacturers and other companies in the industry. (Cindy was one of the first designers in the industry to see the importance of working with manufacturers on a consulting basis, and it was her membership in SCD that helped her build a network of designers and sparked the idea that ultimately led to her successful business.)

Little did Cindy know when she headed off for the SCD seminar that a chance encounter with one of the designers there would actually prompt the formation of a second company. As Maureen put it later, "Once again, I am reminded of the way networking makes things happen in this industry. One never knows what contact or what chance meeting will lead to good business down the road."

When Cindy returned to her office after the seminar, she talked with Lee and Dean, showing them the sculpture she had bought, saying she thought there was an opportunity here. "We started looking for a company that would represent Maureen well, feature her as a key designer, and give her the spotlight she deserved,

but we found no one. All of a sudden, we realized that we could do this. So we started looking into resin casting and before we knew it, we had formed a sister company to produce Pippsywoggins®. We have now done four lines of Maureen's products and two of another artist."

Note: Cindy wants to be helpful to budding designers, but her company is not set up to handle a flood of calls and letters. She does, however, offer a free Artist's Guideline Sheet to professional designers who send a request on their business letterhead and enclose a self-addressed stamped envelope for a copy. "This is a letter that outlines specifically how we operate and how the licensing process works," says Cindy. "It describes the amount of work an artist must do to actually bring a product to market." (See Resources for the address of Gift Connections.)

DESIGNS USED ON PRODUCTS

Annie Lang is currently negotiating to sell her designs to several manufacturers she has connected with through networking and membership in professional organizations such as ACCI and the Society of Craft Designers. She confirmed something I learned as I was writing my last book—that there are no standards in the licensing industry. Everyone operates differently, and the policy of one licensing agency may be totally different from the policy of another. Every deal a manufacturer makes directly with an artist or designer will be different, too. Although it's difficult to negotiate your own licensing contract, Annie is going this route because she happens to like being in control. "I'm writing in clauses I want and asking for others to be changed or deleted," she says. "It's stressful work, and not something beginners in business should attempt."

Another reason Annie is negotiating her own contract is because her research indicates that most agents in this field take from 25 to 40 percent of the total royalties in return for their services. (This seems outrageous when you consider that book agents generally take only 15 to 20 percent.) Prior to signing a licensing contract, Annie will have it checked by an attorney who specializes in copyright/patent/trademark law to make sure she hasn't overlooked anything important.

Something Annie has learned as a beginner in this field is the importance of thinking in terms of "cross-marketing" because the trend today is toward designs that can be used on a wide variety of products. The lines between decorative art, crafts, home decor, clothing, and giftware are growing thinner all the time. Annie's designs, for example, will be used as iron-on transfers and on buttons, lapel pins, and an entire giftware line. She is

currently negotiating to get her designs on fabric, too. The elf shown here will end up as a Christmas ornament.

© A. Lang 1996

LICENSING ROYALTIES

When a product or design is licensed, the designer names the creation and the manufacturer licenses the name and design, producing products for sale, just as a book publisher produces and sells books for an author. In both cases the creator receives a royalty on sales.

Because the licensing industry is in a constant state of change, it's difficult to provide more than general guidelines here. Annie's research indicates that the royalties on an artist's designs can be as low as 2 percent and as high as 10 or 12 percent (although the higher royalties are rare). Every sale has a different contract, and the percentage of royalties and what they will be paid on (net or gross sales) can vary considerably depending on the size of the company, what you're licensing and how it's going to be used. Cindy Groom Harry's research indicates that royalties generally range in the 3 to 7 percent range, but may go as high as 10 percent of net sales. "The amount a designer receives depends in part on the amount of participation he or she contributes after the licensing agreement has been made," she says. "For example, to promote the sale of Pippsywoggins®, Maureen writes the *Pippsywoggins® Gazette* (which we publish) and also participates in trade show promotions."

The Society of Craft Designers

N OW I WANT to tell you how membership in a single organization can make all the difference in your ability to earn serious income from your design talents. The most successful designers in the crafts industry are members of the Society of Craft Designers (SCD), and it's important to remember they were all amateurs at one time. Society members receive an informative newsletter, but their greatest opportunity for learning comes at the annual educational seminar, which is held in a hotel conference center in a different city each year. For many designers and craft editors, this five-day seminar is the highlight of their year. Here, beginners and professionals alike find business doors opening to them as they meet leading editors, publishers, and manufacturers who explain their needs. Experienced designers take beginners in hand, sharing trade secrets they won't learn anywhere else. After an intense day of workshops, everyone gets together in groups for informal evening networking sessions. Here specific problems are discussed and everyone has a chance to contribute "off the cuff" advice and ideas.

"If you're a designer, you simply must attend SCD seminars," says Nancy Bell Anderson. "As a member, I had the opportunity in 1997 to travel to England for a three-day seminar in London sponsored by England's equivalent of SCD. After the seminar, we toured through Belgium and ended up in the Netherlands for a European trade show. This gave us a good overview of what the northern European market was for crafts. It was here that I and several other SCD members made connections with foreign magazines, and where I met the editor of *Popular Crafts*, who asked me to do a monthly Peg Doll column."

Did you know clothespins in England are called "clothes pegs" and the dolls made from them are called "peg dolls"? Nancy said she got this column because the editor thought her contemporary design ideas would revitalize this old English craft. "The nice thing about it is that I don't have to sell all rights to my projects, so it enables me to reuse old designs in a different way, test new ideas, and still have the right to put them into a book or new kit package."

"Membership in SCD catapulted me from a regional artist to a national polymer clay authority," says Maureen Carlson. "When a member of SCD saw the first videotape Dan and I produced, she urged me to join the organization and attend a seminar. I'd never heard of her or the organization, but our tape wasn't selling well and we needed publicity, so a month later I was in San Antonio. I didn't know anything about the craft world—what was hot or how the distribution system worked, or who the celebrities were. I had never read anything written by the main speaker, Barbara Brabec (I only read books and magazines dealing with polymer clay), but I did gather that she must be respected because people were delighted that she (you) were there. And I remember that you encouraged—and chided—us as you implied that we were not demanding enough respect and money for our talents. Well, I made contacts at that seminar that changed my life, and in 1995 I was chosen Craft Designer of the Year—all of which to me seems pretty incredible."

I have attended several SCD conferences in years past, both as a speaker and interested "watcher." I've seen the wonder in a beginning craft designer's eyes as she realizes *this* is exactly what she needs. Through the years I've encouraged

Designed for Laughs

Elizabeth Bishop sells patterns of Victorian cloth dolls through her Seams Sew Creative catalog, and she also writes how-to articles for magazines. She says some people will never understand the creative concept of originality.

"In trying to describe to a neighbor exactly what I do, I explained that I created totally original projects, copyrighted them, and sold them to publications as how-to articles. Pointing to a magazine cover featuring one of my dolls, I displayed the actual project beside it to illustrate my point. My neighbor studied both intently, then exclaimed: 'That's so good—you made yours look just like the picture!'"

"Victoriana"
© EB Designs

creative people to join this organization, just as I and the designers profiled in this chapter now encourage you.

Annie Lang recalls the impact SCD made on her career. "When I stepped off the plane to attend my first seminar, I felt very intimidated, unworthy, and really anxious. What I found waiting for me was a group of very warm, helpful, and fun-loving professionals who encouraged, guided, and challenged my creativity. An important aspect to SCD is that our networking files seem to multiply as we designers keep in touch throughout the year. When a manufacturer calls with specific needs outside my area of expertise, it's easy to find a fellow designer to refer them to. Likewise, fellow designers do the same for me. At each seminar, editors, manufacturers, fellow designers, and authors from every facet of the industry come together for a few days, not in competition, but by mutual interest in making the industry more exciting and accessible through classes, open discussion and conferencing. This is truly a group of dedicated professionals working together, striving to build the industry."

Writing and Publishing

For the kind of fame that sticks until the grandkids have grandkids, short of being President of the U.S. or curing cancer, there's little like a book with your name permanently plunked on the author line.

GORDON BURGETT, author of *Empire-Building by Writing and Speaking*

ILLIONS OF PEOPLE enjoy putting their thoughts and ideas on paper (or computer, as the case may be) in the form of letters, journals, or personal diaries. Because crafters are naturally creative, they tend to enter the field of writing and self-publishing more readily than the average individual. Now that so many have computers and desktop publishing capability, even more are entering this field. Today, hundreds of newsletters, newspapers, magazines, directories, and how-to books are being published from home base by crafters-turned-publishers. Some, like Linda Ligon of Interweave Press (whose story appears later in this chapter), have grown a home-based publication into a publishing empire. (Even *Reader's Digest* began on a kitchen table.)

In the small space of a chapter, I can only touch on the topics of writing and publishing as a home-based business. I can, however, share some perspective on the profitability of certain types of writing and publishing and introduce you to a few artisans who have diversified their businesses by

➤ Writing magazine articles or a column

➤ Publishing information of one kind or another

➤ Publishing a periodical

➤ Writing a book

➤ Publishing their own books

Yes, once again, I'm trying to push you into new waters. If you can't swim yet, just stick your toe in and see how it feels.

Writing Magazine Articles

L IKE MAKING AND selling crafts, writing well and being able to sell what you write are two different things. Thus you must approach the sale of your writing the same way you would go about selling crafts: First look for a good market, then offer something editors want to buy. The more professional your finished product, the more likely it is to sell.

There are numerous opportunities to be published in dozens of craft and home-business periodicals. Only the larger ones are listed in directories, however, so you'll have to build your own list through reading and research. (Read the classified ads of larger magazines or search the Internet.) Writing for small craft and home-business periodicals doesn't pay much—about 3 to 15 cents a word, tops—but there is nothing quite as exciting as

seeing your words in print for the first time. Newsletters don't pay anything for articles, but you do get tear sheets that prove you're a published writer. In the beginning, the important thing is just to get into print somewhere. If you decide you like the writing business, approach it as something you will be able to do for the rest of your life and strive to constantly improve your skills through practice and self-study.

PROMOTIONAL ARTICLES

Most of the editors in the crafts and home-business fields encourage the contribution of articles by readers, offering free advertising space or a generous publicity "blurb" (or "resource box") at the end of an article (comparable to a classified ad). If you have published a book, one of the easiest ways to get publicity for it is to pull some excerpts from the book and offer them as free articles. (If you write a book for a trade publisher, be sure to add a clause to your contract that allows you to do this.) The blurb at the bottom of a promotional article might tell readers to send a check to order, call your toll-free number, or log onto your Web site for more information.

Crafts business writer Barbara Massie writes articles for several print and online newsletters and magazines, not all of whom can pay for her material. "Crafters need the kind of information I can offer," she says, "so when a publisher can't pay me for an article, I'm happy to share what I know in return for advertising space or publicity." A typical blurb at the end of one of Barbara's articles might read: "Barbara is the owner of Massie's, a company that describes itself as 'The Crafter's Helper.' She is the author of *Craft Malls—Do a Craft Show Everyday* and *Basic Bookkeeping for a Small Business.* For more information . . ."

TECHNIQUE OR INFORMATIONAL ARTICLES

If you are a professional crafter who has gathered hard-to-find information, knows how to do something the average person doesn't know, or has mastered a complicated craft technique and can explain it clearly, you'll have no trouble selling your articles. In talking with fiber artist Charlene Anderson-Shea, I learned about the last three articles she had sold. One was a how-to article that included not only the instructions for knitting her originally designed shawl, but also explained how to buy the fleece and wash it, dye it, and spin it prior to knitting. It sold to *Spin-Off,* a magazine for spinners. Another article, which sold to *Shuttle, Spindle & Dyepot,* explained how to write a newsletter for one's local weaving guild. The third article was especially interesting to me.

"I proposed an article to *Interweave Knits* (Winter 1997/98), saying that I and two others would personally test all the knitting needles on the market, and I would then write a review of all of them and the types of materials they were best suited for," Charlene explained. "The article paid well and I ended up with a nice bonus: 339 pairs of knitting needles— about a thousand dollars' worth—contributed by needle manufacturers. I personally knitted on 113 different needles, as did my friends who lived in different parts of the country. What was interesting to me is that all three of us liked the same needles best—ebony ones made by Muench."

I used to knit years ago, but I had no idea there were so many different kinds of needles today, made from so many different materials besides plastic, including steel, brass- and gold-plated metals, fiberglass, bamboo, birch, rosewood, and ebony. Does this article suggest ideas on things you might write about? For example, how many different kinds of crochet needles are there? What kinds and types of carving tools are available to wood-workers? How many different kinds of threads can one use for cross-stitch embroidery? What exotic yarns are available to knitters and crocheters? What are the best scissors for each type of craft work people do? Or glues? Or teddy-bear stuffing tools? Are your wheels spinning yet?

A COLUMN OF YOUR OWN

If you have a lot to say about a particular topic, you may be a columnist waiting to be born. Like magazine articles, payment for a column can vary greatly from practically nothing to several hundred dollars per article. While a column may sound like a lot of fun, it is also demanding, in that you must meet regular publishing deadlines and you must be reasonably sure you won't run out of ideas for what to write about. Many newsletter publishers and home-business periodicals would welcome a business-oriented column, but craft consumer magazines are more likely to be interested in how-to articles.

When I proposed my "Selling What You Make" column to *Crafts Magazine* in 1979, I never dreamed I'd still be writing it twenty years later. The editors have changed twice, but the beat goes on, and so far I haven't run out of anything to write about, thanks to the wonderful feedback I always get from my readers.

Without their sharing of information, my columns and books would not exist. I like what Jim Rohn, author of *The Treasury of Quotes*, says about sharing: "It makes you bigger than you are. The more you pour out, the more life will be able to pour in."

Identifying Your Markets

To DEVELOP A list of possible markets for articles you have in mind, first obtain a copy of the latest edition of *Writer's Market* (Writer's Digest Books). This annual directory is the marketing bible of all serious freelance writers. It lists the editorial needs of hundreds of magazine editors (book publishers, too) and tells how to order sample issues so you can get a clear understanding of the kind of articles each magazine publishes.

I also recommend *Making $$$ at Home—Over 1,000 Editors Who Want Your Ideas, Know-How & Experience* by Darla Sims (Sunstar Publications). In the late 1970s, Darla turned her love of knitting into a lucrative career as a freelance designer, publishing hundreds of designs and written instructions that later led to this book on how to sell articles of all kinds. "The book was a natural result of the research I had done as a designer, always on the lookout for new magazines," Darla told me. "The longer I did this, the more aware I became of all the little niche magazines out there. Most people don't realize that the special little things they do every day or for special occasions are worth money to magazine editors. My book simply helps people find paying outlets for their good ideas."

As a crafts designer herself, Darla understands the crafter's mentality. "Many are so focused on their work—like having blinders on—that they've lost their vision of the possibilities. There are so many topics they could write about—and sell—if they only made the attempt."

Another book I particularly like is *The Silver Pen—Starting a Profitable Writing Business from a Lifetime of Experience*, by Alan Canton (Adams-Blake Publishing). In his book, Alan emphasizes that editors want articles that offer information readers can take away with them. "If you can write about an experience that taught you some lessons, gave you new viewpoints, or changed your life in some way, editors are going to be interested," he says, adding this warning: "Well-meaning people are likely to discourage you from writing, but don't listen to them. You have to adopt the belief that you can do anything you set your mind to do. Don't accept outside advice or input that tells you otherwise." (I liked Alan the mo-

ment I read the "About the Author" page. It said: "As an active writer on technology issues, Mr. Canton has been published in numerous magazines and journals. He is married with four cats.")

Publishing Booklets, Directories, and Reports

IF YOU SELL anything by mail, adding booklets, directories, or reports to your line could put thousands of extra dollars in your pocket. If you have a computer, high-quality printer, and information likely to be interest to others, you can literally start an information-based mail-order business overnight. The print format you use can be as simple as a brochure (8½ by 11-inch sheet of paper folded in thirds to fit a business-size envelope); several pages of information stapled together; or a stapled (what printers call "saddle-stitched") booklet.

If you have a mailing list of people who have bought your handcrafts, supplies, or patterns, use this as a base from which to start. By using classified ads and press releases, you can tap a national market of people likely to be interested in what you have to sell. Depending on the

Selling Poetry and Nostalgic Reminiscences

Because poetry and nostalgic writing is difficult to sell, most of it is self-published. Artist Ruby Tobey has developed quite a following of customers through the years who are quick to buy the little poetry booklets she has illustrated with her drawings. "I have always printed booklets a thousand at a time to get a good price," says Ruby, "but after you have three or four in print, it gets expensive to keep them all in print and find a place to store everything."

Now older and not quite as ambitious as she once was, Ruby is thinking smaller these days, and may have discovered something equally as profitable as her 36-page poetry booklets. "I'm now doing little 12-page booklets (counting front and back covers) of poetry and art that I sell for $2 each," she says. "A friend puts the whole booklet on computer for me and prints out the color covers on cardstock. I print the black-and-white inside sheets at a local printer, doing fifty or a hundred copies at a time and folding and stapling booklets together myself."

Given the increased cost of regular greeting cards now, Ruby could easily get $3 for this product if she included an envelope with a bit of color art on it and packaged the booklet as a greeting card or little gift item. By adding about 15 cents to the cost of this product, she could make an extra 45 cents profit on each booklet.

Designer Susan Young, who has several magazine articles to her credit, has increased the profits of her Peach Kitty crafts and pattern business by publishing a growing line of article reprints, tip sheets and charming booklets. A nostalgic soul, Susan writes not only poetry, but short stories. She has published *Tea for Grandmother* and *Tales from a Celestial Prairie—Memories, Contemplations, and Dreams,* a book coauthored with her great aunt. "Both books are trips down memory lane," she says, "and both have sold very well to the same people who buy my crafts or patterns."

Susan has had no difficulty in getting $6.95 for *Tea for Grandmother,* a 53-page booklet (5 1/2 by 8 1/2 inches), and $15 for the 75-page book (8 1/2 by 11 inches), proving there is a market for this kind of writing.

type and format of your information, it might be priced anywhere from a couple of dollars to $10 ppd. (Information priced higher than this is unlikely to sell through a classified ad or publicity mention.)

Of course there is a knack to writing a good classified ad or press release that will be published by national magazines—topics beyond the scope of this book but discussed at length in my *Homemade Money* book. (This "home business bible" includes all the strategies I and others have used to build successful home-based businesses of all kinds.)

The Profitability of Booklets

As shop owner and catalog marketer Janet Burgess has learned, sometimes the market for a simple booklet can be astounding. Through her Amazon Vinegar & Pickling Works Drygoods business, Janet has sold tens of thousands of copies of *Clothing Guidelines for the Civil War Era,* a 42-page, $4.95 booklet first printed in 1982. "We reprint in quantities of 5,000 at a time," Janet says, "and we've sold so many booklets over the years that I've lost track of total sales to date."

This is a perfect example of the old saying about necessity being the mother of invention. Janet says the only reason she published this booklet was because she got tired of giving the same little lecture over and over again to Civil War reenactors, people doing plays, managers of historic houses, museums, and so on. "There are other books on this topic, but my little booklet presents a simplified overview in response to questions asked by people who are interested in living history."

Janet specializes in sewing patterns of the past—clothing from early Medieval up to 1950, and she markets clothing patterns, accessories, and patterns for Victorian window treatments through three separate catalogs. Her business certainly sounds interesting—and, if the following story is any indication, it's often good for a laugh. Janet relates this story about a customer who bought one of her Victorian corsets and laced it too tight: "She called me in total bewilderment saying, 'I don't know what happened—I sneezed and the whole thing blew up!'"

Although Janet has sold thousands of her booklets one at a time to individual catalog buyers, she has also wholesaled thousands to gift shops connected to museums, historic houses, and other living history places. Thus, in pricing any booklet you decide to sell, be sure to keep the price high enough to allow for wholesaling in case the opportunity presents itself. Also, get several quotes before you have it printed because one printer's estimate can often be twice as high as another's, and the prices you get from a local printer are apt to be highest of all. (For a list of printers you can work with by mail, see the resource chapter for *Directory of Printers.*)

Interesting side note: Remember Mary Lou Highfill? A while back, when Mary Lou advertised her sunbonnet patterns in a sewing magazine, Janet Burgess responded to her ad, saying she wanted to add her sunbonnet patterns to her catalog. "I was just getting started and didn't know the first thing about how to do this, so Janet took me under her wing and helped me more than I can say. I couldn't draw, so I just sent her several sunbonnets and she made line art drawings of them for her catalog and for my own advertising purposes. I also use these drawings on my business envelope to stimulate interest in what's inside."

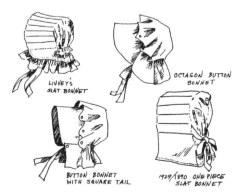

LIUVEY'S
SLAT BONNET

OCTAGON BUTTON
BONNET

BUTTON BONNET
WITH SQUARE TAIL

1929/1890 ONE PIECE
SLAT BONNET

DIRECTORIES: A LITTLE GOLD MINE

Prior to starting her own crafts business, Adele Patti says her main skill was that of "speed typist." Sixteen years of office work had also taught her discipline—being able to meet deadlines and deliveries. These skills were a perfect base on which to launch Front Room Publishers in 1983. Today, Adele is the largest publisher of craft directories in the industry.

Her focus has always been on providing information to help professional crafters sell with greater success. Her first publication was *Directory of Craft Shops and Galleries,* followed by *Creative Crafters Directory,* which lists the offerings of crafters nationwide. Craft shop and gallery owners use this directory to find new suppliers, and craft mall owners are buying it to round up vendors or advertisers for online sites. These two directories work hand-in-hand because Adele is always promoting the second directory as she gathers updated information for the first. Other guides include *Directory of Seasonal Holiday Boutiques* and *Directory of Craft Malls and Rent-a-Space Shops.*

Although directory publishing can be quite profitable, it's also demanding and time-consuming. Don't even think about this kind of publishing unless you are going to make a concerted effort to keep information up to date. To do otherwise is a disservice to buyers, and anyone who continues to sell information known to be outdated will ultimately ruin their reputation as a reliable information provider.

"I try to update all my directories annually and usually issue update sheets in mid-year, including them with all orders for the directory," says Adele. "But keeping directories up to date is difficult—almost impossible at times—even with computer technology. People don't always return update questionnaires on time and there are always mail problems."

Adele has priced all of her directories at $12.95 to allow for wholesaling to other publishers. She cautions publishers never to print or reprint without getting a new quote because printing prices are always changing.

MONEY FROM A SIMPLE BROCHURE

While doing some publicity work for authors and small publishers, Darla Sims collected a series of tips to help them promote and publicize their books. "I translated these tips into a little brochure titled "101 Ways to Publicize Yourself or Your Business," she says, "and on a whim sent it to *Bottom Line/Personal,* a newsletter whose circulation base is the largest in the country. I offered to send their readers a copy for $1.50, they gave it a 1-inch mention, and I was astonished to get over 2,000 orders for it. This told me that there are a lot of people out there who are struggling to compete. They don't have money for advertising so they are looking for creative ways to promote their business."

Crafters and other home-business owners are in the same boat, of course, so if you're a successful business owner who can help others succeed, put your information in printed form and offer it with a press release to small and large magazines and newsletters alike. As Darla's experience proves, any format will work so long as the information is valuable. Her "brochure" was nothing more than a legal-sized piece of paper folded twice to fit a #10 standard business-size envelope.

Periodical Publishing

IT SEEMS EVERYONE wants to publish a newsletter these days. But can this be as easy as it sounds, and is this a good way to make extra money at home? Yes . . . and no. As an ex-newsletter publisher who realized good profits from publishing for nearly fifteen years, you might think I'd encourage others to start newsletters, too. But things are changing, and I and many

The Profitability of Tip Sheets

Sometimes you can make more money selling a $2 tip sheet than a $20 book, provided you take the time to learn how to write a good press release and mail it to a few hundred publications.

If you sell to crafters themselves, there is no limit to the kind of information they will buy if it costs only a few dollars. Anything you've learned from experience can be shared in printed form and sold to this vast audience. (The best way to get ideas for the kind of information that sells is to read the classified ad sections of several magazines.)

If the names on your mailing list are people who have bought your handcrafts in the past, some may be crafters, too. Most, however, might respond better to information related to their use of handcrafts—yours and others'. For example, if you make quilted products, you might offer a $2 tip sheet on how to care for both new and antique quilts, or how to repair an old quilt or display quilts as art. If you restore antiques or make antique reproductions of a certain type, you might share tips on how to tell a fake from the real thing. A list of where to find museum exhibits or displays of particular crafts when traveling would also appeal to many people.

others feel the Internet has greatly devalued the worth of print newsletters because there are now so many free newsletters online.

The world is literally drowning in information, and now that we all have free access to thousands of informative articles and online newsletters, why would anyone pay for similar information in print? I don't think they will . . . unless they can get information, ideas, or insight not readily available elsewhere or, if available, too time-consuming to gather it themselves.

SHOW-LISTING PERIODICALS

The most successful subscription-based craft publications today seem to be show-listing periodicals that include advance information about where artists and crafters might sell their work. Because we are now seeing a growing number of Web sites offering show-listing information, the Internet may also impact the profitability of show-listing publications in time.

Often a cross between a newsletter and a magazine, show-listing periodicals may list events nationwide (like *Sunshine Artist, Arts 'n Crafts ShowGuide,* and *SAC Newsmonthly*), or focus on a particular state or region. For example, Christel Luther has been publishing her *Hands On Guide* since 1988. For ten years, whenever Christel displayed her appliqued sweatshirts and other crafts at a fair, crafters would always ask how she found out about shows. Like Janet Burgess, who got tired of saying the same thing over and over, she decided to launch a publication to help local artisans, crafters, and interested shoppers find the best arts and crafts fairs, antiques, and collectibles shows in California and ten other Western states.

Across the country, Rita Stone-Conwell has also turned years of experience in selling her crafts into a newsletter called *Crafts Remembered*, which offers a comprehensive listing of events in the New York state area plus articles and business information. Rita's 3,500 subscribers receive quarterly three-hole-punched pages they can keep in a binder for easy reference. "I hope to eventually turn my newsletter into a bimonthly magazine," she says. Rita cautions beginners,

however, that publishing a newsletter requires "research and more research. Don't think you can just throw something together overnight. Unless you have thousands of dollars to spend on advertising, it's difficult to get subscribers, and once you have them, it's difficult to keep them."

The Financial Realities of Newsletter Publishing

IN ADDITION TO publishing directories, Adele Patti has published *Craft Marketing News* since 1984. She agrees that newsletter publishing is a lot of work. "And those publishing deadlines come awfully quick. Before you realize it, it's time to start another issue. Getting renewals is a constant battle, too. Big-time newsletter publishers say you have to send a string of notices to get renewals, but I've found this a waste of time and money. Crafters are either going to renew on the first or second notice or they're not going to renew at all."

Make sure you fully understand the economics of newsletter publishing before you commit yourself to this kind of business. Newsletter novices tend to start by picking a subscription rate—let's say $18 for a bimonthly—figure their printing and postage costs, and subtract them from gross income to estimate their potential profit. This sounds good in theory but doesn't work in practice. Let's say it costs 40 cents to print an issue. Multiplied by six issues, this is $2.40. Add first-class postage (currently $.32 but subject to change) and you've got a total production/mailing cost of $4.32. (You may think you can save money by mailing at bulk rates, but I no longer recommend this. The difference between first class and bulk mail is only a few cents, and bulk mail can take up to forty-five days to be delivered. Although the post office claims bulk mail is delivered in ten days, I and many other publishers have learned this is not true.)

In the above example, it appears you might make $13.68 on every subscription you can sell, but that isn't how it works. From this "profit," you must now subtract:

➤ The cost of your time to design all the printed materials needed to solicit subscriptions, including promotional flyers, subscription forms, direct mail brochures or catalogs, envelopes, office forms, invoices, and so on—not to mention the writing of classified ads and press releases.

➤ The cost of advertising—classified ads, publicity, or direct mail promotions. (You can't sell more than a handful of subscriptions with classified ads or publicity mentions. All you can do is offer sample issues to get the names of prospects who *might* subscribe if you send them a terrific brochure that outlines all the benefits of your publication. Even when you do this, you will be lucky to get more than a 3 percent subscription response to any mailing.)

➤ The time it takes to write and produce each issue. (It took me an average of sixty hours to write and format each issue of my eight-page newsletter. Rewriting and tightening copy to make it fit the cramped confines of a newsletter's format is often the most time-consuming work of all.)

➤ Labor costs of labeling and bundling issues for mailing.

➤ The cost of maintaining your subscriber and prospect mailing lists—all those additions, deletions and corrections on a continuous basis.

➤ The cost of your time in answering reader mail and sending letters or making phone calls to get articles and information for each new issue.

➤ The cost of getting renewals. By the time you add all the expenses involved in getting new subscribers, you may find you're paying more for each one than you're charging for a year's subscription, so now you hang your hopes on renewals. But subscribers are just like commuters: Some are always getting off while others are getting on. Count yourself lucky if 30 percent of your first-year subscribers renew. Half of those might renew the second year, and so on, until by the fifth year, you may have only a handful of those original subscribers left. Believe me when I say that people are lethargic about renewing subscriptions, even to periodicals they claim to love. There are just too many places where dollars need to be spent these days, and one way to save is to cut back on subscriptions.

Am I trying to discourage you from publishing a newsletter? Yes . . . and no. Although a newsletter with a low subscription rate is not likely to be profitable in terms of dollars, producing it could give you a great deal of satisfaction while enabling you to polish your writing skills. You will connect with all kinds of interesting people who will add interest and excitement to your life, and somewhere along the way you might connect with someone who will change the course of your business. A newsletter will also give you a kind of credibility you can't get in any other way, even as a published author. If your goal is to draw added attention to other things you've written, or other

products and services you offer, a newsletter can be a great promotional tool.

At the very least, newsletter publishing broadens one's horizons—not to mention hips, with all that sitting in front of a computer and no time to exercise. Whether profitable or not, a newsletter is absolutely guaranteed to be stressful. In the end, it was the relentless publishing deadlines that finally did me in—that, and the fact that I finally wised up to the fact that I could write a whole book in the space of time it would take me to write six newsletters, and earn royalties from that work for years to come.

After several years of doing a newsletter, one woman who was totally stressed out commented in a letter about the frustration she was feeling at that time: "I keep promising myself one day I will have time for me. Time to sew, do my crafts, teach again, read a book, work in the garden, and a lot of other things. I feel as though I'm on a merry-go-round that just never stops. As it goes round and round, I see posters listing all the things that must be done, and I try to grab one off each time I go round. But as one poster comes down, another takes its place."

Without question, a newsletter runs your life because there is always one more deadline to meet, one more job to do, one more new problem to cope with. It can be exciting, but it's not for everyone, and crafters rarely stay in this game for more than a few years. Be warned that it's easier to start a newsletter than stop it because you either have to refund the money people have paid you for subscriptions you aren't going to fulfill, or be clever enough to figure out how to give them something of equal value in return. Before you start, know how you're going to stop. It's easy to get on a merry-go-round that's just sitting there, but jumping off once it's started is hard to do without getting hurt.

From Little Acorns . . .

- -

Linda Ligon's success story was featured in the first edition of this book. Now, twenty years later, I am delighted to have the opportunity to share "the rest of the story," as Paul Harvey would say. Today, Linda describes herself as "a publisher who loves making books and magazines." Back in 1975, however, she thought of herself as an ex-teacher, mother of three, and someone who loved to weave.

"When Day was born, I had two other children aged six and eight. Day was ill for a long time after his birth, so there was no way I could think of going back to my job

teaching high school English," she recalls. "Straight housewifing was not for me, nor production weaving. And I didn't have the art background to feel like I could weave museum pieces or brilliant commissions. I decided that what I needed was a challenging job at home, and I got the idea for publishing a weaving magazine because I was dissatisfied with the periodical literature available for weavers at that time."

Except for some experience on her high school newspaper, Linda had no background in journalism or publishing, so she began an intensive period of self-study. "I bought magazines that I thought were well done and tried to figure out what it was about the writing, design, and format that made them appealing. I found a sympathetic printer (his bid wasn't the lowest, but he didn't ask me who my boss was, either) and asked a lot of questions."

Using her teacher's retirement fund money (about $1,700) to start with, Linda bought a converted linotype that punched paper tape for typesetting, and a photo enlarger she set on top of the washing machine. She scrounged mailing lists from guilds and from one friendly mail-order supplier. From the very beginning, the magazine she called *Interweave* operated in the black. By the middle of its second year, circulation had reached 1,600, an impressive figure for so young a periodical. At that time, Linda told me she was optimistic about the magazine achieving financial viability, not just hand-to-mouth existence. But she didn't have a clue then where that magazine was leading her.

Like all new publishers, Linda had too little time for everything, and no time at all for weaving. She just dreamed of the day when she could afford full-time help, wouldn't be three months behind in the mail, and could get back to the loom. "Much of my time problems in those days were of my own making," she says. "I was a Brownie Scout and 4-H leader and a parent-teacher council member because those things were important to me. I had to make some deliberate choices about my time that I could change if I chose to. My family was extremely supportive and very nice to me during my quarterly frenzy. The older kids helped prepare mailings and my husband gave me a sympathetic ear and good advice on occasion."

After a while, Linda moved from the dining room to her own office in the basement and was only one month behind in her correspondence when she decided to cease publication of *Interweave* and roll its subscriber base over to a new magazine called *Handwoven*. "Whereas the first publication was oriented more to weaving techies, *Handwoven* was the only weaving magazine at that time to offer how-to projects. It found an immediate and very appreciative audience."

In 1979 Linda diversified her business by launching a book publishing division that now includes over 120 fiber-related titles. Anyone who starts a publishing business needs to be space-oriented, because it is the nature of this business to hog every inch of space it can find. Five years after she began, Linda had outgrown the basement of her home and moved her operation to an old Victorian home in town. In 1990, when those quarters also became too crowded, she bought a charming 1920s bank building that offered the necessary room for comfort and growth. So far, her business hasn't outgrown this space, in spite of the fact that Linda now publishes seven magazines with a combined circulation of over 100,000. They include *Piecework* (historical textile and needlework crafts with projects); *Interweave Knits; Herbs for Health* (medicinal herbs); and *Beadwork* (launched in 1997). All publishing activities are done under the Interweave Press umbrella, and of course there is a Web site called interweave.com.

In looking at Linda's accomplishments over the past two decades, I am both impressed and astonished by all she has done on an initial investment of $1,700 and no prior experience in publishing. From a staff of one, she has grown her little home business to an economy-impacting corporation that now provides work for sixty-five people. Beginning with equipment now found only in museums, today Linda's publishing enterprise is totally dependent on computers. "We don't use layout boards and film anymore," she says. "Everything goes out of here on disk—we go to press computer-to-plate." She laughs as she recalls *Handwoven's* fifth birthday, when she commented in an editorial that the business had grown from a card file of subscribers to a computer with 64 megabytes of customer records.

Linda still loves to weave for pleasure, but it's clear she was born to be a publisher, and home never could have contained her ambitions. "My original goal was to be at home as long as the children needed me, and I met that goal. Then it was time to move on," she says. "I've always wanted to grow—not be so vertical."

Linda started her business the way she quit smoking—just said, "I will do it"—and never gave herself a chance to say, "Yeah, but . . ." She says success is more likely if you build on something you love to do, and then do it not for your own ego gratification but to help others in some way. She believes that people—dependent women in particular—need to be told about the possibilities that exist for them. "I regret that I was thirty-two years old before it occurred to me I could

do anything besides be a teacher. But no one ever told me."

Writing a Book

SOME PEOPLE SLIDE into the writing of a book as naturally as a duck takes to water. Once they have established themselves as a professional artist, crafter, designer, teacher, or writer, a book is the most natural thing in the world to do. Even so, the idea of writing a book can be intimidating.

Although I had published a crafts magazine for five years, I never thought of myself as a writer until a publisher asked me to write a book for homemakers who wanted to make money at home from crafts. After saying I'd think about it, I found myself wondering if I could actually write a book. "How hard can it be?" the publisher had asked. "All you have to do is string a bunch of your magazine articles together and you'll have a book." As an avid book reader, however, I knew there had to be more to writing a book than that. By then, my name was well known in the crafts field, and all I could think about was how embarrassed I would be if I did a poor job with my first book. The day I signed the contract to write *Creative Cash* was the day I vowed to become a professional writer.

The first thing I did was go to the library in search of books on the topic of how to be a good writer. I selected three books at random, went home, and literally devoured them, reading well into the wee hours of the morning. I didn't learn until years later that I had accidentally selected one of the best books ever written for beginning writers. It was *On Writing Well,* by William Zinsser (HarperPerennial). That book changed my life by changing the way I thought about myself. It convinced me I could be a professional writer *if I chose to be one.* The most important lesson I got from this book was that the most successful writers are people who write about things they know best. Zinsser also emphasized the use of short words and sentences, which encouraged me greatly. Prior to that, I thought good writers were the ones who used flowery words and wrote paragraph-long sentences, like the book reviewers in newspapers.

The next (and smartest) thing I did was subscribe to *Writer's Digest,* the monthly bible for writers, and buy several years' back issues. Every day I'd work on my book, and every night I'd read an issue of the magazine and discover I was doing something wrong in my writing. The next day, I'd go back and rewrite what I'd written before. This went on for the whole year it took me to write the book, and by the time I'd finished, I'd rewritten every sentence, paragraph, and chapter of *Creative Cash* a dozen times or more. In the process, I learned a lot about the craft of writing. The book was published just as I wrote it, with only minor copy editing, making me think I'd done a good job of writing it. When I decided to do this all-new edition, however, I looked at my first writing effort with a critical eye and was embarrassed by what I saw, much as some crafters are embarrassed to remember the work they sold when they first got started. What started out as a revision of the old book quickly became a totally new book instead. With twenty years of writing under my belt, and word processing software (*WordPerfect*) that makes it easy to organize a mass of information, my ability to turn out a helpful book has naturally improved. With time and practice, your writing will improve, too, so don't give up if you think your work is amateurish now. Just keep working to make it better.

Like professional crafters, good writers aren't born overnight. The only way to move from "amateur writer" to "professional writer" is first to educate yourself on the craft of writing through intensive self-study, then improve your writing skills through constant practice. You must also familiarize yourself with the way editors and publishers work to learn what they want to receive from writers. (Resources includes books that will help you do this.)

"Just DO It!"

Artist Laura Donnelly Bethmann says it was serendipity that led her to write her first book, *Nature Printing with Herbs, Fruits & Flowers.* "Once when I was doing a water color of a river scene, I retrieved a leaf from the bottom of the river that had been dyed a rusty brown from the cedar content of the water. I pressed it to my watercolor paper and made my first print. After that, I continued to incorporate leaf prints into my watercolors of rivers."

One day, an herbalist Laura was corresponding with suggested she write a book about the art of nature prints. Prepared for rejection, she decided to begin with an article for *Herb Companion* and was surprised when it was immediately accepted. Encouraged, yet still feeling a bit insecure, Laura submitted a book proposal to Storey Communications.

Laura's drawing of herself at work in her "secret garden," clipped from her business brochure.

"I let go of the fear of making mistakes long ago," Laura told me. "Still, I was reluctant to send my first book proposal off to a publisher. After six months of reworking, it was finally packaged up and ready to do. Thinking of what to redo, I considered putting it off for another month and said out loud, 'Maybe I should include more artwork.' My daughter, ten years old at the time said, 'Just *send* it, Mom!' She was right. It would never be *perfect.* But the first publisher I sent it to loved it and published it in a hardcover edition in 1996. A note now tacked up in my studio reads, JUST DO IT!"

Working with Trade Publishers

THERE ARE SEVERAL differences between "trade publishers" and publishers of the "floppy books" discussed in the previous chapter. Although some trade publishers market aggressively by mail or sell to special markets, most sell only through bookstores, libraries, and book clubs. Unlike craft publishers, who often buy book ideas outright or work on a cooperative basis with authors, trade publishers work only on a royalty basis, paying authors a small percentage of either the retail price or their net earnings from the book. Upon signing a contract, authors receive an advance against royalties, the size of which is entirely up to the publisher (or your agent's ability to negotiate a higher amount for you). Whether a book comes out in a hardcover or paperback edition is also up to the publisher and dependent on the market for each type of edition.

RESEARCHING YOUR BOOK IDEA

Before you start to write a book, you need to answer these questions. How many other books similar to yours are already in print? Is anyone currently using the title you plan to use? What will your book offer readers that other books do not? If you're connected to the Internet, you can gather a wealth of information in minutes simply by going to Amazon.com, the largest online bookstore. It lists 2.5 million book titles, both in and out of print. You can search this database looking for specific titles, key words in titles, subject content, author, and more. (If you can't do this from your home computer, you may be able to access the Internet through a computer in your library.) Manual research can also be done by browsing

bookstores or directories at the library, such as *Books in Print* and *Forthcoming Books* (R. R. Bowker).

Don't be discouraged if you find that several others have written books on your topic. This is no reason not to publish a book. I actually laughed the day a publisher asked me to write the book that would later become *Creative Cash*. "But there are at least a dozen books on this topic already," I said. "That doesn't matter," the publisher countered. "I think you can write a better one, and we're sure we can sell thousands of copies." He was right. The first edition of *Creative Cash* was a selection of five book clubs and quickly sold 30,000 copies. My ability to get publicity for this book in such magazines as *Family Circle* and *Woman's Day* increased sales dramatically. Through the years, more than 100,000 copies of *Creative Cash* have been sold, and it has outlived all its original competition. Thus, if you discover that several books on your topic have already been published, don't despair. Just write a book that gives readers something they can't find in any other book and then work like the dickens to promote it.

Note: Even when you are published by a trade publisher, you must aggressively promote your book, constantly drawing people into bookstores to look for it. After the publisher's initial "push" for a new book, sales are generally dependent on favorable reviews, author interviews, and word-of-mouth advertising. Authors who sit back and wait for a publisher to do all the selling are likely to find their book out of print in a couple of years.

IDENTIFYING THE MARKET FOR A BOOK

What's the market for your book? Write a description of the people most likely to be interested in reading your book and how they can be reached. For example, what organizations are they likely to belong to? Are mailing lists or directories available for use in doing direct mailings? What magazines or newsletters do they read? For publicity purposes, you'll need a list of all of them for your publisher or for your own marketing plans.

SENDING A BOOK PROPOSAL

Don't write the whole book before you start looking for a publisher; write a proposal instead and send it to several publishers who might be interested. For help in doing this, check the resource chapter for *How to Get Happily Published* by Judith Appelbaum (HarperPerennial). This book, one of my all-time favorites, presents a marvelous overview of one's options as a writer, from how to sell both articles and books to publishing your own books.

Some writers find an interested publisher on their first try, while others struggle for months or years without success, so be prepared for rejection. Timing is everything in the publishing game, whether you're a rank beginner or an author with several books to your credit. I may have what I think is a great book idea; but unless I offer it to a publisher who also thinks it's a great idea and happens to have a spot for that kind of book in its line, it will be rejected. Sometimes a book is rejected because a publisher thinks the market for it is too small (which is usually what prompts authors to publish their own work). It does help to have an agent who knows what each publisher is currently looking for, but unknown authors may also have a hard time finding an agent who wants to take them on. (See the sidebar "Tips for Beginning Writers.")

Publishing Your Own Book

IN MY LIMITED space here, I cannot begin to discuss this topic in any detail, but I can at least give you a bit of perspective. If you have a following in your field and several outlets through which to sell a

Tips for Beginning Writers

BY BARBARA DOYEN, Doyen Literary Agency

1. Start with articles, building up a portfolio of published pieces that will give you a big boost when you're ready to do a book for a trade publisher. Target a variety of publications.

2. Always polish, revise, and edit your work until every word shines.

3. Seek an agent before you approach any publishers. While you will be marketing articles yourself, a book should be handled by a literary agent. Get the names of agents from a current directory (there are several available) and write to a handful at a time, enclosing a stamped self-addressed envelope for a reply. *Do not call and do not send any of your material*—only a one-page letter describing your project and telling something about your background. If your letter is well received, you'll be asked to send more. If not, reevaluate your letter to ensure that it's your very best writing, and send out another round of query letters.

4. Do remember that rejection letters often have nothing to do with you or your writing, so don't take them personally. My most important advice of all is to *stay positive!*

self-published book—in your classes, at fairs and shows, in your craft mall booths, holiday boutiques, mail-order catalog, or Web site—you may profit greatly from publishing one or more of your own books, particularly if you write for a niche market.

BOOKS FOR DECORATIVE PAINTERS

Norwegian rosemaler Pat Virch says she didn't know the first thing about writing the day an editor asked her to write a magazine article, and she knew even less about publishing when she first dipped her toes into these waters. Yet through the years she has sold between 20,000 and 40,000 copies each of her various color portfolios and design books because she found a wonderful niche market and a way to get her books into special outlets throughout the United States, Canada, and several foreign countries.

"I spent a lot of money advertising my books in craft and consumer magazines in the early days—around $3,000 a year— but my advertising decreased through the years as I gained a word-of-mouth following from my teaching and got publicity in major consumer magazines," Pat remembers. "My husband, Niron, loaned me $5,000 to cover the printing and advertising costs of my first book, *Traditional Rosemaling,* and the first 2,500 copies were gone in six months. I had enough money then to pay for another printing, so we got brave and printed 5,000 copies that time. It sold in less than a year and we went on from there and have been reprinting the book ever since."

Before you get the idea that publishing and selling your own book is as easy as I've just made it sound, let me emphasize that self-publishing has its pitfalls and problems like everything else. As with selling handcrafts, having the best product is useless unless you also have a market for it, so the most important question to consider before trying to publish your own book is: *Will it sell?* Do you really have something of interest to write about, and are there people who will want to buy your book? You'll have to do some market research to find out.

Two big pitfalls in book publishing are printing more books than you know how to sell and trying to compete in the bookstore market (see story on next page). Instead of thinking only about the number of books you should print to gain an economical per-book cost, think instead of the number of books you can reasonably expect to *sell* in nine months or a year.

Personally, I'd rather print fewer books at a slightly higher per-book cost than have an extra 500 books sitting in the basement, tying up my business capital. (Many book printers specialize in small press runs of as few as 100 to 500 books and work with publishers by mail. Request quotes from several of them to find a printer who can deliver the book you want at a price you can afford.)

APPLIQUE AND SEWING BOOKS

After years of searching for the right job, Mary Mulari discovered it at her fingertips, finding her niche in designing appliques, writing creative sewing books, and teaching under the name of Mary's Productions. She has been very successful at selling her sewing and applique designs in the form of $5^{1}/_{2}$ by $8^{1}/_{2}$-inch books about fifty pages in length. Through the years she has published eight titles, selling over 200,000 books by mail to individual customers, at wholesale to shops, and through distributors who sell to independent sewing stores. Each book, priced from $7.95 to $12.95, includes nearly a hundred designs. "I found distributors for my books by reading trade publications such as *Craftrends/SewBusiness* and *Craft and Needlework Age,*" says Mary, who has always been a whiz at marketing and getting publicity for her work through press releases and visibility on television shows such as *Sewing with Nancy.*

Mary is winding down her self-publishing business now because her success in this area attracted the attention of Chilton Book Company, which asked her to write for them. "My first trade book, *Sweatshirts with Style,* has sold over 50,000 copies," she says, "and I've done two other books for Chilton since then: *More Sweatshirts with Style* and *Mary Mulari's Garments with Style.*"

Mary continues to give seminars across the United States and Canada, has taught on cruise ships to the Caribbean, developed ideas for new publications, and tested and designed products for the sewing industry. Most recently, she has designed appliques on an embroidery card for the Viking Sewing Machine company. As you can see, Mary has stitched quite a niche for herself over the years, and the road she has taken has plenty of room on it for others who might want to follow in her footsteps.

PUBLISHING TRADE BOOKS

James Dillehay, a weaver-turned-book publisher, shared keen insight on the problem facing small book publishers today. "I published my first book, *Weaving Profits,* because I felt the market was too small to attract a larger publisher and I had such a burning passion to see it in print. Rather than deal with being rejected by publishers, I decided to publish it myself. Threw myself into the study of self-publishing, what it would involve, what it would cost, what I would have to do to carry it off successfully. Dan Poynter's *The Self-Publishing Manual* and John Kremer's *1,001 Ways to Market Your Books* were my bibles."

To make a long story short, James got good reviews for his book and sold 2,000 copies at $19.95 in the first couple of years. Then he decided to convert the book to a general crafts marketing guide, retitled it *The Basic Guide to Selling Arts & Crafts,* and lowered the price to $14.95 to be more competitive with trade publishers. With 8,000 copies sold, James then published *The Basic Guide to Pricing Your Craftwork.* This certainly sounds like a success story, but there is always a story between the lines.

"If I were doing it over again," says James, "knowing everything I know now," I wouldn't try to self-publish. I've had some terrible experiences, such as three wholesalers going bankrupt and owing me a lot of money. I had problems getting a bookstore distributor (which required a 63 percent discount) and I have lost a lot of money from bookstore returns. (Although bookstores commonly return books to publishers, it's very difficult for a small publisher to absorb this expense.) In the end, my actual profit on my first trade book was only about a dollar per book. My big mistake was in trying to be a publisher in a world where you need literally thousands of dollars to sustain yourself. It's one thing trying to sell books by mail; quite another to try to compete with trade publishers in the bookstore market. I do not recommend that any small publisher attempt this."

At this point, James is taking a hard look at cash flow problems, assessing prior mistakes, and considering projects that might be more profitable in the future— "a more expensive product, perhaps, or a more targeted type of information rather than general. An entrepreneur must always have an eye open to the next thing," James emphasizes. "There is a natural cycle to business, and every four or five years things change, and we must change too."

Profit from Special Know-How

All of us, regardless of our age or station in life, are good at something, and that something is likely to be of interest to others.

DARLA SIMS, author of *Making $$$ At Home* (Sunstar)

PEOPLE TEND TO have narrow vision when it comes to making money from a particular art, craft, or needle skill. Their first thought always is, "I will make this and sell it." But, as you probably know, certain forms of art, craft, and stitchery are so labor intensive that it is literally impossible to make a good profit from the sale of them. If and when you run into this brick wall, try turning your thoughts to the many other ways you might profit from your years of creative experience and know-how.

As you have learned in the last two chapters, there are many opportunities for turning creativity into cash through designing, writing, and self publishing. As you will learn in this chapter, people who become involved in one of the aforementioned fields often glide into one or more of the following high-profit areas as well: (1) teaching an art or craft; (2) speaking or lecturing about a favorite topic; and (3) offering special services.

Sometimes things happen in a different order (for example, one may teach first and write or self-publish later), but there is a pattern here I don't want you to miss: *The most successful people in the crafts industry generally combine one or more of the activities discussed in this and the last two chapters—and few would have been able to develop this kind of "success package" if they hadn't first started selling handmade products at craft fairs.*

As the examples in this chapter illustrate, there are several different ways to approach the general topic of teaching and speaking. You can teach or speak about a wide variety of topics in a wide variety of places in your own area, across the nation, or in a foreign country. Teaching and speaking become even more profitable when coupled with the sale of one's books, tapes, or related items. (Many teachers eventually write books, often publishing their own work. Some sell the books of others or increase profits by selling their own pattern packages or kits, audiotapes or videotapes, and special or hard-to-find supplies and materials.)

Teaching How-To Techniques

IF YOU'VE EVER taught a friend how to use a particular skill she didn't know she had, you know the joy that comes from sharing what you know. A crafts teacher once told me that, in addition to being highly proficient in one's subject, a good teacher must also have (1) good organizational skills; (2) a strong voice; (3) patience; (4) a sense of humor; and (5) the ability to clearly explain processes and theories.

"Successful teachers must begin with good communication skills," says home-business teacher and speaker Sylvia Landman in her book, *Crafting for Dollars* (Prima Publishing). "Expertise alone is not enough. It is one thing to be a proficient technician and quite another to communicate it clearly, sequentially, and in a manner that is beneficial to students."

Since people learn in many different ways, explanations may need to be repeated several times, each time saying it in a different way. Good visual aids and large-scale demonstration materials are also necessary in teaching manual skills to large classes.

LEARNING HOW TO TEACH

If you've never taught before, how do you know where to begin? I generally tell people the best way to learn how to do something is read a book, but aside from a couple of books I've listed in Resources, there seems to be little published information on how to become a teacher. The fact that there are thousands of self-taught teachers in the arts and crafts field, however, proves that formal training is not necessary for success. Often it is the students themselves who teach a teacher how to teach. Certainly this was true in my case. Every time someone asked me a question or told me they didn't understand what I was saying, I was alerted to something I should or should not do the next time around.

"My advice to beginning teachers is simply to share what works for you," says self-taught teacher Karen Combs. "In quilting, there are a hundred ways to do something, and I've tried them all, but many things didn't work for me so I don't teach them." Karen, who made her first quilt at sixteen and then taught herself quilting techniques by studying books and magazines, is the author of two books for quilters. The fact that she was nominated Teacher of the Year in 1995 by *Professional Quilter Magazine* offers evidence that self-taught teachers are often the best teachers after all. Adding to my list above, Karen says a good teacher must also be willing to keep learning and be able to take criticism.

"I always learn from my students. If someone tells me she has found a different way of doing something, I always ask her to show me because she might have come up with something I haven't thought of. If the idea is a good one, I encourage sharing it with the whole class. If I receive criticism on the class evaluation sheet, I try to remember that some people may have come to class with excess baggage that makes it difficult for them to learn or accept what I happen to be say-

ing. Because criticism is always hard to take, I never read evaluation sheets when I'm tired, and I try to look at each critical remark objectively to determine is a person is whining or offering a real suggestion for improvement."

Most of today's best teachers began on shaky legs and gradually improved their techniques as they went along, proving the old adage that experience is the best teacher after all. Pat Virch is another case in point. This internationally known rosemaling artist, author, and speaker began to teach rosemaling while she was still learning the art herself. Her career began the day someone passed her a plateful of cookies at a homemaker's meeting. On the plate under the cookies was the first example of Norwegian rosemaling she had ever seen. "I fell in love with it and resolved to learn how to do this particular kind of painting," she recalls.

After taking only a few lessons, Pat moved to an area where there were no classes. Although she continued her self-study by doing research in the Norwegian American Museum in Decorah, Iowa (home to the largest collection of Norwegian rosemaling in America), she yearned to meet others who shared her interest. One day a friend encouraged her to offer classes herself.

"But I'm no teacher, and I'm still learning the art myself," Pat protested. "If you want to find someone to paint with, you'll have to teach them how first," her friend argued.

Although Pat felt inadequate to teach, she found the courage to try. She began by copying down all the notes she had taken as a student and digging out all the patterns her own teachers had used. She mixed the colors the way she had been shown, told her new students to purchase quality brushes, and proceeded to give them all the good advice she could. Before long, she was not only an excellent rosemaler, but a good teacher as well. In the years that followed, Pat went on to write and self-publish six rosemaling books, selling them in classes held all over the United States and in Canada, Switzerland, Norway, and the Netherlands. Her advice to beginners: "Make sure you are worth more than what you charge, and you will never disappoint your students."

Finding Places to Teach

O PPORTUNITIES FOR TEACHING are everywhere, as the following list suggests. Payment for classes or work-

shops will vary depending on the demand for what you want to teach and what the going rates are in your area. Once you get started teaching, word-of-mouth advertising will automatically bring new students and other opportunities to teach or speak.

TEACHING AT HOME

Rita Stone-Conwell teaches both at home and in local shops and stores. At home, Rita offers one-on-one lessons in business bookkeeping, for which she charges $45 per two-hour session. (This includes forms, samples of different ways to set up a bookkeeping system, and answers to all questions.) She also gives a variety of two-hour craft classes. "I provide the supplies and charge students for the cost of them plus a class fee, usually $5 to $7," she says. "These are informal affairs that usually end up being a coffee klatch. Actually, this is a great way to socialize without losing money, especially in the winter months. If your husband is a sports fanatic and you're a Sunday sports widow, take a class at Rita's, I always say."

Needlework designer Merrilyn Fedder (one of the "Christmas at the Blacksmith Shop" sellers you met earlier), currently lectures, teaches, and writes a weekly garden column for her local newspaper. As you may recall, Merrilyn lives in a small town, and she might still be teaching in her home if she hadn't run out of

Teaching Mentally and Physically Challenged Children

Weaver Lyndall Toothman says her favorite teaching job was the time she spent with mentally challenged children at a school in California. "This experience taught me to be very creative in teaching," she said. "This was when I began to use colors instead of numbers or letters when showing children how to weave patterns. I found the best way to teach was to just put a child on the loom and get them going. Sometimes it took six weeks to pull a thread, but when they finally got it, they didn't want to stop for dinner, they didn't want to stop to play, they didn't want to stop for anything. They wanted only to work on the loom. Once they got it, it was right there. It was the greatest thing in the world for them to know they could really do something special."

people interested in classes. "While they lasted, however, they were very successful," she says. "I would usually have twenty or twenty-five people in a class that would be on a particular theme, such as creating an herb garden, cooking with herbs, arranging fresh flowers, and so on. Weather permitting, the class would be in our covered patio adjacent to the herb garden. The problem with giving herb classes is that they need to be offered prior to the planting season so people can grow herbs that year. Unfortunately, the weather in Illinois in April is not always conducive to outdoor classes and I don't have enough room indoors to teach more than a dozen people at a time."

Merrilyn encourages others in small towns to consider giving classes in their home on any topic in which they excel. "You may eventually run out of people interested in taking classes, but in the interim period you will be building your reputation as an expert in your field, and this may lead you in other directions such as writing, speaking, or designing."

LOCAL SHOPS AND STORES

There are many opportunities to teach in neighborhood craft, needlework, or fabric shops and large chain or franchise stores. Teachers who live in small towns are unlikely to earn as much as teachers in larger cities, but the benefits of teaching go far beyond just earning extra money. First, teaching is personally satisfying because it leads to new friendship, broadens one's knowledge, and spurs creativity. Offering classes in a shop also means being able to buy supplies at a discount.

If you have a shop or store in your area that doesn't offer classes at the moment, call the owner and describe a class you'd like to teach. Rita Stone-Conwell told me about a small craft shop in her neighborhood whose clientele was always looking for new things to do. "The owner loved the idea of being able to offer classes, so I rounded up half a dozen teachers for her, including myself. She provided space in the store and we all benefited." (Students here were charged only $5 for a two-hour class that featured supplies they could buy in the store, and teachers received $4 per student for their pay.)

Depending on where you live, you may find chain or franchise craft stores such as Michaels, Ben Franklin, A. C. Moore, or MJ Designs that offer craft classes. Since each store may charge differently for classes, teacher's fees vary accordingly. When Rita teaches painting on wood shapes or Paper Twist dolls in a store such as A. C. Moore or MJ Designs (in the Troy, New York, area), she receives $3 per hour, or $6 per person for a two-

hour class, and she can set the limits of the class as she wishes. "If a store supplies the materials I use to make a sample, I can either leave the sample or pay for the cost of materials less 20 percent. I can also buy all other needed supplies at this discount."

Susan Young, who teaches folk painting in Michaels and Ben Franklin stores (in the Madison, Illinois, area) gets a 25 percent discount on store merchandise on top of a good hourly wage. "Being able to get my supplies this way is a big advantage of working with stores in my area," she says. "I've received between $8 and $12 per student for an hour's class, and you can offer more than one class if you wish." (Classes are generally in the evening or on weekends, and stores take 20 percent of each student's fee.)

Mary Lou Highfill, the sunbonnet/pincushion expert, teaches sewing classes in Pfaff and Bernina sewing centers in the McLoud, Oklahoma, area. "I never tried to sell myself as a sewing teacher," she says, "but one shop owner who heard me speak invited me to give classes and I got the second job when I was buying material in one of the Bernina stores and just happened to mention that I was going to use it to make sunbonnets. This started a conversation that led to my speaking to members of the Bernina Club and giving classes in how to make pincushions."

Mary Lou's classes are four hours in length. She sets the fee she wants and the limit for size of class. The sewing center usually keeps 20 percent of the class fee ($20 to $35) and gives Mary Lou a 30 percent discount on her fabric purchases.

In talking with Anna (the anonymous shop owner who offered such helpful information on selling patterns in chapter 8), I learned that she works with her teachers on a salaried basis. Day-long classes are held on Saturdays, or perhaps two evenings in a row, for which students might pay $35. Classes are limited to eight or ten at most to make sure each student gets maximum attention from the teacher.

"Because I want the people who attend classes in my store to be delighted with the instruction they receive and continue to come back to me for all their supply needs in the future, I hire only the best teachers I can find," says Anna. "Part of my agreement with teachers is that they cannot teach at any other store in my area, and for this consideration I pay them up to $20 per hour."

CONTINUING EDUCATION CENTERS AND COMMUNITY COLLEGES

Decorative painter Donna Brady, who specializes in restoring old trunks, also teaches knitting at a local college. She had taken the latter talent for granted until she spotted an ad in the local paper saying a knitting teacher was needed for a continuing ed class at a local college. "I was surprised to find I suddenly had a needed talent," she says, "and since I had just moved into the area and wanted to get out and meet people, the class proved to be a double blessing. I started with seven students, four of whom were total beginners. We did a small project of two basic stitches—a knitted dishcloth—that could be finished within three weeks. I've been doing this class for four years now and we're up to sixteen students." (Because this is a state program, Donna is paid on a per-hour basis.)

A former librarian, quilter Karen Combs got her first teaching job by calling Continuing Education and asking if they would be interested in someone to teach quilting classes, then spent her whole summer working up the lessons and handouts for her first class. Today she lectures on a variety of topics using slides, quilts, and handouts to effectively communicate with students. Her workshops for quilt guilds and conferences nationwide focus on specific techniques such as hand dying fabric, use of scraps, color, texture, and optical illusions. For example, her "Twist on Tradition" workshop teaches how to make traditional quilt blocks look three-dimensional (per illustration shown here), and how color can enhance the effect.

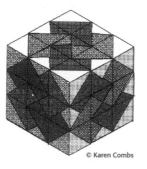

© Karen Combs

CRAFT SUPPLY MANUFACTURERS

Many companies that manufacture supplies for the arts and crafts industries now offer classes and workshops in their plants because they have found this to be a great way to promote their products. "Many invite shop owners and teachers to come in and run a series of classes," says Pat Virch, who has worked for companies that make tinware, oil and acrylic paints, and artist brushes. Designers who join the Society of Craft Designers are likely to make connections with several manufacturers for whom they might teach. Or, if you happen to love the line of products, supplies, or materials made by a particular manufacturer, simply write to that company and tell them about your enthusiasm for their products and your interest in teaching classes or workshops for them. (Refer back to chapter 8 for tips on how designers work with manufacturers to create project sheets.)

ELDERHOSTEL ORGANIZATION

Founded in 1975, this nonprofit organization provides educational adventures throughout the world to adults aged fifty-five and older. Its network of 2,000 educational and cultural sites in the United States, Canada, and seventy countries includes colleges and universities, conference centers, state and national parks, museums, theaters, environmental/outdoor educational centers, and more.

Note that this is *not* a market for general how-to classes, but an educational program that educates and enriches those who participate in it. To qualify as a teacher here, you would need to be well versed in the historical or social aspects of your art or craft and demonstrate basic how-to techniques in the process. For example, in the programs Pat Virch has done for Elderhostel, she explains the different kinds of decorative painting common to different countries while also demonstrating the different painting techniques.

Additional information about Elderhostel's classes is available on its Web site at www.elderhostel.org. Libraries everywhere also have a current copy of classes being offered. Interested teachers should contact the organization's headquarters in Boston (see Resources) and ask for the name of their state director. Contact that individual, explaining the skills you have and the kind of educational/how-to program you could offer. It is completely up to each host site/institution to select and hire lecturers. Usually they use their own faculty or staff, but some do approach experts from the local community. Each institution has its own arrangements for payment or honorarium. A typical week's worth of learning in a U.S. location may cost participants around $350, including room and board, and teachers might receive up to $500 for twenty-two and a half hours of teaching over a five-day period.

TEACHING IN PRISONS

Through the years, I've received many letters from inmates who have found my books in the prison library. Recently, I heard from a fellow who said *Creative Cash* had changed his thinking about crafts as a business. "Hobby craft is a great equalizer in prison," he wrote. "I've never been able to do anything with my hands before I started latch-hook rugs, but I've made over a hundred rugs now, using my own patterns and designs. I hope to continue this work when I am released."

My mail tells me that prisons across the country offer classes to inmates in all types of arts and crafts, but I found it impossible to get basic guidelines on how to get this kind of teaching job. Although I made countless calls to several different

people within the correctional system, I found no commonality in the way this program is operated nationwide. Each state correctional department works differently; but it appears to me that if classes are offered as part of a prison's educational program, teachers have to be state certified to qualify. If a program is offered as a recreational activity, however, this may not be a necessary requirement. One contact did give me the names of two men she knew who were teaching within the prison system, but I was unable to connect with either of them. One taught photography; the other worked with native Alaskans, teaching them how to make a living after they get out of prison.

I wouldn't have included this topic at all if not for knowing Lyndall Toothman, the spinner and weaver whose entertaining story closes this chapter. She told me how she accidentally fell into this kind of teaching toward the end of the Depression, when she applied for a job as a correctional officer at Alderson Reformatory, a women's prison. After being there a short time, the warden showed Lyndall some handwoven things the inmates were doing in an Oklahoma prison. Lyndall said, "I can do that," and was immediately appointed weaving teacher.

"I worked there for twelve years," she said, "and taught three ex-spies how to weave. One of them was Lily Stein, formerly the head of a German spy ring whose experience was the basis for the movie *The House on 92nd Street.*" After she left Alderson, Lyndall found a job in Washington teaching weaving at a reformatory for juveniles. "Teaching crafts to inmates was both profitable and personally satisfying," she says, "and I never felt safer than when I was inside a prison."

One of the prison directors I spoke with said she has often heard teachers say how much they enjoy this kind of teaching and how safe they feel when teaching within a prison. Clearly, this is worthwhile work. If there is a prison near you, and you are intrigued by this idea, contact the warden's office and try to get the name of the person in charge of that prison's craft or leisure interests program.

Speaking About Your Art or Craft

NANCY MOSHER STARTED Nan-Craft in 1982, first selling her crafts and later beginning to teach, write, and self-publish. Today, she presents seminars and writes business articles for many publications. Her seminars for professional crafters were the first to be presented at the Association of Craft & Creative Industries (ACCI) trade shows. Nancy has increased her income by publishing a series of business and record-keeping materials (ledgers and craft show schedule sheets), a long-distance telephone log book, and a line of display signs for use at craft fairs. She also offers private consultation to individual crafters and is always working within the crafts industry on their behalf. "My goal is to help raise the respectability and integrity of professional crafters so they may be accepted as part of the industry as a whole," she says.

Many creative people who excel at a particular art or craft, or acquire special knowledge about the history of it, sort of "fall into speaking" accidentally when someone invites them to give a little talk. If you do a good job the first time out, business will automatically come to you. My experience in presenting musical programs for arts clubs back in the sixties, and doing home-business workshops in the 1980s and 1990s, taught me that one job always leads to another. I never advertised my availability as a speaker beyond networking with business associates and listing upcoming engagements in my newsletter, but I had all the work I could handle during those years.

Without advertising, Mary Lou Highfill is invited to speak about three dozen times a year for civic groups, churches, museums, historical societies, and various organizations. As a genealogist, she has been speaking on Colonial cooking and clothing for over fifteen years, so when she got interested in making and selling

Oklahoma sunbonnets and Victorian pincushions, she naturally added those topics to her list of programs. Although Mary Lou sells her crafts and patterns at fairs and shows, she doesn't like to sell after her talks, preferring instead to just give people her card so they can order later if they wish. This kind of speaking will never make Mary Lou financially rich— she generally gets around $50 and a free meal for a short talk—but at sixty-four, she has her own definition of "rich."

"I am having the time of my life!" she says enthusiastically. "I love to share my interest in preserving the history of sunbonnets, display my bonnet collection, and talk about how different bonnets were used for different things. People seem to like the fact that I bring back memories of a time gone by, and there is always someone in the audience who has a sunbonnet tale to tell. Once, when I was at a convention, one woman said she used her bonnet while milking the cow because it kept the tail out of her face. Another woman piped up, 'And those tails had burrs!' I make new friends every time I speak, and every speaking engagement leads me to yet another new bonnet pattern. It's hard to put a price on the value of all this."

Publicity is a natural byproduct of the kind of speaking Mary Lou does because the groups that hire her usually arrange for some kind of media coverage. Headlines on two clippings Mary Lou sent me read, "Living history event attracts record crowd" and "McLoud woman preserves history in bonnets." I have encouraged Mary Lou to write and publish a booklet about the history of Oklahoma sunbonnets, including photographs of the different bonnets, some of her patterns and all the colorful sunbonnet tales she has collected. This would not only further her goal of preserving Oklahoma history, but would give her a wonderful product suitable for sale after a talk on this topic.

Adding Pizzazz to Your Presentations

IN THE FIRST EDITION of this book, I wrote about cornshuckery artisan Margo Daws Pontius. I've lost touch with Margo now, but she had given over 500 lectures and eighty all-day workshops by the time I'd met her, and the topic of professionalism was high on her list of success tips for speakers. "Be a responsive business person," she urged. "Confirm all details about the speaking engagement. Don't bring products for sale without checking on whether this is okay or not,

and be sure to arrive to speaking engagements on time." Margo's special tips for making any presentation more interesting are as timely now as they were when first published:

➤ Be an authority. Know your art or craft—its background and all its techniques. Supplement your talk with poems that fit in with the theme, or pleasing stories of the era your craft originated in.

➤ Be daring. If you do your craft similarly to someone else, then display it differently. Add music to create an unusual mood or try unusual lighting techniques.

➤ Be enthusiastic in your presentation. If you truly love your art, just let the "glow" out for others to see.

➤ Give your talk a definite message or theme. For example, you might lecture on your art through one or more seasons, a certain era, or a place in history. Or use folklore, nationality, ecology, nature, or even song titles to provide a theme.

➤ Use well-designed displays so your audience can visualize what you're saying. Use colored mats and tagboards to create a setting. Backdrops can be fastened to cemetery wreath tripods, which are easily obtained, lightweight, and collapsible. Instead of setting up your whole display before a talk, you might hold audience attention better if you set up parts of it as you talk about it.

➤ Interact with your audience. After speaking, stay long enough afterwards to mix with the audience and answer questions.

What I remember most about Margo is where she got all the cornshucks needed for her dolls. Initially, I figured she got them from the cornfield, like everyone else, but then she told me she was a city gal who had to resort to using the husks of Wisconsin sweet corn from the grocery store. I wasn't surprised to learn that it had taken Margo a while to figure out a good method for drying and storing sweet corn shucks, but I was startled to learn how much corn the Pontius household was consuming in those days when Margo's business was at its peak. In order to keep her supplied with sufficient shucks for all the dolls she was making for sale, Margo, her husband, and three teenagers somehow managed to gnaw their way through eighty dozen ears of corn a year—almost 200 ears apiece.

That may not have been a world's record, but back in 1976 it was enough to capture the attention of the Wisconsin State Committee, which asked Margo to represent Wisconsin during the Bicentennial. She sent a series of her colonial dolls to the White House and was understandably proud of the letter she received from President Ford. "I hung it over my ironing board to inspire me to greater things," she told me.

Margo later wrote to say she had written her first book, titled *American Corn-shuckery in Action*. Because she had already written several articles on her craft, a book was the logical thing to do at that point. (Margo's children wanted her to title the book *What Mother Does in the Cornfield*, but she decided making the bestseller list wasn't all that important.)

The last time I heard from Margo, she was still lecturing, only now she had added a new topic: International Eggery.

How to Become a "TV Personality"

MARIA NERIUS BEGAN as a hobby crafter in 1984. Today she hosts "Creative Chat with Maria Nerius," an hour-long segment on *Aleene's Creative Living Show* on TNN (currently on Wednesdays, at noon E.S.T). "I feel right at home here," she says, "but if someone had asked me fifteen years ago to speak to 500 of my peers, I would have desperately looked for the exit door."

Between the time she started to sell her crafts at fairs and 1997 when she became a television personality, Maria gained not only confidence but experience in all areas of the crafts industry. As a designer, she has worked for several manufacturers, representing their products on television. As a writer, her articles and columns have appeared in many magazines and can be found all over the Internet on one craft site or another. Prior to doing this television show, Maria was editor of *The Craft Supply Magazine—The Independent Journal for the Professional Crafter.*

"I love doing this show," she says, "because I can talk about anything I want and report on what's happening within the industry. There are so many new products, and consumers are hungry for this kind of information. Aleene's show is the highest rated show on TNN, with an audience following even greater than that of Martha Stewart. There is also a companion magazine published by Oxmore House, and a phenomenal companion site for crafters on the Internet (Aleenes.com)."

I grant that there aren't many jobs like the one Maria has, but her experience certainly underscores everything I've told you in this book. "No one knows what your talents are unless you tell them," Maria stresses, "and you have to make your own opportunities. No one is going to invite you to do a television program. You have to present yourself and come up with an idea for a segment that will fit into a network's format. Initially, I submitted a magazine column idea to Aleene, and later translated that column idea into what I thought would make a great segment for television."

Doing television is not for everyone, of course. Being able to demonstrate a craft or speak to a live audience is one thing; demonstrating or speaking to a heartless camera is another. "But you don't have to have a magnetic personality or look great to succeed on television," says Maria. "My viewers don't seem to mind that I look like the average person who talks like their sister. Initially, I was worried that my dry sense of humor might not convey over a broadcast medium, but I've been amazed by the warm response I've received."

After telling me this, Maria proved she has a good sense of humor by sharing this moment in time. After speaking at a conference, a woman came up to her and said, enthusiastically, "You look so much better in person than you do on television!"

Although she is now a "television personality," Maria is still just a crafter and designer at heart. "The reason I'm a crafter is because there is no right or wrong," she says. "When I was studying art, there was always a right or wrong. The idea behind crafting is that you create. There's never a mistake, there's just a new technique to be learned."

That just about sums up Maria's philosophy of life. For the rest of her success story—how she made the journey from hobby to profession—see "What Goes Around Comes Around" in the last chapter.

DOING A LOCAL CABLE SHOW

As SueAnn Antonini nears the age of forty, she looks forward to retiring from her corporate job so she will have more time for her crafts career. After years of selling at craft fairs and home shows, she eventually grew tired of mass production and decided to do something else. "I have always had confidence in my crafting skills," she says, "but about a year ago, I suddenly became obsessed with the idea of creating new ideas instead of products."

After reading one of my "Selling What You Make" columns in *Crafts Magazine,* SueAnn found the encouragement she needed to query several magazines to see if they would be interested in buying her how-to projects. The interest she received from magazine editors fueled her enthusiasm for selling her ideas and prompted her to contact a local California television network. Before she knew it, she had sold her "Craft Crazy" segment to TSPN local TV.

"I show viewers how to make usable items and gifts," she says. "Some projects on my show have featured bathroom bunnies made from hand towels, designer pails made from ordinary paint buckets, decorating techniques for fruit jars, angel projects, and handmade ornaments."

With each show being cablecast fourteen times weekly, SueAnn is reaching nearly 19,000 viewers while gaining experience that may someday prove invaluable. To sell her show, she prepared a marketing presentation that showed the station how her craft projects would attract new advertisers and benefit local merchants who sold the supplies she used. The success of the television show led

SueAnn to create a cartoon strip around the adventures of Krafty (see illustration) and her sidekick, Kit. Now, using her favorite segments from the TV show, she is currently working on two books as well.

© Sue Ann Antonini

"So many crafters underestimate their skills," says SueAnn. "They have talent, but lack confidence to do something with their ideas. I would encourage such people to build a support network. It's amazing how many people want to help others succeed. Letting people know my interests, desires, and goals has opened many doors for me."

Selling Needlework or Stitchery Services

I F YOU LACK the ability to create original designs, but have fine needlework or stitchery skills, there are several ways you might make money from them.

CUSTOM NEEDLEWORK

Millions of women love to do needlework, myself included, but few can make a good profit by selling finished needlework because it involves too many hours of labor. There is good money to be made in custom stitchery, however. When I checked a new needlework shop in my area shortly after it opened, asking if there really was a demand for custom needlework, I got an enthusiastic yes! In fact, the first week this shop was open, three customers had inquired about the availability of custom services. One wanted an antique footstool refurbished with fresh needlepoint, another wanted a humorous cross-stitch sign made for her kitchen, and a third needed a small clutch bag to complement a new evening gown.

Also check with needlework shops about the possibility of stitching samples for them. Any shop that offers a variety of needlework kits might like a few finished samples to display.

CHARTING NEEDLEWORK PATTERNS

Can you turn a picture or photo into a cross-stitch or needlepoint pattern? If so, this talent may be of special interest to shops that occasionally get special requests from customers who have a de-

sign they would like charted so they can stitch it.

FINISHING NEEDLEWORK PROJECTS

Connie Stano, a designer featured in the first edition of this book who later sold her thriving needlework business, said a woman working by herself in her own community could stay busy merely by running an ad in her local paper offering to finish kits, frame, or design custom pieces. "There really is a market for embroidering kits for money," she told me. "Not just for people who are too lazy or inept, but more often for people who are just too busy, or not interested in doing it themselves. It is a unique operation and word-of-mouth advertising works well on a local level. Some of your best customers will be women who started a kit and lost interest, or found they couldn't do it. Others will be people who bought a kit and then never had time to start it."

QUILTING SERVICES

Quilters may be able to pick up some jobs by letting local fabric and needlework shops know of their quilting services. "People sometimes ask us if we know of anyone who can finish a quilt they've made," says the owner of a fabric shop in my area. "Before I would recommend any quilter's services, however, I would have to see several samples of her work. I couldn't recommend just anyone who tells me she can do this kind of work. Many people would like hand quilting, but when they find out how much it costs, they settle for machine quilting. The few quilters today who will do hand quilting charge by the hour and it can cost several hundred dollars depending on whether they are just quilting or marking the design, basting the quilt together, binding it, and so on."

Kay Hineman has been quilting for profit since 1985, selling mostly in local consignment shops and fairs. Through ads in national quilt magazines, Kay also found a market for her quilt tops. "Although some people who answered my ads wanted finished quilts, most did not like to piece quilts but wanted only to do the hand quilting," she says. By selling some of her quilts at Amish auctions held twice a year in her area, Kay met several Amish who wanted quilt tops too. "A lot of people would rather quilt than piece," she concludes, suggesting a niche market other quilters might like to tap. Although she's never been stung on a custom order,

Kay says she always requires 50 percent down before doing this kind of work.

CUSTOM FINISHING

Professional blocking and framing of needlework—all kinds—can bring in money, too. This is a skill you can learn by studying needlework instruction books and from simple trial-and-error experience. (Practice on your own work first, of course.)

Offering Special Business Services

SOMEONE ONCE SAID that an expert "is someone who doesn't know more than most people, but has it better organized and runs a slide show." You don't need to run a slide show to share your expertise, of course, but what you know or have learned from hands-on experience could be the perfect foundation for a new business, as the following examples show.

LASER CUTTING SERVICES

Remember Rita and Gary Villa (chapter 1), who went from making dollhouse furniture by hand to starting their own laser-cutting business? As the Villas exhibited in miniatures trade shows, worked with sales reps, and sold their products through a catalog, Gary began to explore the possibility of having Rita's dollhouse furniture parts cut by laser. It took a great leap of faith to buy that first laser cutter at a cost of $92,000 and move their home-based business into a shop, but it proved to be the right thing to do. Two additional laser machines were purchased in following years and now the Villas's company, Smidgens, Inc., employs nine people and generates sales of nearly a million dollars a year.

By offering affordable laser-cutting services to other craftspeople like themselves, the Villas have not only increased their own income, but enabled countless others to move into wholesaling or start whole new businesses based around a product that can be mass produced at low cost.

SHOW PROMOTER

All of Anita Means's past experience has neatly positioned her for the show promotion work she is now doing. This kind of business is not for business beginners, but if you have been presenting successful craft boutiques for years, know many crafters and work well with them, this might be a good business idea for you.

Anita got her start in 1983 when she started a home-based craft boutique business that featured the work of fifteen area crafters. In those days she was presenting spring and Christmas boutiques and also doing a "Christmas in July Festival." Six years later, she and husband Tom decided to buy a 150-year-old church in Holmdel, New Jersey, that had National Historic Landmark status. "Making the commitment to buy the church and run my Cottage Crafts business on a year-round basis was one of the biggest decisions of my life," Anita recalls, "but we were spurred on by our mutual interest in the history and preservation of the area, and my dream of turning the building into a cultural event center."

In time, the old church became a year-round craft shop and place where people could take lessons in various arts and crafts. Special events and craft boutiques were scheduled throughout the year and this was a happy and satisfying time in Anita's life. After nine years of retailing, however, Anita felt burned out and was ready to move on to something else.

"I had started to promote shows in 1995 and, after a very successful event, I decided there was potential for growth in this field," she says. "A couple of years later, we decided to close the retail operation of Cottage Crafts, renting the store space in the church to an interior designer. By then, I had developed three of my own shows and was also serving as a craft consultant for a foundation that produces two festivals of its own. I really love this work. It has given me personal freedom (at fifty-three, with grown children, my husband and I can pick up and go wherever we want). I have utilized my past experience and good reputation in the craft industry to develop the craft shows in an area where my customers can still shop. In a way, I am returning on a different level to where I began my business, which was organizing craft boutiques."

Being a show promoter is hard work and not without financial risk, as Anita has learned. "Outdoor shows must always contend with weather problems," she says. "I once had to cancel a large craft show when a northeaster blew through our area, destroying large craft tents and saturating the grounds."

Anita also stresses the importance of planning. "You have to go before the parks and recreation committees and do a lot of negotiating on the agreement to rent the grounds. Then you have to design a professional brochure and attract crafters. Having a retail show for nine years gave me a jump on market research because I knew the market I had to target, and I had a good list to start with. Even so, I had to buy additional names while I was waiting to get listed in all the show publications crafters received. I also went to many craft shows, personally talking to people and inviting them to participate in my shows. I got a good response, but the big obstacle for the new show promoter is that you have no track record. It's like trying to get your first job with no experience. No one will hire you unless you really sell yourself. Even then, there will be people who refuse to do first-time shows no matter what. Fortunately, my attendance at first-year shows has been good."

SALES REP BUSINESS

Do you love crafts, like to travel, and have a knack for selling? If so, you might make a good sales representative for people who love to produce but hate to sell. Your know-how and sales expertise could be put to work for you in one of two ways: (1) as a sales rep who exhibits the lines of several sellers at trade shows, or (2) as one who calls on retail shops and other buyers. In both cases, you would be working on a commission basis. As a full-fledged sales representative, you would need to travel extensively, doing one trade show after another. As a part-time sales rep, you could work on a schedule of your own making, in a sales territory as limited or extensive as you care to make it. For example, you might represent several artisans who live in isolated, rural areas by setting up a display in a gift mart and showing samples of their work to shops in several cities.

Sharon Olson of Northwoods Trading has been representing crafters at trade shows since 1993, usually taking about eight lines to a show. (Crafters pay a fee of around $100 per show and must supply Sharon with necessary samples.) Currently, her product lines include primitive and country folk art, collectibles, miniature redware, antique gameboards, and reproductions of antiques. "I will look at anything people send me," she says, "but I don't want samples—just pictures and an SASE for a response."

Sharon may do seven or eight shows a year all over the country, including the Beckman shows, Market Square in Philadelphia, and Americana Sampler. This isn't easy work, but Sharon seems to thrive on it. "You have to have everything well organized," she emphasizes. "I usually ship in twenty boxes or cases of sample products and display materials. Every city and state has different rules for setting up at a trade show, but union labor must often be used. I drive to some shows, fly to others, always shipping materials ahead. I have had no problems in doing shows alone because exhibitors always take care of each other's booths when breaks are needed."

To help crafters everywhere find good sales reps who understand the nature of the crafts business, Sharon also publishes *The Directory of Wholesale Reps for Craft Professionals*, updating it from time to time (see Resources). In the process of compiling this directory, Sharon asked reps what advice they would give to craftspeople who were using a rep for the first time. Over and over, they commented on the lack of good promotional literature from crafters, lack of communication, and the inability to fill orders promptly and pay commissions on time. Thus you need to pay attention to these things if you hope to establish a profitable relationship with a sales rep. "When looking for a good rep," adds Sharon, "check out other lines a rep carries for compatibility with your products, and don't hesitate to ask for a resume and references."

A Teacher Turned Entertainer

I F YOU THINK you're too old to do anything interesting with your life, think again. Lyndall "Granny" Toothman didn't hit her stride until her late sixties when, after years of teaching both weaving and spinning, she finally found her special niche in life as a crafts demonstrator and entertainer. In those days she was traveling to festivals in a bright yellow van, sometimes with her granddaughter, Lee, also a demonstrating spinner, and always with a dog whose fur she collected for spinning.

When Lyndall turned seventy, she wrote, "I'm still working four months a year at Cedar Point, Ohio, and the rest of the time I am here and yon. Spent last winter in Texas and loved it! I don't know how I get myself in so many different situations, but it seems like I am never doing the things people expect a seventy-year-old to do. P. S. I just bought a blue van with a gray turtle top."

When Lyndall celebrated her eightieth birthday, she astonished everyone by buying a new red-and-white Pontiac Trans Sport Van. In a letter then, she wrote, "After I'd driven to Georgia to do the Foxfire Festival, an *old* woman of seventy asked me if I drove when I told her I had come alone. I told her no, the LORD was doing the driving, I was just holding the wheel." Eight years later when I called Lyndall for an update for this book, I was amazed to learn her birthday van had over 90,000 miles on it. "And I drove nearly every mile of it myself," she says. Lyndall has now traveled to all fifty states and Canada, going unaccompanied to Alaska when she was eighty-four.

When I first met Lyndall back in the 1970s, she was working the annual crafts festival at Silver Dollar City, Missouri. By her side, sharing the spotlight as she demonstrated how to spin dog hair, was Sammy, a Samoyed (a breed from Northern Siberia whose fur has been a favorite of spinners since 1804). Spinning dog hair has long been Lyndall's specialty—her gimmick—and it seldom fails to command attention. Through the years, she has spun the fur of more than a hundred different breeds of dogs, as well as cats, llamas, bison, camels, wolves, rabbits, the manes of a lion and a Clydesdale horse, belly fuzz from a penguin, and the beard of an electrician whose auburn hair she admired. You can imagine how much all this gives her to talk about, and talk she does!

As adept at telling a good story as she is at spinning a fine yarn on her old Saxony wheel, Lyndall—who, when performing, is known as "Granny"—delights in answering the many questions asked by a curious crowd and generally embellishes her replies with country wit or wisdom. She is always a surprise to those who stop to watch her work, and a diamond in the rough to those who are privileged to know her as a friend.

There she sits, spinning away with all the casualness of a shoplifter about to make her move, looking not at what she's doing, but at the gathering crowd instead. (She's sizing them up, that's what she's doing.) No one suspects that Granny— so cute in her pink Colonial dress, white apron, and crocheted cap—actually pre-fers blue jeans to dresses and is a strong and energetic worker who, after the age of sixty, designed and built her own log cabin almost singlehandedly. Bystanders are seldom prepared, either, for Granny's sharp wit and ready sense of humor, which comes into play the moment anyone speaks to her.

"What's that you're spinning?" someone in the crowd will ask.

"This is dog hair," she replies firmly, with a strong emphasis on the last two words that sound like "dawg hair."

"Nah," another will argue, "you're kidding."

"No, I'm not," she says, pointing to her green display board hanging nearby. It's literally covered with photographs of animals—mostly dogs—and stapled to

each picture is a small hank of yarn. Lyndall explains this is yarn she has spun from each animal's fur. She speaks in a high-pitched, crackly voice perfectly suited to her Granny character, and just when the crowd is beginning to believe everything she's telling them, she sets them up for a fall with a line like this:

"There's only one kind of dog hair I've been unable to spin so far," she says with great seriousness. After a slight pause for effect she adds, "and that's the Mexican hairless."

She chuckles pleasantly with the crowd, which now realizes what a delightful entertainer she is. And a good spinner, too! A few people move closer for a better look at her hands, which have never stopped moving for a minute. By this time, of course, she has completely captured the attention of everyone within earshot and is ready and waiting for the two questions most frequently asked along about now: "Do you kill the dog?" and "Does your foot get tired?"

"No, my foot doesn't get tired," she assures them, "and I don't kill the dog, for heaven's sake! He's sleeping right over there." Then she explains how one simply washes and brushes a dog to get its fur, and several people may sigh with relief to learn she doesn't practice cruelty to animals. Soon, someone will inquire about the furry garments hanging on the tree or wall behind her, and she will tell them it's a coat, or a shawl, or a poncho she has made by weaving or knitting the yarn spun from various kinds of dog hair.

"How long did it take to make that coat?" another may ask, and Granny will

Green Thumb Program

Lyndall Toothman has been working with Green Thumb for several years. This federally funded program finds part-time work for people with low incomes. Lyndall said she was the only one in this program in the field of crafts, yet they found work for her in several different places, including festivals, schools, and museums. Her best job was being Artist in Residence at Morehead State University in Kentucky from 1985 to 1993. (Green Thumb won't keep people in the same place for more than four years, so at the end of Lyndall's four-year period, Morehead simply put her on their payroll, providing an apartment as part of her wages.)

answer with a twinkle in her eye, "I'm not sure. All I know is, the dog wore it one year and I wore it the next." The crowd roars with laughter—they love her! When she tells people, "Yes, you can wash and dry the coat in the machine," someone is bound to look at her incredulously and say (as I did years ago), "But won't it shrink or something?"

"Of course not," Granny answers snappily, "does your dog shrink when you leave him out in the rain?"

Occasionally, someone will make a remark that annoys her, in which case she's apt to spit out a reply that leaves the person at a complete loss for words, like she once did to the fellow who came up to her and said, critically, "That's not the way my grandmother used to spin." She looked at him for a moment and then said with subtle sarcasm, "Well, then, your grandmother just wasn't a good spinner."

Few people could duplicate Lyndall's "act," but many could use it as an example on which to base their own entertaining demonstration or program. Now eighty-eight, Lyndall expects to drive another 10,000 miles this year, doing craft fairs and festivals or just visiting friends. "I've never had any difficulty getting $100 a day to play at my spinning wheel," she says. "It's a great life. I've always just packed up my costume, spinning wheel, and display board and gone wherever I felt like going."

Crafters and Computer Technology

I believe the next decade will truly be the most entrepreneurial time period in the entire history of this earth. It's going to be a wonderful time to be active, with loads of opportunity for anyone who wants it. I can't wait to see where the Internet takes us.

EILEEN HEIFNER, Create an Heirloom

ARTISTS AND CRAFTSPEOPLE haven't changed much in the past five decades, but the world in which we now live changed so dramatically in the 1990s that few of us have been able to comprehend what happened, let alone adjust to it. Recently, I heard on the evening news that four out of every ten families in the United States now own a computer, and there are now more computers in the workplace than employees.

The experts were right years ago when they predicted that computers would put thousands of people out of work. What they didn't tell us then, however, was that computers would someday be as common and affordable as television sets, and that we would be able to use both of them to promote and sell our products and services to the whole wide world.

While this chapter is addressed mostly to computer novices, some of you "old computer pros" out there may chuckle as you read about others and remember your own computer beginnings. I've shared some of my thoughts and computer experiences along with the comments and

229

viewpoints of several craft business own-ers, including examples of how computer technology is helping them. A brief intro-duction to the benefits of going online and setting up your own Web site rounds out the chapter.

Why Some People Don't Buy Computers

I F YOU ALREADY use a computer in your personal life or home-based busi-ness, I don't need to tell you about the wonders of technology and how it makes one's life easier. If you're still stalling about buying a computer, however, you probably have several reasons why you shouldn't do this now.

THE COST FACTOR

You may think you can't afford one. You may feel overwhelmed by all the work you're trying to juggle now and can't imagine how you'll ever find the time to learn "computer stuff." You may even fear you won't be able to learn at all, and oth-ers will laugh at your stupidity. During the first six years of my present business, I was using all of these excuses to delay my own computer purchase.

Saying you can't afford a computer today, however, is a poor excuse. The way prices are dropping, before long even the most powerful computers are apt to cost only a couple of thousand dollars. Used computers are already being sold for a pittance. In fact, I just paid only $400 for a second computer system I could use as a backup in case my hard drive crashes when I'm on a tight deadline. I told the clerk at the Computer Renaissance store in my neighborhood that I wanted a clone of my present system that had the same kind of color monitor and tape backup system I now have. He tried not to laugh when I told him I wanted a 486 machine, however, saying "I'm not sure we have anything that slow." *That slow?* A couple of years ago, a 486 was considered state-of-the-art, offering more speed, power, and disk space than most home-based businesses would ever need. What's really interesting is that my 486 "clone" not only cost six times less than what I paid for the original, but has twice the RAM, double the megahertz speed, more hard disk space, extra ports, a sound card, a mouse, and a CD-ROM drive besides.

As my experience proves, you can buy a lot of computer power today for a few hundred dollars. What's important is to just get started. You can upgrade later when you know what you really need to keep growing—and what you *need* will de-pend entirely on what you want to *do* with

Technology Overload

The Internet, which many people find wildly exciting, is frightening to many older people who are now being made to feel they are missing something important in life if they're not digging around online for hours every days. "Technology scares me," says a crafts wholesaler. "Everything seems too fast (as I get older, more so). I know I will have to investigate being on the Web, but currently I'm just playing and using e-mail." A craft shop owner in her sixties says she's too old to try to keep up with all this modern technology. "We will have to go on the Internet and I really don't want to," says another shop owner who has been in business for nearly thirty years, "but my business will be left behind if we don't." A successful needlework designer realizes the importance of staying on top of technological developments and being aware of changes and trends as everything becomes increasingly competitive, but is resisting a move in that direction. "I will eventually, I suppose, have to invest in a fax machine, go online, and so on, whether I want to or not," she says, reluctantly.

Clearly, many people are having a hard time coping with all the new technology they are being forced to accept, and wondering what other changes are looming on the horizon. In her book *The Popcorn Report* (Doubleday, 1991) Faith Popcorn talked about the trend of "cocooning" and how people were retreating to the safety and comfort of their home. She continues to comment on how we're all suffering from technology overload, and as a result have simply burrowed deeper into our homes, "building ourselves a bunker, cocooning for our lives." She says now that cocooning is no longer about a place (the home), but about a state of mind—self-preservation.

a computer. Some readers may wonder why I want a second 486 machine when more powerful computers are available at low cost. It's because all the new computers run on Windows software, which I hate, and which won't allow me to use the DOS-based software I've grown up with.

At my age, when all I want to do is write articles and books and keep using my old *dbaseIII+* software, I see no reason to switch to a Windows computer system as long as I have a choice. Of course, if you happen to be a designer or anyone who uses powerful graphics-based software programs, you may well need a Pentium CPU to operate at maximum efficiency.

THE TIME FACTOR

If you're feeling overwhelmed with work and have no time to learn, just take it small bites at a time and keep thinking about all the time you're going to save once you get past the learning stage. Actually, it's much easier to learn how to use a computer today than it was ten years ago. I learned by reading several books that explained the software programs I was trying to master. Subscriptions to computer magazines broadened my education considerably. At first, everything was just so much gobbledegook but, bit by bit, I learned the computer jargon and began to understand the technology. Today, a variety of how-to videotapes and cable television shows make learning at home easy and fun; but if you learn better in a class atmosphere, check to see what computer classes are being offered at nearby colleges or adult education centers.

I won't bore you with the details of my computer-learning experience, except to say that I had a long talk with my equipment as soon as I plugged it in and turned it on. "Listen," I said, "I haven't got time to learn all this stuff because I've got a business to run and deadlines to meet.

I've got to get my subscription list on computer in just one month, so don't give me trouble, okay?" Seriously, I believe my positive approach to learning, coupled with the knowledge that I *simply had to do this thing—or else*—made all the difference. Later, after I'd accomplished my first goal of getting my subscriber list on computer and was feeling comfortable at the keyboard, my husband said he never could have done what I'd done in only a month with no help from anyone. I told him he was right—not because he wasn't bright enough to learn, but only because he lacked a reason to do so. From experience, I can assure you that if you *need* a computer in your business, and *want* to learn how to use it efficiently, learning will be an exciting and satisfying experience. All it takes is time, patience, and perhaps some help from an eight-year-old. (The kids of today already know more about computers than we adults will ever learn.)

What a Computer Can Do for You

IN WRITING THE computer chapter for *Homemade Money*, I interviewed seventy-five computer users in my home-business network who shared their start-up experiences with me and explained how computers had sparked business ideas or changed their personal lives.

A new home-business owner said using a computer made her feel younger. By keeping up with computer technology she had, in her words, "conquered my own mythical beast by learning how to use this machine to do me some good. That is a major confidence-builder for me. It means the brain cells will still accept new concepts and skills and that's exciting for the entrepreneurial housewife." Another business owner discovered unknown artistic talents when she began to play around with the graphic capabilities of her computer. She went on to publish a book of computer cartoons and said the computer actually unlocked her sense of humor.

WRITING AND ORGANIZING INFORMATION

One woman who said she had failed typing in high school, and was a poor speller to boot, found the computer unleashed all sorts of ideas she could at last put on paper. "My typing problem was keeping them locked in," she told me, "and my word processing software helped me discover that I could write articles or do a newsletter." Several individuals, while trying to work with computer programs inadequate for their needs, learned how to write programs from scratch, thus launching themselves into the business of helping others as computer consultants or programmers. Some people, on finding how easy it was to gather and organize certain kinds of information for printing, began to sell that information in the form of newsletters, special reports, directories, or books.

After reading the computer chapter of my *Homemade Money* book, Carol Carlson realized that she had to get computerized, too, and she helped the learning process along by taking classes at a community college. "What a difference the computer has made in my business," she says. "I knew I had to change my thinking from small-time worker (everything done by hand, like handwritten addresses) to professional worker. I had to join the computer age in order to do bulk mailings to customers. Before the computer, people would call for info of some sort and I'd be looking through my stacks of papers and notebooks. It had to change, but I fought it for a long time because it was going to require a lot of work. I used to cut-and-paste all my catalogs, but my latest one has now been done mostly on computer. And with the help of a scanner, my next catalog—which will have hundreds of illustrations of my originally designed hangtags—will be done entirely by computer. My business has become very dependent on my machines. I am now able to do custom work for people without white-out and rubber cement. Mailings are easier and I do the work of numerous people myself."

© Carol Carlson

MANAGING TIME

Even the smallest crafts business will find computer technology a boon to their personal and home-business lives. Among other things, a computer saves time, improves office efficiency, gives any business a more professional image, empowers one to accomplish things heretofore impossible, and enables one to speed through routine tasks such as bookkeeping, accounting, record-keeping, correspondence, invoicing, tax returns, the design of printed materials, and so much more.

To me, the saving of time is the greatest benefit of computer technology. I grant that it takes a lot of time to learn to use new computer software; but once you've mastered it, the time it will save you will increase your productivity ten-

fold, and you can begin to actually do some of the things you've only had time to dream about in the past.

In looking back, I cannot believe I actually published a newsletter for several years—not to mention two books—using only an electric typewriter, tons of white-out, rubber cement, and patience. Keeping my mailing lists up to date was even more stressful. By the time I bought my first computer in 1986, I was trying to manage thousands of names on 3 by 5 cards and paper masters that had to be photocopied for each mailing. Once I began to do all this work on computer, my productivity skyrocketed because at least 30 percent of my time had previously been wasted by doing everything the hard way.

"Before I computerized my business, my only real obstacle was the unbelievable amount of paperwork consuming my time," says Annie Lang. "In an average forty-two-hour work week, I figured I was spending nearly eighteen hours doing record/bookkeeping and answering customer needs by mail."

DESIGNING AND PRINTING BUSINESS MATERIALS

Adding a computer to your life is like suddenly having a couple of helpful employees at your beck and call, and the value of suddenly being able to design and print everything you need to run your business is beyond measure. Overnight, you will begin to save money on printing, save time by eliminating trips to print shops, and lower your stress accordingly. Being able to create promotional flyers, press releases, and catalogs on computer is an incredible boon to mail-order sellers like myself. It used to take me two weeks to cut-and-paste up a typeset catalog to sell my publications; but with the graphic capabilities of my *WordPerfect* software, I can design a new catalog in a day, once I've written the copy for it.

Many crafters now scan photos of their products into a file that can be used with a word processing software package. Once a master catalog has been created, copies can be printed either with a laser or inkjet printer or by other photocopy methods offered by office centers such as Kinko's. (Color printers are now so affordable that even the smallest business can afford one.) If you don't have a scanner, many printers and office centers can scan your photos and artwork for you at reasonable cost and put them on a disk you can use with your software or incorporate into your Web site.

"How I wish I'd had my computer in the beginning for all those small-scale printing jobs," says Carol Krob. "I continue to study and learn, and I will upgrade my system as necessary to produce top quality materials and save time that can be devoted to designing and writing." Carol now creates all her printed materials on computer, including a promotional newsletter and her 36-page catalog of stitchery graphs and needlework kits illustrated here. "With only a little help from my teacher in the preliminary and final stages, I was able to produce this catalog after having my computer for only a few months. This was undoubtedly one of the biggest challenges of my entire professional career—definitely a learning experience. The artwork was all drawn by hand and scanned into the computer. A commercial printer did the actual printing."

I like the way Carol has shown the personal side of her business on the catalog cover. "My personal physical fitness regimen, an important part of my daily routine, was the inspiration behind the exercise motifs; the florals and geometric shapes represent elements of many of the needlework designs featured in my books and kits."

DESIGNING ON COMPUTER

Designers everywhere are now using computer software to create patterns and designs, graph needlework charts, and more. Susan Young uses her computer to design the inserts for her pattern packages. She also publishes a promotional newsletter and little books of poetry and other writing. Kathy Cisneros, "The Bottle Cap Lady," wrote and illustrated two books, teaching herself how to draw the graphics on her computer. If you're still not ready for a computer of your own, however, maybe you can benefit from the technology by working with a friend who has one. Artist Ruby Tobey, for example, says she hasn't found time to learn much about working with a computer, but is collaborating with a friend. "She doesn't draw," says Ruby, "but she enjoys the creative part of working with a computer. Besides doing the typesetting for my promotional newsletter, she scans my little

Designing on Computer

Professional designers everywhere are using their computers these days not only to manage their businesses more efficiently, but to actually design on them. If this is a topic you'd like to know more about, check out Judy Heim's book, *The Needlecrafter's Computer Companion— Hundreds of Easy Ways to Use Your Computer for Sewing, Quilting, Cross-Stitch, Knitting & More.* This is a terrific aid for anyone interested in creating patterns and designs. The book comes with two disks of Shareware and demo software and explains how to electronically link up with hundreds of thousands of stitchers now networking on the Internet and commercial online services. You will find this publisher's Web site at www.nostarch.com.

Another book that will be helpful to fiber designers is *Software Directory for Fibre Artists*, which discusses over 275 fiber software programs for knitting, quilting, needlework, sewing, and weaving. Updated information on programs and new versions since the directory was published can be found on the publisher's Web site at www.studioword.com.

drawings and prints note paper, business cards, and other little things for me."

Jacqueline Fox designs her Waxing Moon Designs needlework patterns on computer, using *Cross Stitch Designer Gold* software by Oxford. "This program took a while to learn, but it sure saves time once you get the hang of it. It allows me to see a design in color as it is being developed. You can work with up to ninety-nine different colors, charting stitches one at a time or using a paintbrush feature to fill in areas."

© Waxing Moon Designs 1997

Jacqueline's designs have been published by Leisure Arts, but she didn't like the idea of having to sell all rights to her designs and thought self-publishing would prove more profitable. Her pattern packages retail for $10 because they include special accessory items such as gold charms. She is marketing to shops across the country by mail and through needlework distributors who buy at 20 percent off the wholesale price. "I connected with these companies by reading trade magazines," she says.

"Surfing the Net"

THE TERMS "INTERNET" and "World Wide Web" are interchangeable. As you know, the Internet is a computer network that connects millions of computers worldwide through telephone lines, fiber optics, and modems. The World Wide Web, or "Web," as most people now call it, is simply a way of publishing and accessing information on the Internet. Anyone with a presence on the Web will have an online address that begins with "www."

"Surfing the Net" has become the catch phrase for what millions of people now do every day. One Internet service provider says that the average person now spends thirty hours a week online, so it's clear to see we're breeding a new kind of addict here. In fact, I recently noticed a book titled *Caught in the Net* (Wiley, 1998), that addresses this problem by offering a plan to salvage one's sanity without disposing of one's keyboard. While some people seem to be spending the better part of their waking hours in front of a computer screen, a segment of our population has definitely "tuned out" on this topic because they feel they're too old to be bothered with it. Unfortunately, if you have any kind of business you're trying to develop, you can't afford to ignore the marketing potential of the Internet, even if you do feel you're too old to learn new tricks.

As one of the older generation myself, I resisted the Internet long after most of my friends and business associates had their own Web sites. I had a whole list of reasons for this, of course. First, I had computer problems—a modem/software communications problem and too little RAM. I was also concerned about accidentally downloading a virus and opening up my computer to hackers (something everyone does when they go online). My biggest objection to the Internet and World Wide Web (initially, and now as well) is that I don't have time to waste surfing the Net, answering e-mail, and chatting with strangers all over the world. I can relate to what self-publishing guru Jerry Buchanan once said in his newsletter: "Joining online chat groups can be like Forrest Gump on the roadside bench waiting for a bus and just talking to whoever happens to be seated on the same bench. I see myself as more focused than that."

I did consider buying a second computer I could dedicate to the Internet, but a more desirable solution presented itself last year in the form of WebTV. For $150 and no stress at all, I connected our big-screen television set to the Web simply by plugging in a couple of things and switching it on. Everything is controlled by a little box that sits on top of the TV. A special printer has been developed for use with WebTV, but so far I haven't seen much need for one. As an avid reader of books, magazines, and newsletters, I much prefer my reading in this form, and already have more to read than I can find time for.

E-mail is clearly the big attraction for most people who have gone online. WebTV comes with a cordless keyboard and e-mail privileges, but since I need information in printed form for my writing, I prefer fax communications at this point. I believe our need for e-mail depends a lot on what we do, where we live, and who we want to communicate with. Certainly, if you need to regularly communicate with business associates or have friends or family members all over the world, you can't beat e-mail for speed, cost, and efficiency. And, as many crafters have discovered, it's also a great little promotional tool.

Online Networking, Research, Promotion, and Sales

THE WORLD WIDE Web is grand and glorious," says Maria Nerius. "I think it will open avenues we never dreamed possible. My heart breaks a bit at the commercialism of it, and there is a lot of hostility online that we need to get rid of, but crafters all over the world are now communicating with one another. I see the Web enhancing and giving us the ability to blend different techniques, supplies and perspective."

Thousands of crafters are now networking through online craft forums, doing research and making marketing connections. Several Web sites now offer listings of shows and fairs across the country, and soon there will be a wealth of such information. With a bit of research, anyone can find "virtual shops and craft malls" through which they may be able to sell their products, but the publicity power of the Internet is just beginning to be discovered by crafters.

PUBLICITY STRATEGIES

Weaver, writer, and teacher Bobbie Irwin is excited about the publicity potential of e-mail. "I just finished a fifteen-day teaching tour organized on short notice, entirely by e-mail," she says. "In a matter of a few weeks, I was able to line up four lectures and three workshops for five California guilds, and it worked out just great. I've had more inquiries in the year I've had e-mail than ever before."

"The Web has turned out to be a really good promotional tool for me," says teacher and author Karen Combs. "Originally, I started out to promote my quilting classes, but now I'm selling my two books and some hard-to-find notions through my online catalog, offering credit card purchase ability to my customers. I've added a bimonthly letter and family page as well. I've had some 14,000 visitors to my site over the past two years. I know something about the 2 percent of them who have accepted my invitation to tell me something about themselves on my 'Sign-My-Guest-Book' page, and I get a lot of e-mail from other visitors."

Although Karen has a good speaker's brochure, she likes being able to refer people to her Web site because it includes the same information plus color images of work she has scanned into the site. Her advice to other teachers? "If you don't have a Web page, you're missing out, big time. As one program director told me, 'I work full time and I don't have time to send out a lot of letters and wait to get information back from teachers who might be interested in speaking at our conference. I simply spend a little time on the Internet, select teachers I want, and send invitations to speak.'"

RESEARCH

"I've done amazing things on the Internet," says Karen Lyons. "There's no excuse for not researching any show/

company/business arrangement you're contemplating." Jana Gallagher, whose Web site serves a large network of crafters, says the Internet is a great way to gather market research information. "My experience has been that if you ask readers for their comments about a certain product or idea, they will drop you a quick e-mail reply."

"The Internet has played a large role in how designers network as individuals and as a collective group," says Annie Lang. "The wealth of information gathered in a few hours over the Web can save us days of research at the library and information gathering over the phone."

I love books and like doing research at the library, but I must agree it's a great time-saver to be able to connect to the Internet at a moment's notice and immediately find needed information. Unfortunately, we cannot assume that everything we find online is accurate or up-to-date. I haven't yet had time to correct all the inaccurate information about my books and newsletter (out of publication since 1996) that I found on my initial search on the World Wide Web. In their zeal to get information on their sites, some Web site owners are simply picking up information from other sources without bothering to check if it's accurate or not. And, as emphasized in the sidebar "Protect Your Intellectual Property," some are also illegally lifting copyrighted material.

SELLING ON THE NET

Although some people are making direct sales on the Internet, I think its greatest value lies in the area of networking and promotion. More artists and crafters than I can count have set up their own Web sites to offer art and hand-crafted items, and countless others are offering products through many of the online craft malls. Whether such products will ever sell on the Web with any degree of success remains to be seen, however. Each time I've asked crafters what kind of sales they're making online, most say they're selling a few things but getting mostly inquiries for the brochures or catalogs they're offering. In most cases, I believe the real selling will always be done through the catalogs and brochures sellers send to interested people who have popped in to their Web site for a look around. This is a topic I will continue to monitor and write about at greater length when I have gathered more success stories about this kind of selling.

Like many other Web site owners, Jana Gallagher is not thoroughly convinced that a storefront Web site is the way for her to go, hence her hesitation to offer handcrafts for sale via the Internet. "I have a classified section on my Web site that is attracting fellow crafters," she says, "but it appears to me that the people who are looking for crafts are not necessarily retail buyers, but rather wholesalers looking for particular items they can resell."

It may well be that craft wholesalers will benefit more from a presence on the Web than crafters trying to sell direct to consumers. Instead of sending out expensive mailers to shops and other buyers, wholesalers can simply send a postcard or promotional newsletter to their shop contacts inviting them to visit their Web site for a look at their newest products.

Although my books have had a presence on the Web since 1996, I have not found this to be an effective way to get mail orders for them. Initially I hoped to be able to generate orders by advertising them on various Web sites, inviting people to call in or fax orders to me on a credit card. This rarely happened, however. I believe this is because people prefer to buy books in bookstores whenever possible—first, to see what they're buying and, second, to save shipping charges on a mail order.

Since bookstore sales of my books are excellent, I conclude that my presence on the Web is helping these sales along. Now, instead of trying to compete for direct sales on the Web, I am promoting the various retail outlets where my books can be found. Self-published authors, however, should definitely explore their options for mail-order book sales on the Internet, either on their own Web site or by advertising on other sites such as www.amazon.com (the Internet's largest online bookstore).

Note: Self-publishers who sell at wholesale can sell their books through Amazon's Web site even though they are not online themselves, provided their books have an ISBN number and the required information can be submitted in electronic format. Lacking regular bookstore distribution, this is a great way for small publishers to capture sales generated through publicity. (See Resources.)

A couple of years ago, I vowed I would never have my own home page on the Internet because I felt I didn't have time to figure out this technology and then maintain a site once it was established. After "surfing the Net" for a few months and writing this book, however, I finally began to see the many benefits of a permanent presence on the Internet. Thanks to Renee Chase, who has designed and set up an electronic home for me on her own Web site, I am now permanently entrenched at www.crafter.com/brabec. Here you'll find information about all my books plus my online newsletter, *Barbara Brabec's Craftsbiz Chat & Personal Reflections*. (Old newsletter editors never die; they just keep looking for new people who want to read what they write.) I am particularly excited about using this Web site to connect with interesting people I can write about in future books or articles.

Jana Gallagher currently uses her Web site for such purposes. "In the past, I've focused on many of the quick and easy crafts I have designed for crafters, parents, teachers, and caregivers, as well as the book and product reviews that I do. I am now writing a book of craft projects and my Web site is a way I can try out projects and see how well they are received. Questions are e-mailed to me on a daily basis about project ideas needed by scout groups, school teachers, parents needing birthday party ideas . . . the list goes on. It has been a wonderful way to spark my creativity."

SELLING SUPPLIES

If handcrafts aren't selling with great success on the Web, patterns, kits, and sup-plies certainly are. "One of the more astounding aspects of our business has occurred since we put a site on the World Wide Web," says Bob Gerdts, a retired Army officer who was drawn into his wife's business. "Carol originally collected egg art. She got me to take lessons in egg artistry with her, and that led to our making items for sale. We didn't know what www meant until we shipped to Sidney, Australia, Yokohama, and Waco City, Japan. We haven't sold but one decorated egg through the Net, but our egg art supply business has exploded. We're a small business, but we're probably the biggest egg art supplier on the Internet. The other suppliers (our competitors) apparently aren't computer-oriented yet."

Jewelry designer Lynn Smythe has a Web site through which she advertises her Dolphin Crafts jewelry creations. She also sells a line of bead supplies, buttons, books, and related materials. To illustrate her catalog and Web site, she scans in finished jewelry pieces such as the one shown here.

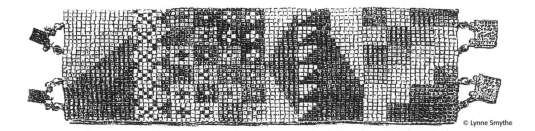

© Lynne Smythe

Protect Your Intellectual Property

The electronic age has greatly compounded the problem related to the pirating of designs, so be cautious about putting your writing, designs, patterns, and other ideas online. "With every country in the world having access to the Web, U.S. copyrights are not necessarily recognized by all," notes Annie Lang. "Any image up on the Web can be captured, clipped, and used by anyone, despite the trademarks and copyright notices, and few individuals have the resources to protect any written materials or images they publish on the Web."

© A. Lang 1996

"I got a lot of inquiries for the supplies catalog," she says. "I used to send it free, but this proved to be too expensive. Now I send a free brochure that gives a brief overview of what I offer, and people can send $2 to receive a complete catalog, getting a $5 money-off coupon they can apply to their first order." Lynn says her catalog is generating an order response of between 3 and 4 percent, which is excellent.

"Many crafters are saving hundreds of dollars using the Internet to find their supplies," says Renee Chase, one of the Web pioneers in the crafts industry. (See "Setting Up Your Own Web Site," at right.) "The educational aspect of the Internet has also helped crafters at our site. I receive e-mails quite often from crafters who have had their questions answered from articles we've included in our electronic newsletter. Files can be attached to an e-mail, which is really neat. This saves so much time! Some of the crafters I know are sending projects, patterns, and other documents via e-mail attachments. Recently, when I started an online scrapbook of the crafters in our chat room, many of them sent their photos via e-mail."

Setting Up Your Own Web Site

RENEE CHASE IS one of the Web pioneers in the crafts field. In 1995 she was the first person to simultaneously publish a crafts marketing magazine in print and online. The *Neighbors & Friends* publication she created, however, is now under new ownership and Renee no longer has any connection with that business. She has, however, developed a new Web site for crafters that offers an electronic newsletter, live chat rooms, resources, shows, malls, suppliers, and downloadable project pages. (Go to www. crafter.com.)

Only a few years ago, Renee's only use of a computer was to write letters to her mom. With some help from her computer-expert husband, Michael, Renee gradually learned how to use desktop publishing software, and then went on to master the basics of setting up a Web site. "Learning is all a matter of attitude," she says. "I believe that if we have the desire to learn about something, be it crafts or computers, we can do it. The trick is not to get hung up on the little problems."

Renee sees online browsing like moving into a new town. "The best way to find out what's available is to get in the car and drive around. Your Internet browser is like your car, and you're cruising through this interesting new community. Some things will interest you and others won't.

The more you're out there, the more comfortable you're going to become with the environment."

In setting up your own Web site, Renee stresses the importance of remembering who you're trying to reach and the kind of computer setup they may have. "Most people don't have high-end equipment yet. If they have a slow modem, a site with a lot of graphics will take too long to load and you'll lose them. Nothing has developed impatience more in me than the Internet, and I'm sure many others feel the same way. That means we have only about fifteen seconds to get someone's attention. With so much else out there to explore, no one is going to wait long for any site to load."

There are now several software packages you can use to set up a Web site. Renee likes *Hot Metal Pro.* "I was surprised by how easy it was to set up a simple Web page," she says. "It's just like putting a page together using a graphics-oriented word processing program."

Technology *vs.* Craftsmanship

T HE THOUGHT THAT I am likely to be living for some time in the Third Millennium, surrounded by technology that boggles my mind, sounds more like sci-

Registering Your Web Site

"I will build a Web site and they will come," many Internet novices think. Unfortunately, it doesn't work that way. "It doesn't do any good to set up a Web site if you're not going to promote it," says Bob Gerdts. "More important, to be found by the various search engines people use when they're looking for information, you either have to pay somebody to register your site with all the search engines or visit each one yourself and put your URL address there.

"For example, go into Yahoo. Add your Web address where it says, 'Add URL.' All the search engines have indexes, so you should list your address under the appropriate index, such as 'Arts and Crafts.' If you need assistance in getting your listings registered, check out the services of a company called WebPromote. Their Web site address is www.webpromote.com."

Renee Chase adds that the majority of the search engines have "robots" that are constantly searching the Internet and grabbing information and key words from Web sites. "To insure that your pages and sites get pulled up, you need to insert what are called 'meta tags' in the heading of your HTML programming—a descriptive paragraph, for example, that tells people exactly what people can expect to find on your site." (The Web site that will write meta tags for your site is http://vancouver-webpages.com/VWbot/mk-metas.html.)

ence fiction to me than real life. Some days I yearn to curl up and escape back to my grandmother's time. Life was so simple then, when the whole world didn't suddenly stop the moment the electricity failed or the computer crashed. As a business person, however, I see that people who elect to remain in the old world by avoiding computer technology are apt to end up on the short end of the stick someday, and that's the last place I ever want to be. The key to survival in any kind of business today seems to lie in one's ability to remain flexible and go with the flow, so even though I hate having technology shoved down my throat, I plan to keep learning a little each day as long as I live.

Actually, because of the rate at which knowledge is increasing, we must all live to learn, according to Laurence J. Pino, Esq., president and founder of The Open

University. "Retraining people for new jobs will be woefully inadequate for the coming century," he says. "More important will be developing an attitude of life-long learning to constantly train ourselves as we develop increased skills and more finely tuned competencies." In other words, we must first understand technology itself before we can access the information we need.

Although computer technology has changed the way we do business and the way handmade products are being designed, developed, and marketed, it isn't likely to hurt the market for high-quality, originally designed handcrafts at any time in the foreseeable future. In fact, many people believe that the more high tech our society becomes, the greater the need for the kind of human touch handmade products can provide.

Amy Detwiler, editor of *Sunshine Artist*, commented on a talk given by *Megatrends* guru John Naisbitt at a conference she attended. "What he said spoke loudly for the future of art and crafts," she told me. "Basically, he said that because we are so high tech, so electronic now, we're all looking for that personal touch—something that hasn't been mass produced, something that gives us the feeling that someone's hands made this. He said that what gives people a kick now is getting a hand-written letter."

TECHNOLOGY'S IMPACT ON HANDCRAFT BUSINESSES

In response to my question about how computer technology might affect the future of certain craft businesses, many crafters said they weren't much concerned. Calligrapher Barbara Schaffer hopes people will continue to appreciate hand-lettered work and will stay away from the computer-oriented calligraphy, "which is dreadful," she says.

"My designs will still likely be hand-crafted and not greatly affected by technology," says Dodie Eisenhauer. "But I think technology will make it easier to communicate or transmit photos of my products and produce better looking printed materials."

"Technology helps me communicate," says Anita Means, "but one of my goals as a craft show producer is to introduce the human element back into gift buying."

"I don't think I'll be impacted because I sell history and nostalgia in small practical items whose purchase can easily be justified and which can also be used in decor," says sunbonnet expert Mary Lou Highfill.

"There isn't a computer program in existence that can paint a Santa face the way I can," quips Susan Young.

"The coming generations are going to be even more submerged into the 'instant everything' and rapidly evolving technolo-

The Popularity of Crafts

Now that MasterCard and Visa have combined their efforts to provide a secure system for on-line credit card sales, crafters have greater sales opportunities. This will be especially helpful to professional crafters who live in rural areas. Fortunately, it is now easier to get merchant status from one's local bank because home-based businesses are viewed with greater respect than they were a decade ago.

A few years ago, I reported in my newsletter that banks were reluctant to give merchant status to any business based at home because such businesses were then on the bottom of bankers' lists as being most undesirable, right after sex merchants. Recently, in researching topics on the Internet, I found thousands of sites under the arts 'n crafts umbrella and was very amused when someone told me that "crafts" was the second hottest topic on the Internet . . . right after sex. Funny, isn't it, how crafts have gone from the bottom of one list to the top of another, both times "right after sex."

gics, so the art and craft of handwork may suffer," says Sherrill M. Lewis, who has named her beaded jewelry and accessories business Eximiously Yours! (with an exclamation point). "The definition of 'eximious' is . . . distinguished, eminent, excellent. The exclamation point signifies my joy of working with such lovely materials and, occasionally, the surprise factor that rewards the creative endeavor. I hope the appreciation for fine things, handwrought and well made, distinctive, and truly one-of-a-kind, will grow even more desirable in the future. We who are artists must strive to teach others and encourage them to pass our craft on."

CHAPTER 12

Endnotes

I've found that everything we do leads to something else. My love of crafting has led me to hundreds of other crafters, and it's wonderful talking shop and encouraging those who feel they have no talents. I am convinced that God places us where we are for a reason, and while we are there, we touch those people's hearts for that season.

OPAL LEASURE, The Apron Strings Lady

YOU WILL RECALL that at the beginning of this book, I emphasized the importance of taking just one step in a new direction to see where it might lead. Throughout the book, I've given you dozens of real-life examples of the kind of things likely to happen if you will only let loose of the reins and give your natural creativity and imagination its head. "You can't just sit and wait for things to happen," says Kathy Cisneros of Recreational Recycling. "I had been waiting for weeks for a potential commercial spot on television when a friend asked if I

had followed up on it. I said no, I was waiting, and she said, 'Nothing ever happens to people who wait for things to happen.' So now I *make* things happen!"

If what you're trying to make happen doesn't actually happen, don't be too concerned about it—you can be sure something *else* will happen in the process of trying. You've noticed, I'm sure, how many people started doing one thing only to end up years later doing something totally different. Take Joanne Hill, for instance, who used to sell information by mail to crafters and at one time designed

248

and sold greeting cards. It took her a while to realize what her greatest talents were. "Without an involvement in the crafts field, I might never have discovered them," she says. "I've finally realized that one of my special God-given gifts is the ability to be a strong resource for people who are grieving."

Joanne has lost more friends and loved ones to death than anyone I've ever known. Although it was a drain on her spirit each time she held someone's hand

Start an Idea Box, Notebook, or File

Ideas don't keep. If they aren't captured as soon as they arrive, they will evaporate from your memory as quickly as this morning's dream. "Creative minds tend to run rampant," says crafter Janet Gurgel. "Instead of putting all our ideas into a logical pattern, we sometimes turn them into a crazy quilt."

If this is how you see all the ideas in your mind, it's time to get them recorded and cataloged so you can do something constructive with them. First plan how you're going to capture your great ideas. An idea box would be good for busy crafters whose best ideas come while in the middle of making something. A notebook is good for people who are always on the run. Since I spend most of my time at the computer, it's easy for me to pull up one of my idea files and add a quick note in it. To capture ideas at other times, I keep note paper and pens everywhere, especially in the kitchen, bathroom, and by my bedside. Many of my "flashes of genius" come when I'm fixing dinner, taking a shower, or reading in bed at night. In fact, my most creative ideas tend to come in the wee hours of the morning, particularly when I've gone to bed with a problem or challenged my subconscious mind to delve into its database for information or insight. (This really works. I got the titles of both *Creative Cash* and *Homemade Money* in the middle of the night.)

From time to time—at least once a year—read through all the ideas you've collected, selecting some to develop now and reserving the rest for later. Don't throw any of them away, however, because it can sometimes take years for a particular idea to jell . . . or for you to grow enough to be ready to do something with it.

as they lay dying, her faith enabled her to grow through it all. What Joanne learned during this difficult period of life has now been captured in her first book, *Rainbow Remedies for Life's Stormy Times.* "I couldn't find a publisher for it," she says, "so I decided to publish it myself. I have two companion books in the works and I'm now presenting self-help/motivational workshops for people who are grieving."

This is a far cry from selling crafts or telling crafters how to do it, but a wonderful example of how life leads us in new directions if we only have the courage to get started. During that period of time when Joanne was still searching for the right road of life, she was growing in wisdom and spirit through traveling. "I've been to Ireland and England twice, Wales once, took a cruise around the Hawaiian Islands, attended a number of storytelling and motivational workshops, remodeled my home, covered nearly 20,000 miles in my RV (with my dogs and guardian angel for company), and finished some college courses. In spite of all the stormy times, I still feel the wonderment whenever God provides rainbows in serendipitous events and loving, helpful people. I'm so glad I took this leap of faith. Win, lose, or draw, I will always be grateful for the opportunity to follow my dreams."

Sometimes people start in one place, go on to other things, and eventually end up back where they started, like Anita

Means. "Over the past fourteen years, my path has gone from craftsperson, to retail store owner, to craft show promoter, and it has brought me back to my home, where I started fourteen years ago," she says. "Along the way, I have learned that you must do what you are passionate about, which I did do. I know that positive energy forces produce positive results and that life and business changes, while seemingly negative or disappointing, can always be turned into a learning/growth experience."

What Goes Around Comes Around

ONCE UPON A time, a hobbyist sent a letter of complaint to a craft supply company. Fifteen years later, the hobbyist ended up working for the woman who answered her letter. In the years in between, the hobby business grew to occupy three rooms of the home plus all of the garage, and the hobbyist became a professional designer, writer, editor of a leading crafts magazine, and finally, a television personality. It happened like this:

Back in 1984, when Maria Nerius lost her job, she invested $25 in felt, fiberfill, and glue so she could make some Christmas ornaments. "They turned out terrible," she said, "and my background in advertising convinced me it was because the glue was bad. So I sent a letter of complaint to Aleene's, the company who made the glue, saying, 'You have a bad batch of glue here, thank you very much.'

"I got a lovely letter back from Aleene herself, saying, 'We're sorry, here's more glue, keep crafting.' I kept crafting, decided I liked it, and wanted to make it a business. Three years later, while at a trade show, I went into this company's booth to thank them and met Aleene, one of the pioneers in the crafts industry. Later, she invited me to be a guest on her television show, but I said no because I was afraid. When she invited me again the following year, however, I said yes and fell in love with the medium."

Today Maria has a regular spot on *Aleene's Creative Living* show on TNN called "Creative Chat with Maria Nerius," in which she talks about various things going on in the industry. Maria says success is measured in many different ways, but one of her greatest thrills was winning the Designer of the Year award in 1996. As one of five nominees for the award (sponsored by Monsanto, Loctite Corporation, and *Craft and Needlework Age*), Maria was the first professional crafter to win it. "I felt this was an acknowledgment that the people in my field are creative, innovative, and know their audience. That I could bring that honor to all professional crafters was a great thrill to me."

If Aleene hadn't taken the time to acknowledge Maria's complaint letter fifteen years earlier, Maria said she probably would have been too discouraged to continue with crafts. "I am so blessed that I lost my job, decided to make some ornaments, and wrote a letter of complaint," she says.

What gave me goosebumps when I heard this story was the fact that Aleene was in the audience when Maria accepted her award—a perfect illustration of "what goes around, comes around." And it was she who started Maria's standing ovation. "There she was . . . my hero . . . standing and clapping for me," says Maria. "The memory of it still takes my breath away."

Believe It or Not

THROUGH THE YEARS, I've come to know and write about hundreds of interesting men and women who have astonished me with their creativity, ingenuity, and personal accomplishments. When I think about amazing women, however, the one that always comes first to mind (after my mother) is Lyndall "Granny" Toothman, now eighty-eight years old. Without question, she is the most interesting, dynamic, and ageless woman I've ever known, and I have long been inspired by her zest for life. If I live to be eighty-eight, I'll be remembering how she was still driving 10,000 miles a year at that age—alone—to entertain people at craft fairs and festivals or just to visit a friend.

It takes courage to reach for one's dreams, live life to its fullest, and keep plugging along when old age finally catches you. In one of her lectures to women across the country, Dr. Joyce Brothers once commented that the only difference between being a neurotic and a creative artist is *courage,* adding that the creative person is capable of turning adversity to advantage, whereas a neurotic would wallow in self-pity. Twice, when arthritis temporarily put Lyndall in a wheelchair, she ignored the doctors who said there was nothing she could do about all her pain and immobility except take aspirin. Instead, she bought a self-help book on how to fight arthritis, followed instructions to the letter, got out of her wheelchair, and went back to doing shows. (She says the book that helped her so much was *A Doctor's Proven New Home Cure for Arthritis* by B. Franklin, M.D., Parker Publishing.)

Books have always been an important part of Lyndall's life. Once, when we had time to muse about life in general, she told me how much she loved to read. "As a child, I loved to go to bed early so I could read and then dream about all the

Author's line drawing of a photograph of "Granny" Toothman and a sample display board similar to those now in Ripley's Believe It or Not Museums.

places I wanted to see. I read everything I could get my hands on, but I couldn't have imagined then the interesting life I would have, nor all the wonderful people and places I'd get to know."

Long after Lyndall is gone, people will remember her and the impact she had on their lives. Her accomplishments appear in two of the *Foxfire* books, and samples of her work are now featured in several of Ripley's *Believe It or Not* Museums. In fact, they have purchased $6,000 worth of Lyndall's products, including one of her human-hair bags and a dog-hair sweater for their museum in England, and several of her fur sample display boards and some of her handspun, handwoven products for other museums in this country. Remember that coat I mentioned in an earlier chapter, the one she spun from Sammy's fur? It's on display in Ripley's museum in Branson, Missouri. "They paid me $500 for that coat," says Lyndall, "which I thought was a fair price, considering this was the first coat I'd ever made and something I wore for thirty-five years."

During the past thirty years, Lyndall has been featured in hundreds of newspaper articles and magazines and has been a guest on numerous radio and television programs. She would have made the Johnny Carson show, too, if her arthritis hadn't flared up at the time they wanted her on the show. Lyndall obviously thrives

on attention (as we all do), but I think her constant connection with the public is what has kept her always so young at heart. Clearly, she has no conception of the words, *old* or *retirement,* and I hope you'll remember her the next time you try to use your age as an excuse not to do something you'd really like to do. "God willing," she says, "I'll still be working when I'm 100 years old. They say old people don't dream—they have visions—but I still dream, so I must not be old yet."

I'll never forget what Lyndall said that summer's evening so long ago when we touched on the topic of dying. "It don't bother me none," she said. "It's just going to be my next great adventure!"

Crafts as Both Work and Therapy

IN AN EDITORIAL for *Crafts 'n Things* magazine, publisher Marie Clapper called crafts the miracle drug of the twenty-first century. "Crafting is powerful," she says. "When we craft, we step outside ourselves. We leave our personal world and enter the world of imagination. We take risks. We learn. We view the world differently. When we craft, we focus on the task at hand—on the canvas, the cloth, the beads. We discard our

The Best Advice I Ever Got

➤ Keep family priorities above business. Without a secure family, business doesn't mean anything.

—Dodie Eisenhauer

➤ Establish your needs . . . present a plan . . . expect results!

—Sondra Lucente

➤ Accept the fact that it's not a perfect world. When business problems arise, turn the stumbling blocks into stepping stones and move on. (And get it in writing!)

—Sue Cloutman

➤ When you do what you love, it's hardly any work at all. This advice comes in most handy when you have to deal with the long, long hours any new business requires.

—Eileen Heifner

➤ You can't get to second base with your foot still on first (advice from Barbara's *Homemade Money* book).

—Annie Lang

everyday thoughts and worries; there simply is no room for them in our minds. We live in the moment. That regenerates us. Lifts us. Fills us with joy. And hope. Crafting gives our souls a chance to catch up with our lives—and in the process heals us from the stress of living at this time . . . in this culture . . . on this planet."

How true! Crafting is the best stress reliever I've ever found. After eight hours of finger work over a computer keyboard, nothing relaxes me more than two or three hours of cross-stitch embroidery or teddy-bear making. I get so absorbed in my work that the world is literally held at bay. I forget that my back aches or my knees hurt, that I'm behind schedule on a book or have a stack of bills to pay. For a few hours, at least, I just lose myself in whatever I'm working on at the moment. Sometimes I think of my mother and the last quilt she ever made. After Daddy died, she told me she couldn't have gotten through his long illness and death without a quilt to work on the whole time. Although making it was wonderful therapy for her, in the end the quilt contained so much grief that she couldn't stand to look at it, so I took it. Still heavy with memories, it makes me wonder how many other women have gotten through the hard times in life by quilting, stitching, or doing some other art or craft.

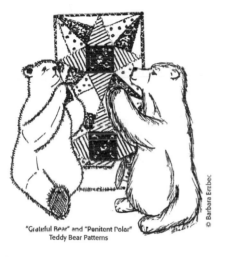

"Grateful Bear" and "Penitent Polar" Teddy Bear Patterns

© Barbara Erebec

Since 1974, Betty Marx's part-time business has been both profitable and therapeutic, helping her through the death of two husbands and her own battle with throat cancer. Now in her seventies, Betty still sells her specially designed jewelry and ascots for laryngectomy patients through a national mail-order catalog, while also doing volunteer work. "I visit schools to speak to children about the dangers and results of smoking and also work as a patient-to-patient volunteer at Sloan-Kettering, visiting new laryngectomies," she says. "This can be a very dis-

figuring type of surgery, not to mention the emotional and psychological effects. It has been a great satisfaction to be able to help other women through this ordeal while also enhancing their appearance."

Making money from your special artistry and creativity is what I hope you'll soon be doing, but don't get so carried away by the idea of financial success that you lose track of your real goals. If in the end you never sell a thing, you'll still have your art or craft, and it will continue to enrich your life.

Although Lyndall Toothman has always been well paid for what she does, money has never been her motivating reason to keep working into her eighties. She simply loves crafts and all the interesting people it has enabled her to meet through the years. Like Jimmy Stewart, she says she has had a wonderful life. "People have often encouraged me to write a book about my life and experiences," she says, "but that doesn't interest me. The fact that I've lived it is enough."

Coping with Accidents and Disabilities

WHEN YOU ARE totally involved in a business of any kind, you will find that you rarely get sick. Insurance statistics have proven that self-employed people have fewer illnesses than others, and the reason is simple. First, we love what we're doing and work even when others in our condition would call themselves "sick" and take the day off from work. Second, we simply don't have time to sit around feeling sorry for ourselves. There are always deadlines to meet, orders to fill, things to do, and places to go. Accidents are a bit trickier, though. You may not be able to prevent them, but you may have to get creative to work around them. To a crafter, nothing is worse than an injured hand. Karen Rioux shares this story about the time she was doing home parties and her orders had just reached their peak. It was then that she caught the middle finger of her right hand in the metal garage door.

"I was lucky to be wearing leather gloves at the time or I might now be called Stubby," she says. "However, I did break it and had a puncture wound. Curiously, my first thoughts were not of the pain but how I was going to get all my orders done on time. Luckily, the break did not require a full splint, and within thirty-six hours I was back painting shirts and ceramics and only missed my last delivery date by a week. I decided I had a choice of either throwing in the towel or going forward. I realized then that this probably wouldn't be the only (or last) obstacle I'd face having a business, so I'd better learn to cope."

Survival in a home-based business has many direct ties to one's health, as Pat and Ed Endicott learned a while back. After working as partners in their House of Threads and Wood home-based business for nearly fifteen years, Ed suffered a massive stoke that left him partially paralyzed and unable to speak. Each time I've called Pat for an update, I've been surprised by the upbeat tone in her voice and the fact that she always focuses on the positive aspects of her life.

"Life has a way of getting you to rethink things, and perhaps some things are meant to be," she says. "All the long hours of a home-based business have given me the most flexibility and drive to keep things going during this trying time. It has created a haven to hide all thoughts and emotions while getting work done at whatever time I want."

It took a while, but Pat finally learned she couldn't be superwoman. "I finally stressed out trying to do everything myself," she says. "Had a few counseling sessions (along with many talks with the Big Guy Upstairs), and am concentrating on taking control of my life, working on self-preservation, and understanding what is and isn't possible in this life I/we have. There's a bit more permission now to take time out for me, and enjoy what the good Lord has given us."

Building on Faith

"The future has two handles: fear and faith," says pastor Adrian Rogers. "In times of trouble, which one are you likely to grab?"

"The three secrets to life," says Dr. Robert Schuller of The Crystal Cathedral, "are faith, focus, and follow-up." Wally Amos could relate to that, I'm sure. Although he lost the right to use his own name in connection with the famous cookie company he started, he bounced back to build a new No Name Cookie Company. "Faith is what you need when you don't have any facts," he asserts. "It's stepping out on nothing and landing on something."

Or, as the Bible confirms, "Faith is the substance of things hoped for, the evidence of things not seen." (Hebrews 11:1)

"Life does force change upon many creative people," says Barbara Sharpe, a lifelong sewer, teacher, and writer who is now facing legal blindness from macular degeneration. While contemplating a less finely defined future, Barbara may be remembering the days when she used to canoe whitewater rivers. She isn't just sitting around waiting for the lights to go out, however. Knowing that she will soon have to modify her computer system to keep working, she has gathered huge amounts of resource materials regarding optical aids, voice-recognition computer systems, closed-circuit TV scanners to increase viewing printed materials, and so on. She continues to teach courses in business discipline at a local college and occasionally presents her Sewing for Profit seminars. "I can still see to sew and thread a sewing machine in good light when I'm not tired," she says, "which is good considering that I have a huge stash of fabrics that needs to be reduced." If Barbara someday tells me she is giving seminars on how people who are losing their eyesight can keep working, I won't be a bit surprised.

Making Changes

IN A RECENT letter, Opal Leasure, The Apron Strings Lady, wrote, "Remember what you once said to me about getting too old to do crafts forever—that someday we wouldn't be able to keep up the pace of a twenty-four-hour-a-day craft business that is bringing in only part-time money? Well, your words have been haunting me because you are absolutely right. It's been very hard for me to work full time at home while also trying to fit in all my daily mothering, busing, cooking, cleaning, crafts designing/manufacturing/selling, and worrying all into one body. As my crafts business grew and grew, my free time diminished and I was still making part-time money, but no longer had part-time work hours, and there was nothing left of *me.* I have now decided I would rather be a full-time *something* than a part-time crafter/author."

©Opal Leasure 1998

It was at this point that Opal began to examine her life, suddenly seeing her lifetime of experience in a new way. "I saw that I had twenty-seven years of volunteering in every preschool, elementary, and high school in a three-county radius," she wrote. "I've chaired events, tested incoming students, been room mother countless times, and volunteered four

years of my life into the Headstart program. Recently, when an ad appeared in the paper for an instructional aide for the country preschool Headstart program, I discovered I had all the qualifications except the certification. So I called around and learned I could become a real teacher within a year simply by taking an examination, filling out some forms, and getting some references from past supervisors. My part-time crafts business, which afforded me the pleasure of raising my children and being home-based, has led to fulfilling my life's dream of becoming a teacher. I am so happy! I still love to craft, but I am slowing down on selling to concentrate on my talent, my creativity—in general, *me.* (And I am going to learn to play the piano!)"

From time to time, it's important to make changes in the way you work or you'll eventually burn out on what you're doing. After publishing a newsletter for fifteen years, I felt controlled by those relentless bimonthly deadlines and was losing all desire to work at all. One day I simply decided enough was enough. The day I made plans to cease publication, the world seemed sunny again. I had renewed enthusiasm for my work and within a month, my blood pressure had dropped forty points. It doesn't matter what your work is—sooner or later, if you don't make changes, you *will* burn out. Crafters are particularly susceptible.

"Many times crafters get so involved in making and distributing their products they forget to also have a life for themselves," says magazine publisher Marsha Reed. "It is important to not only take time for our families and loved ones, but also for ourselves. If we don't do this, we get into a self-neglect or self-destruct mode and begin to resent our work. Once crafting is in your heart and soul, it is extremely hard to totally discard it, but change may be just what we need to start the creativity flowing once again."

As we grow older, things change and we must adjust. If we don't become ill or suffer a physical handicap, we may simply tire of working as hard as we once did, or get bored and begin to look for ways to stay active in our work by doing different things, or doing old things in a new way. Now in their seventies, Pat and Niron Virch still like to travel. Pat goes out a couple times a year to teach, takes a few students, and thinks she might phase out her self-publishing and do some video-tapes instead—a product she could easily wholesale. She's no longer interested in looking for shop markets for her work, but continues to supply a few gift shops with boxes of all sizes (painted inside and out). Mostly, however, she has moved into doing commission work.

"Word-of-mouth advertising and publicity about our home, which is decorated throughout with rosemaling, has brought me a lot of business from people who want me to decorate a wall, ceiling, cabinets, or interior of their homes," she says. "I also get quite a few requests to restore the decorative painting on old furniture people want to pass on to their children as family heirlooms." Pat adds that she plans to paint until she drops, or "until my little finger dies. My hand pivots on that finger when I'm stroking and doing brush work, so if it gets arthritic and painful, I'll either have to stop painting or figure out a whole new way of doing it. So far, no arthritis, so I figure I have at least ten years of painting yet, which is good because I probably have that much wood in inventory waiting to be painted."

Barbara Sharpe's comment about having a stash of fabrics to get rid of, and now Pat's remarks about her wood inventory, makes me think that old crafters never die . . . they just keep looking for ways to get rid of all the supplies they've accumulated through the years.

As the crafters I've written about in this book continue to make changes in their lives, I will be making changes, too. After writing only business-oriented articles and books for the past twenty years, all the technology in my life seems to have thrust my nostalgic yearnings to the forefront, and I am now beginning to write on other topics unrelated to business. In the spring of 1998 I was thrilled to find a home for my new column, "Making

Memories," with *Crafts 'n Things* magazine. The first three articles included nostalgic craft projects of my own—some memory boxes I'd made of my family and myself—and now I'm writing about others who have created one-of-a-kind nostalgic keepsakes for themselves or loved ones. Suddenly, I find I have a knack for writing instructions for craft projects, something I've never done before. And, as a designer of mini-teddy bears, I'm getting the bug to do something with my patterns. Clearly, writing and crafts will always be a part of my life, but my focus is changing and I'm curious to see where new roads may lead me in the future.

The Truck Stops Here

- -

SPEAKING OF ROADS, I have an amusing story about one—but first, a couple of introductory comments. As part of my research for this book, I asked people on my interview list to give me a brief description of what they made or did for a part- or full-time living. The prize for the most original response goes to Dodie Eisenhauer, Village Designs, who wrote, "*Living* is a loose interpretation for cutting, bending, and twisting wire into shapes that people consider aesthetic

enough to purchase, and I consider worthy of the all the Band-Aids I must purchase. If I were doing it all over again, I would design a product with less ability to penetrate skin."

In response to the question, "How have you changed or grown since you started your business," Dodie replied, "I've grown ten pounds, thank you for asking," then suddenly became serious by adding, "God has placed me in some unique situations to teach me lessons I needed to learn."

One of the most important lessons Dodie has learned is that laughter is the best first aid for the stress of running a production crafts business. I first met Dodie a few years ago when I was giving a workshop in her area. When it was her turn to share an interesting crafts business experience, she broke up the whole room with this story:

"We get our screen wire delivered by a semi because it comes on pallets," she said. "Since we live in a remote area on a secondary road, we don't have street signs, so delivery trucks can easily miss us. On this particular day, I heard the semi barrel on past our place. What the driver didn't realize, or course, was that the road was about to narrow and turn to gravel. Knowing the road was only going to get worse, the driver decided to back up and turn around in our neighbor's hog lot. But it was muddy, and he got stuck.

"When our neighbor called to ask if we were expecting a shipment, she said the front end of the truck was sticking out in the road, and people coming home from work couldn't get by, so they were trying to route cars back behind the hog lot. Traffic was stopped for over an hour, and everyone in town could hear the truck motor revving as the driver worked to get unstuck. They finally had to unhook the cab and hook it at a different angle along with the farmer's tractor before they could budge it," Dodie explained.

By now, I was in stitches as I visualized the scene: neighbors inconvenienced on their way home from work; a farmer who didn't appreciate this noisy intrusion into his day and ended up with big mud ruts in his hog lot besides; a truck driver in a state of panic because he had fallen so far behind in his delivery schedule; and Dodie, totally amused by the whole thing.

"I felt so sorry for the driver when he finally got to our place," she said. "He didn't say anything, but he sure looked disturbed. I had visions of him calling back to headquarters trying to explain his delay. 'Well, you see, uh, I missed the customer's place and couldn't turn around because the road narrowed and turned to gravel and, uh, I tried to back up in a farmer's hog lot—yeah, that's what I said . . . a hog lot—and, uh, it was pretty muddy, and, uh . . .'"

I couldn't hold back a minute longer. "What you need to do, Dodie," I said, "is put a big sign by your place of business saying THE TRUCK STOPS HERE. Just think of all the stress you'll save the next truck driver."

You *Can* Change Your Life!

YOU MAY BE surprised to learn that earlier editions of this book have been on the market since 1979. There is quite a story behind this book, but it's too long to tell here. Suffice it to say that *Creative Cash* has had five publishers to date, and I've been one of them on three different occasions. Like a cat with nine lives, this book has simply refused to die, thanks in large part to thousands of satisfied readers who have given it word-of-mouth advertising through the years. Now, with over 100,000 copies sold, this new edition of my "baby" has found a wonderful new home with Prima Publishing, and I hope it will continue to have a positive impact on the lives of thousands of new readers.

In interviewing various craft business owners for this edition, I was surprised to find how many of them had actually launched their business with an earlier edition of this book in hand. When Yvonne Ward decided to start her Country Garden Designs business, she told her mom about her plans, saying she didn't know the first thing about starting a business or what kinds of handcrafts she could make. "At that point, Mom enthusiastically pulled a book off her shelf and gave it to me," she said. "It was *Creative Cash*. This book gave me the information I needed to consolidate my background and allowed me to spin my wheels about the kinds of handcrafts I could make with expertise."

"I have been involved in all facets of the miniatures industry, both as a retailer and a wholesaler," says Nancy Van Horn. "I am a collector, a craftsman, and an author. I have written articles for trade magazines, been on television for Ben Franklin stores and on the Home Shopping Network, explaining how to do porch and dollhouse projects. Who would have thought all of this would develop from reading *Creative Cash* and deciding I could start all of this?"

Nancy received her first dollhouse for Christmas over fifty years ago and has been playing with miniatures ever since.

She never could have imagined then that her love of dollhouses would lead to such an interesting career. She owned her own miniatures shop for several years and, at sixty-eight, still wholesales her own hand-crafted items at miniatures shows while also serving as sales manager for House-works, the world's largest dollhouse component manufacturer in the world. Nancy's former entrepreneurial experience and knowledge about the miniatures industry has made her so valuable that her employer won't let her retire. "You never know what is going to happen as the days go by," she says. "I will probably never retire because I love my work so much."

Countless other readers have written to tell me how earlier editions of this book changed their lives, and this is easy for me to believe because this book has certainly changed my own life. "We never know how far our sphere of influence reaches," says clay artist Maureen Carlson. "We regularly get letters from people thanking us for inspiring them to find out they could be creative and make wonderful things of which they are proud. Some even say their success with clay has allowed them to make some changes in terms of their jobs. The circle does keep getting bigger and bigger."

I thought about Maureen's comment recently when I rolled over one of my IRAs and got confirming paperwork back from the insurance company. The woman who handled this transfer added a little handwritten note at the bottom that said, "Love your books, thanks for writing them." In my wildest dreams, I never would have imagined that the stranger handling my IRA transfer was actually one of my readers. When this message registered, I suddenly found myself won-

Dreams Do Come True: Letters from Earlier Readers of *Creative Cash*

➤ "I started my crafts business six years ago with $22 and *Creative Cash.* The business has done so well I am now expanding."

➤ "*Creative Cash* was the inspiration and stimulus for my decision to become a crafts direction writer. The ideas in it just seemed to open the door to creativity."

➤ "I have been making and selling crafts for five years, and you have been with me every step of the way. In fact, you have been my 'fairy godmother' all these years, and I thought it was time to let you know. As I developed my business, I about wore out *Creative Cash.* I give myself credit for doing the work, but you get the credit for giving me all these ideas to work with."

➤ "*Creative Cash* has really changed my life! One chapter inspired me to write and publish my own books. I will be forever grateful to you for your inspiration"

➤ "After reading your book, I got up the courage to present my designs, came away with seven assignments, and was on my way. I love what I'm doing now, and owe a good deal of it to you."

➤ "I am sending you the first edition of my catalog as a thank you for your book, *Creative Cash.* Your no-nonsense advice, resource guide, and obvious experience combined with humor offered me a most enjoyable way to get my homework accomplished."

➤ "Your enthusiasm leaps out of the pages and grabs me up into the fun! What began as just a hobby is now a money-making hobby."

➤ "You have changed my life! I suppose you get this type of letter often, but I just had to write. After reading *Creative Cash,* my mind could not stop dreaming."

dering how many other people out there are working full-time jobs, reading my books and dreaming of the day when they can leave their job and strike out on their own. If you're one of them, I'd love to hear from you when you start your own business. Like some of the folks profiled in this edition, you may end up a success story in one of my next books.

In the sidebar "Dreams Do Come True," you will find a small sampling of letters from my files that illustrate how you, too, can expect to profit from this all-new edition of *Creative Cash*. "The big challenge in life is to become all that you have the possibility of becoming," says Jim Rohn, America's foremost business philosopher. "You cannot believe what it does to the human spirit to maximize your human potential and stretch yourself to the limit." My wish is that this book will energize you, stretch your mind, and open so many new doors of discovery that it will take you the rest of your life just to explore the possibilities. Please tell me about your accomplishments when you write to me at:

Barbara Brabec Productions
Creative Cash Feedback
P.O. Box 2137
Naperville, IL 60567-213

Resources

The only things worth learning are the things you learn after you know it all.

— Harry S. Truman

Guide to the Resource Chapter

Section I. Periodicals

(For publisher addresses, see Section VI, Address List #1)

Following is a selected list of business-oriented periodicals. Unless specifically mentioned in the text, consumer magazines have not been included here. To find other publications of interest, check newsstands or library directories such as *The Standard Periodical Directory*, *Ulrich's International Periodicals Directory*, *Hudson's Subscription Newsletter Directory*, and *the Oxbridge Directory of Newsletters*.

265

➤ *Arts & Crafts Show Business.* This monthly, published by LaVerne Herren, includes articles and listings of shows, festivals, trade shows, and competitions in Florida, Georgia, North Carolina, and South Carolina.

➤ *Arts 'n Crafts ShowGuide.* Dan Engel publishes this magazine. Devoted entirely to the business side of craft fair exhibiting, it includes business-related articles and a comprehensive national show list.

➤ *Choices for Craftsmen & Artists—"The Yellow Page Directory of Craft Show Information."* Betty Chypre publishes this quarterly, which includes articles and detailed information about shows in Connecticut, Massachusetts, New Jersey, New York, Pennsylvania, and Vermont.

➤ *Craft Marketing News.* Feature articles and other information for professional crafters, with listings of shops, malls, and other markets for art or craftwork.

➤ *Craftmaster News.* A show-listing periodical published by Marsha Reed for professional craftspeople on the West Coast.

➤ *The Crafts Fair Guide.* Lee Spiegel publishes this show-listing periodical for craftspeople on the West Coast. It features in-depth reviews and critiques of shows by exhibiting artists and craftspeople.

➤ *Crafts Magazine.* Miriam Olson, editor. Available on newsstands or by subscription, this monthly has carried the author's "Selling What You Make" column since 1979.

➤ *Crafts 'n Things.* Nona Piorkowski, editor. Available on newsstands or by subscription, this magazine is published eight times a year. It has carried the author's "Making Memories" column since March 1998.

➤ *Crafts Remembered.* A show-listing periodical with articles and other business information, published by Rita Stone-Conwell for artisans in the New York state area.

➤ *The Crafts Report—The Business Journal for the Crafts Industry.* Bernadette Finnerty, editor. This monthly magazine focuses on contemporary art and crafts. Each issue offers industry news, feature articles, show listings, competitions and classified ad sections that enable sellers to connect with buyers.

➤ *The Dream Merchant.* Published by John Moreland, this magazine is directed to inventors and small business owners interested in marketing their inventions. Articles and departments address legal issues, patents, trademarks, and marketing strategies.

➤ *Hands On Guide.* This show-listing guide published by Christel Luther directs artisans and interested shoppers to the best arts and crafts events in California and ten other Western states.

➤ *The Independent Patternmaker.* This newsletter, published by Patricia Nielsen, is especially for the independent pattern producer. It features timely exhibitor information on trade and consumer shows, product and service suppliers, marketing techniques, legal matters, and more.

➤ Interweave Press. This company, owned by Linda Ligon, publishes a line of fiber-related books and seven magazines, including *Piece-*

work, Interweave Knits, and *Beadwork* (as referenced in the text).

➤ *The Professional Quilter.* Edited by Morna McEver Golletz, this quarterly business journal provides business and marketing information for quilters, designers, and teachers interested in making a career in quilting.

➤ *Quilter's Newsletter.* Bonnie Leaman, editor. This full-color monthly magazine includes valuable perspective on the quilting industry, profiles of successful quilters, articles, patterns and more.

➤ *The Ronay Guides.* Three separate volumes list nearly 1500 art/craft shows, fairs, and festivals for Georgia, the Carolinas, and Virginia. Through their "It's Happening! EventsLINK" site on the Internet, the Ronays offer artists and crafters a way to learn about thousands of shows throughought North America.

➤ *SAC Newsmonthly.* Wayne Smith publishes this monthly newspaper featuring national news and thousands of art and craft show opportunities each month. (Many smaller show-listing publications have merged with SAC.)

➤ *The Sewing Sampler—Business Edition.* Kathy Sandmann publishes this newsletter for the small manufacturer/designer interested in business and marketing information.

➤ *Sunshine Artist.* Amy Detwiler, editor. This monthly magazine offers timely articles and detailed descriptions of over 2,000 art/craft events throughout the nation, with critiques of shows from working artists and crafters.

➤ *Teaching for Learning.* This newsletter, edited by Charlene Anderson-Shea, is for fiber teachers interested in networking and success strategies.

Section II.
Trade Publications and Organizations

- -

(For addresses, see Section VI and the specific Address List indicated in parenthesis at the end of each listing.)

The following is a selected list of trade magazines, resource directories, trade shows and organizations likely to be beneficial to a crafts business. Directories in your library will lead you to others.

➤ ACC Trade Shows. The American Crafts Council presents ten of the country's major retail/wholesale marketplaces in West Springfield, MA, Charlotte, NC, Tampa Bay, FL, St. Paul, MN, Atlanta, GA, Baltimore, MD, Chicago, IL (2 shows), New York, and San Francisco, CA. These markets are open to craft sellers nationwide but the standards are high. (#2)

➤ Association of Crafts & Creative Industries (ACCI). This organization serves suppliers in the crafts industry through two trade shows: The International Craft Exposition and The Professional Crafters Trade Show. Although the latter show theoretically enables professional crafters to buy needed supplies at wholesale prices, it appears to be difficult to qualify as a buyer here. Membership in this organization offers access to shows at a lower cost, a group medical insurance program, and merchant credit card services. (#2)

➤ Beckman's Gift Shows. For show-entry information, contact Industry Productions of America. (#4)

➤ *Craft and Needlework Age.* Monthly issues of this magazine emphasize particular aspects of the crafts industry, with trade show news and product information. (#1)

➤ *Craft Supply Magazine.* Edited by John Tracey, this is the only national magazine written exclusively for the professional crafter. Subtitled "The Industry Journal for the Gift Producer," it includes business articles, news and trends, trade show calendar, and a product show. The supplier information and advertisements in each issue offer one solution to the problem of where to find wholesale suppliers who will sell to home-based craft businesses. One issue a year serves as a directory of hundreds of craft wholesalers, with cross-references to over a thousand product categories. (#1)

➤ *Craftrends/SewBusiness.* This monthly trade magazine serves craft, needlework, and sewing retailers, but many professional crafters and designers rely on this magazine for industry news and trends. Subscription includes an annual *Buyer's Guide* that lists all manufacturers, importers, distributors, and publishers in the crafts industry. (#1)

➤ *Gift Basket News.* Published by Margaret M. Williams, this trade magazine is directed to gift basket retailers, but helpful to home-based businesses in this field because of its marketing and supply source information. (#1)

➤ *Gifts & Decorative Accessories.* This monthly magazine for retailers provides an overview of what's hot in the gift industry. A subscription includes the annual *Gifts & Decorative Accessory Buyer's Guide,* which lists thousands of manufacturers, importers, distributors; plus sources for manufacturing and assembling materials, gift boxes, bags, tags, and so on; trade names, trade show information, industry associations, and more. (#1)

➤ Gift Shows. "Handmade" is a unique and upscale forum that features juried artisans, designers and manufacturers of handmade merchandise at three well-established wholesale gift markets: The Chicago Gift Show, the Boston Gift Show and the Washington Gift Show. All three shows are managed by George Little Management, who will send a prospectus on shows of interest. (#4)

➤ Hobby Industry Association (HIA). A major trade association in the hobby/crafts field. Produces annual trade shows in which manufacturers, publishers, and service companies market to wholesalers, retailers, institutional buyers, and professional craft producers. (#2)

➤ Miniatures Industry Association of America. This organization promotes the interest of those engaged in buying, selling, and manufacturing miniatures, dolls, dollhouses, and collectibles. Membership includes *MIAA Industry News,* listing in a trade show directory, and access to The International Miniature Collectibles Trade Show and the National Dollhouse and Miniatures Trade Show and Convention. (#2)

➤ The National Needlework Association. A nonprofit association formed to advance needlework quality, understanding, and marketing in the U.S. Membership includes manufacturers, distributors, importers, and retailers. TNNA produces three major trade shows annually, and publishes *National Needlework News*. (#2)

➤ *Niche—The Magazine for Progressive Retailers*. Published by The Rosen Group, this trade magazine is edited for retailers of contemporary American art and craft. Includes industry news, business articles, artist profiles, and advertising showcases. (#4)

➤ *The Yellow Pages of American Crafts*. A directory companion to *Niche Magazine* published by The Rosen Group. Professional craftspeople can receive one free listing in this directory in a crafts category of their choice (baskets, fiber, gifts, miscellaneous, wood, and so on). Additional listings are extra. (#1)

Section III. Art/Craft and Home-Business Organizations

(For addresses, see Section VI, Address List #2.)

Each organization on this list publishes a periodical for its members and some offer special insurance programs, merchant credit card services and other business benefits. Write to each organization of interest, requesting a brochure. To find the names of other national and regional organizations, check the *Encyclopedia of Asso-*

ciations in your library. (See also the sidebar "Craft Organizations," page 277.)

➤ The American Association of Home-Based Businesses. Headed by Beverly Williams, AAHBB is one of the best organizations of its kind with chapters across the country. Its members have access to merchant status, discounted business products and services, prepaid legal services, informative "Taking Care of Business" tip sheets and a *Connector* newsletter.

➤ American Craft Council (ACC). This organization offers a broad range of insurance plans, including group health insurance and a Studio Policy that protects against loss to both unfinished and finished works, at home or away. Members receive *American Craft* magazine. (See also Section II for ACC trade show information.)

➤ The American Quilter's Society. Offers industry news and show information in its magazine, *American Quilter*.

➤ Arts and Crafts Business Solutions. This organization offers a bankcard service specifically for and tailored to the needs of the arts and crafts marketplace. Members also have access to major medical insurance.

➤ Embroiderer's Guild of America. This American offshoot of the Embroiderer's Guild of England has chapters nationwide. It offers educational opportunities for members, sponsors exhibits on the local, regional, and national levels and publishes *Needle Arts Magazine*.

➤ Handweavers Guild of America, Inc. Nonprofit organization of weavers, spinners, and dyers; publishes a *Suppliers Directory* and U.S.

textile collections directory. Members receive *Shuttle, Spindle & Dyepot* magazine.

➤ Home Business Institute, Inc. Offers merchant card services and group health insurance plan. Members receive *Inside Home Business* newsletter.

➤ Home Office Association of America. This organization offers insurance programs, merchant card services, discounts on travel and office supplies and the *Home Office Connections* newsletter.

➤ International Guild of Candle Artisans. Members have access to workshops, the national IGCA convention, round-robin groups, and a subscription to *The Candlelighter*.

➤ The Knitting Guild of America. Membership includes the quarterly journal, *Cast-On*, and opportunities to exhibit in retail markets and the annual National Convention and Knitting Market.

➤ Montclair Craft Guild. Serves crafters in New Jersey and the Northeast. Membership includes a subscription to *Showcase* newsletter.

➤ National Association of Enrolled Agents (NAEA). Taxpayers may dial this toll-free number 24-hours a day for a referral to a tax professional in their hometown who is trained and qualified to answer complex tax questions: 1-800-424-4339.

➤ National Craft Association. This information and resource center offers a variety of directories to help professional crafters find supplies and locate new marketing outlets. NCA members also have access to insurance programs, discounts on business services and products, merchant card services, and the *NCA Arts & Crafts Newsletter* (available both in print and online).

➤ National Mail Order Association. Founded in 1972, this organization offers information on starting a mail order business, helps small-to-midsize firms use mail order and direct marketing techniques to achieve business goals, and publishes *Mail Order Digest* newsletter.

➤ National Quilting Association, Inc. Membership benefits include workshops at the annual quilt show and subscription to *The Quilting Quarterly*. The association has also published a book, *Teaching Basic Quiltmaking*.

➤ Ohio Arts & Crafts Guild. A nonprofit service and informational organization for practicing artists and craftspeople at all levels of achievement. Members receive *Creative Ohio* newsletter, directory of Ohio festivals/competitions, and insurance options (business, property and liability).

➤ Ontario Crafts Council/Craft Resource Centre. This organization has established Canada's largest and most comprehensive crafts reference library. Members receive the magazine *Ontario Craft*.

➤ Society of Craft Designers. A professional organization for designers, writers, book and periodical publishers, editors, teachers, and others who wish to sell in the crafts and needlework industries. The Society's newsletter and annual educational seminar enables beginners to learn from the experts and make valuable editorial, publishing and manufacturing contacts.

➤ Society of Decorative Painters. They hold an annual convention and publish an annual directory. Members receive a quarterly, *The Decorative Painter.*

➤ Volunteer Lawyers for the Arts. A non-profit legal aid organization that provides free arts-related legal assistance to artists and arts organizations in all creative fields who cannot afford private counsel. Has affiliate offices in forty-two cities nationwide.

Section IV.
Business Books
and Directories

(For addresses, see Section VI and the specific Address List indicated in parenthesis at the end of each listing.)

Many of the books and directories in this section have been self-published and are not available in bookstores. In that case, publisher names are shown in parenthesis so you can contact them for ordering information. To find other business-related or how-to books of interest, check the *Books in Print* directory in your library along with its supplemental volumes, *Guide to Forthcoming Books.* To search the Internet's largest online bookstore, go to www.amazon.com.

➤ *The Apron Strings Lady Did It . . . So Can You,* by Opal Leasure. Complete guide to starting and operating a successful party-plan (home parties) business, published by the author. (#3)

➤ *Artist's Market.* Published annually by Writer's Digest Books, this directory lists 2,500 buyers of graphic and fine art. (#1)

➤ *Art Marketing 101—A Handbook for the Fine Artist,* by Constance Smith (ArtNetwork). (#3)

➤ *Basic Bookkeeping for a Small Business,* by Barbara Massie (The Magnolia Press). (#3)

➤ *The Basic Guide to Pricing Your Craftwork,* by James Dillehay (Warm Snow Publishers). (#1)

➤ *The Basic Guide to Selling Arts & Crafts,* by James Dillehay (Warm Snow Publishers). (#1)

➤ *Business Forms and Contracts (in Plain English) for Crafts People,* by Leonard D. DuBoff (Interweave Press). (#1)

➤ Books for self-publishers by Gordon Burgett. Gordon is the author and publisher of three books of possible interest to this book's readers: *Empire Building by Writing and Speaking, Niche Marketing for Writers and Speakers,* and *Publishing to Niche Markets* (Communications Unlimited). (#1)

➤ *The Business of Sewing—How to Start, Maintain, and Achieve Success,* by Barbara Wright Sykes (Collins Publications). (#1)

➤ *The Consignment Workbook,* by Sue Harris (Scandia International). A spiral-bound manual on how to start and operate a general consignment shop. (#1)

➤ *The Copyright Handbook—How to Protect and Use Written Works,* by Attorney Stephen Fishman (3d. ed., Nolo Press).

➤ *The Crafter's Guide to Pricing Your Work,* by Dan Ramsey (Betterway Books). (#4)

➤ *Crafting as a Business,* by Wendy Rosen (Chilton).

➤ *Crafting for Dollars—How to Establish and Profit from a Career in Crafts,* by Sylvia Landman (Prima Publishing). (#4)

➤ *Craft Malls—Do a Craft Show Everyday,* by Barbara Massie (The Magnolia Press). (#3)

➤ *The Crafts Business Answer Book & Resource Guide,* by Barbara Brabec (M. Evans). Answers to hundreds of troublesome questions about starting, marketing, and managing a home-based business efficiently, legally, and profitably. (#3)

➤ *The Crafts Business Encyclopedia,* by Michael Scott (as revised by Leonard D. DuBoff; 5th ed. (Harcourt Brace Jovanovich).

➤ *Crafts Market Place—Where and How to Sell Your Crafts,* edited by Argie Manolis (Betterway Books). Includes more than 575 listings of shows, craft malls, cooperatives, and other places to sell crafts. (#4)

➤ *The Crafts Supply Sourcebook,* by Margaret Boyd (4th ed., Betterway Books). Includes mail-order suppliers for all types of art, craft, hobby, needlework, sewing, and fiber arts tools, supplies, and books. (#4)

➤ *Creative Crafters Directory,* compiled by Adele Patti (Front Room Publishers) to aid shopowners and other buyers in finding products for resale. (#1)

➤ *Directory of Craft Malls and Rent-a-Space Shops,* compiled by Adele Patti (Front Room Publishers). (#1)

➤ *Directory of Craft Shops & Galleries,* compiled by Adele Patti (Front Room Publishers). Includes catalog markets, sales reps, and craft home-party organizers who accept handcrafted items. (#1)

➤ *Directory of Printers,* by Marie Kiefer (Ad-Lib Publications). Lists nearly 800 printers who specialize in bound publications—from catalogs to cookbooks to consumer guides and directories—and can work with publishers by mail. (#1)

➤ *Directory of Seasonal Holiday Craft Boutiques,* compiled by Adele Patti (Front Room Publishers). Descriptions of boutiques nationwide through which crafters can sell their work. (#1)

➤ *Directory of Wholesale Reps for Craft Professionals,* compiled by Sharon Olson (Northwoods Trading Co.). Lists companies interested in hearing from craftspeople with wholesale product lines. Includes crafts wanted, commissions taken, and tips from sales reps themselves. (#4)

➤ *Earn a Second Income from Your Woodworking,* by Garth Graves (Betterway Books). (#4)

➤ Dover Publications, *Pictorial Archive Books.* These books include thousands of copyright-free designs and motifs that can be used in any manner or place desired, without further payment, permission or acknowledgement. The perfect solution for people who claim they "can't draw a straight line." Request a free catalog. (#1)

➤ *Empire-Building by Writing and Speaking,* by Gordon Burgett (Communication Unlimited). (#4)

➤ *Handmade for Profit—Hundreds of Secrets to Success in Selling Arts & Crafts,* by Barbara Brabec (M. Evans.) Focuses exclusively on how to price and sell handcrafted/handmade products in sixteen different retail markets, with numerous illustrations, crafts marketing tips, checklists, worksheets, and success formulas. (#3)

➤ *Homemade Money—How to Select, Start, Manage, Market and Multiply the Profits of a Business at Home,* by Barbara Brabec (5th ed., rev., Betterway.) The most comprehensive home-business guide in print—covers all aspects of running any kind of business at home. Includes special A-to-Z "Crash Course in Business Basics" section, several marketing-oriented chapters, and a 300-listing resource chapter. (#3)

➤ *How to Get Happily Published,* by Judith Appelbaum (5th ed., HarperPerennial). Excellent overview of the whole publishing world, including information on self-publishing and a great resource chapter.

➤ *How to Show & Sell Your Crafts,* by Kathryn Caputo (Betterway Books). (#4)

➤ *How to Start Making Money with Your Crafts,* by Kathryn Caputo (Betterway Books). (#4)

➤ *How to Start Making Money with Your Sewing,* by Karen Maslowski (Betterway Books). (#4)

➤ *How to Start and Run a Successful Handcraft Co-Op in Your Own Community,* by Cathy Gilleland (Front Room Publishers). (#1)

➤ *How to Survive & Prosper as an Artist,* by Caroll Michels (4th ed., rev., Owl Books/Henry Holt). Subtitled "Selling Yourself Without Selling Your Soul," this book includes the names of hundreds of arts-related organizations, publications, audiotapes and videotapes, and software programs.

➤ *The Law (In Plain English) for Craftspeople,* by Leonard D. DuBoff with Michael Scott, (Madrona Publishers). Covers issues of concern to craftspeople who need to acquire business skills and a grasp of legal principles relating to the sale and use of their work.

➤ *Make Your Quilting Pay for Itself,* by Sylvia Ann Landman (Betterway Books). (#4)

➤ *Making $$$ at Home—Over 1,000 Editors Who Want Your Ideas, Know-How & Experience,* by Darla Sims (Sunstar Pub.).

➤ *Marketing Online,* by Marcia Yudkin (Plume).

➤ *The Needlecrafter's Computer Companion—Hundreds of Easy Ways to Use Your Computer for Sewing, Quilting, Cross-Stitch, Knitting & More!* by Judy Heim (No Starch Press). (#1)

➤ *Newsletters from the Desktop—Designing Effective Publications with Your Computer,* by Roger C. Parker (Ventana Press).

➤ *On Writing Well,* by William Zinsser (HarperPerennial).

➤ *1,001 Ways to Market Your Books,* by John Kremer (Ad Lib Publications). (#1)

➤ *Professional Teaching Techniques: A Handbook for Teaching Adults Any Subject,* by Elizabeth Nelson (WE Unlimited). (#1)

➤ *The Self-Publishing Manual,* by Dan Poynter (Para Publishing). The most comprehensive and informative book beginning self-publishers can read. (#1)

➤ *Selling in Craft Malls,* by Patricia Krauss. How to find and select good malls and maximize sales. (#3)

➤ *Selling Your Dolls & Teddy Bears,* by Giguere & Waugh (Betterway Books). (#4)

➤ *The Silver Pen—Starting a Profitable Writing Business from a Lifetime of Experience,* by Alan Canton (Adams-Blake Publishing).

➤ *Small-Time Operator—How to Start Your Own Business, Keep Your Books, Pay Your Taxes, and Stay Out of Trouble,* by Bernard Kamoroff, CPA (Bell Springs Publishing). (#1)

➤ *Software Directory for Fiber Artists,* by Lois Larson, 3d ed. (Studio Word Processing). Includes reviews of over 275 fiber software programs for knitting, quilting, needlework, sewing, and weaving (with heaviest emphasis on weaving programs). (#1)

➤ *The Teddy Bear Sourcebook for Collectors and Artists,* by Argie Manolis (Betterway Books). (#4)

➤ *Trademark: How to Name a Business & Product,* by Attorneys Kate McGrath and Stephen Elias (Nolo Press).

➤ *The Treasury of Quotes,* by Jim Rohn (Jim Rohn International). (#1)

➤ *The Woodworker's Guide to Pricing Your Work,* by Dan Ramsey (Betterway Books). (#4)

➤ *Writer's Guide to Book Editors, Publishers, and Literary Agents,* by Jeff Herman (Prima Publishing). (#4)

➤ *Writer's Market.* The professional writer's bible, published annually by Writer's Digest Books. (#1)

Section V: Selected Suppliers

(For addresses, see Section VI, Address List #4.)

➤ Craft Hangtags. The following crafter-owned companies offer catalogs of originally designed hangtags for handcrafts. Write to each, enclosing SASE for information about the current cost of a catalog and sample labels: E & S Creations, Kimmeric Studio and Wood Cellar Graphics.

➤ Fabric Labels. The following companies offer custom designed fabric and care labels and will send free samples on request: Charm Woven Labels, Sterling Name Tape Co., and Widby Enterprises (enclose large SASE).

➤ Office Supply Catalogs. Save money by doing some comparison shopping. On Address

List #4, you will find toll-free numbers for the following companies, all of whom offer office and computer supplies, furniture and equipment: NEBS, Office Depot, OfficeMax, Quill, and Viking.

➤ Packaging and Shipping Supplies. Add these catalogs to your reference file (toll-free numbers are on Address List #4): Action Bag Company (zipper bags, corrugated boxes, bubble wrap); Chiswick (poly bags, boxes, mailers, labels, tape); Fetpak, Inc. (cotton filled jewelry boxes and displays, other gift boxes, bags, tissue, zipper bags, merchandise tags, tagging and pricing guns, custom labels).

➤ Preprinted Papers for Laser/Inkjet Printers. These companies offer colorful preprinted and designer papers so you can make your own business cards, stationery, brochures, flyers, and other printed materials. Their toll-free numbers appear on Address List #4: Great Papers, On Paper, Paper Direct, Premier Papers, and Queblo.

Section VI. Addresses

ADDRESS LIST #1: PUBLISHERS

Ad-Lib Publications, 51 1/2 W. Adams, Fairfield, IA 52556

Arts & Crafts Show Business, P.O. Box 26624, Jacksonville, FL 32226-0624; (904) 757-3913

Arts 'n Crafts ShowGuide, ACN Publications, P.O. Box 25, Jefferson City, MO 65102; Web site: www.acnshowguide.com

ArtNetwork, P.O. Box 1268, Penn Valley, CA 95946; (916) 432-7630

Bell Springs Publishing, P.O. Box 640, Laytonville, CA 95454

Choices for Craftsmen & Artists, The Yellow Page Directory, P.O. Box 484, Rhinebeck, NY 12572; (914) 876-2772

Collins Publications, 3233 Grand Ave., Suite N-294, Chino Hills, CA 91709; (909) 590-2471

Communications Unlimited, P.O. Box 6405, Santa Maria, CA 93456; (805) 937-8711; Web site: www.sops.com

Craft and Needlework Age, 225 Gordons Corner Plaza, Box 420, Manalapan, NJ 07726

Craft Marketing News (See listing for Front Room Publishers)

Craftmaster News, P.O. Box 39429, Downey, CA 90239-0429

The Crafts Fair Guide, P.O. Box 688, Corte Madera, CA 94976; (800) 871-2341; Web site: www.virtualbazaar.com/craftfairguide/

Crafts Magazine, P.O. Box 1790, Peoria, IL 61656

Crafts 'n Things, Clapper Publishing Co. Inc., 701 Lee St., Suite 1000, Des Plaines, IL 60016

Crafts Remembered, 1046 Madison Ave., Troy, NY 12180; (518) 272-4064; Web site: www.taconic.com/crn

The Crafts Report—The Business Journal for the Crafts Industry, Box 1992, Wilmington, DE 19899; (800) 777-7098; Web site: www.craftsreport.com

Craftrends/Sew Business, 2 News Plaza, Box 1790, Peoria, IL 61656

Craft Supply Magazine—The Industry Journal for the Professional Crafter, Hobby Publications, 225 Gordons Corner Rd., Manalapan, NJ 07726; (800) 969-7176

Dover Publications *Pictorial Archive Books,* 31 E. 2nd St., Mineola, NY 11501

The Dream Merchant—How to Make Money from Good Ideas, 2309 Torrance Blvd., Suite 201, Torrance, CA 90501; (301) 328-1925; Web site: www.dreammerchant.net

Front Room Publishers, P.O. Box 1541, Clifton, NJ 07015; Web site: www.intac.com/~rjp

Gift Basket News, 9655 Chimney Hill Ln., Suite 1036, Dallas, TX 75243; (214) 690-1917

Gifts & Decorative Accessories, Geyer-McAllister Pub., Inc., 51 Madison St., New York, NY 10010

Hands On Guide, 1835 S. Centre City Pkwy., #A434, Escondido, CA 92025-6544; (760) 747-8206

The Independent Patternmaker, 804 Forest Park Blvd., Fort Worth, TX 76102; (817) 338-0025

Interweave Press, Inc., 201 E. Fourth St., Loveland, CO 80537; (970) 669-7672; Web site: www.interweave.com

No Starch Press, 401 China Basin St., Suite 108, San Francisco, CA 94107; (800) 420-7240; Web site: www.nostarch.com

Para Publishing, P.O. Box 4232-175, Santa Barbara, CA 93140-4232; 1-800-PARAPUB

The Professional Quilter, 22412 Rolling Hills Ln., Laytonsville, MD 20882; (301) 482-2345

Quilter's Newsletter, Box 394, Wheatridge, CO 80033

Jim Rohn International, 6311 N. O'Connor Blvd., Suite 100, Irving, TX 75039; (972) 401-1000

The Ronay Guides, A Step Ahead, Inc., 2090 Shadowlake Dr., Buckhead, GA 30625-2700; (800) 337-8329; Web site: www.events2000.com

SAC Newsmonthly, P.O. Box 159, Bogalusa, LA 70429; 1-800-TAKE-SAC

Scandia International, 133 Olney Rd., Petersburgh, NY 12138; (518) 658-3754

The Sewing Sampler, P.O. Box 39, Springfield, MN 56087

Sunshine Artist, 2600 Temple Dr., Winter Park, FL 32789; (800) 597-2573; Web site: www.sunshineartist.com

Studio Word Processing, Ltd., 5010-50 Ave., Camrose, Alberta T4V 0S5; Web site: www.studioword.com

Teaching for Learning, P.O. Box 3154, Jackson, WY 83001; (307) 734-8207

Warm Snow Publishers, P.O. Box 75, Torreon, NM 87061

WE Unlimited, P.O. Box 120633, St. Paul, MN 55112; (612) 783-0345; Web site: www.teachadults.com

Writer's Digest Books, 1507 Dana Ave., Cincinnati, OH 45207; (800) 289-0963

Yellow Pages of American Crafts, Suite 200 Mill Centre, 3000 Chestnut Ave., Baltimore, MD 21211

Craft Organizations

Art and craft organizations exist on all levels—local, state, regional, and national. While some have full-time staffs and permanent headquarters, others operate through volunteers. In cases like this, an organization's address is likely to change every year as new officers are elected. For this reason, no one has ever been able to compile a complete list of all the organized craft groups in America, which include associations, leagues, guilds, and clubs. One of the best lists appears in *The Craft Supply Sourcebook,* by Margaret Boyd (Betterway Books). You can also compile your own list by using association directories in your library and reading a variety of craft books and periodicals. Professionals in all fields recognize the value and importance of association membership, and readers of this book will benefit from membership in one or more of the regional or national organizations listed in this chapter.

Why join an organization? "The environment of an association," says Margaret Boyd, "provides an impetus, a thrust into crafts participation that excites the imagination. It aids craftspeople in gaining a sense of awareness of themselves in regard to their craft work—helps them determine where their work stands in terms of talent, originality, and quality."

ADDRESS LIST #2: ORGANIZATIONS

The American Association of Home-Based Businesses, P.O. Box 10023, Rockville, MD 20849; (800) 447-9710; Web site: www.aahbb.org

American Craft Council, 72 Spring St., New York, NY 10012. For membership information: (800) 724-0859; for information about the ACC trade shows: (800) 836-3470.

American Quilter's Society, P.O. Box 3290, Paducah, KY 42002-3290; (502) 898-7903

Arts and Crafts Business Solutions, 2804 Bishop Gate Dr., Raleigh, NC 27613; (800) 873-1192

Association of Crafts & Creative Industries, P.O. Box 2188, Zanesville, OH 43702; (614) 452-4541

Embroiderer's Guild of America, 335 W. Broadway, Suite 100, Louisville, KY 40202; (502) 589-6956

Handweavers Guild of America, Inc., 2 Executive Concourse, Suite 201, 3327 Duluth Hwy., Duluth, GA 30096-3301; (770) 495-7702

Hobby Industry Association (HIA), 319 E. 54th St., Elmwood Park, NJ 07407; (201) 794-1133

Home Business Institute Inc., P.O. Box 301, White Plains, NY 10605-0301; 1-888-DIAL HBI; Web site: www.hbiweb.com

Home Office Association of America, 909 Third Ave., Suite 990, New York, NY 10022; (212) 980-4622; Web site: www.hoaa.com

International Guild of Candle Artisans, 867 Browning Ave. So., Salem, OR 97302

The Knitting Guild of America (TKGA), P.O. Box 1606, Knoxville, TN 37901-1606; (615) 524-2401

Miniatures Industry Association of America (MIAA), P.O. Box 2188, Zanesville, OH 43702-2188; (614) 452-4541

Montclair Craft Guild, P.O. Box 538, Glen Ridge, NJ 07028

National Craft Association, 1945 E. Ridge Rd., Suite 5178, Rochester, NY 14622-2647; (800) 715-9594; Web site: www.craftassoc.com

National Mail Order Association, 2807 Polk St. N.E., Minneapolis, MN 55418-2954; (612) 788-1673; Web site: www.nmoa.org

The National Needlework Association, Inc. (TNNA), P.O. Box 2188, Zanesville, OH 43702-2188; (614) 455-6773

National Quilting Association, Inc., P.O. Box 393, Ellicott City, MD 21041; (410) 461-5733; Web site: www.his.com/~queenb/nqa

Ohio Arts & Crafts Guild, P.O. Box 3080, Lexington, OH 44904; (419) 884-9622

Ontario Crafts Council, Craft Resource Centre, 35 McCaul St., Toronto, Ontario M5T 1V7

Society of Craft Designers, P.O. Box 3388, Zanesville, OH 43702-3388; (740) 452-4541

Society of Decorative Painters, 393 No. McLean Blvd., Wichita, KS 67203-5968; (316) 269-9300; Web site: www.decorativepainters.com

Volunteer Lawyers for the Arts, 1 E. 53rd St., New York, NY 10022; legal hotline: (212) 319-2910

ADDRESS LIST #3: INDIVIDUALS MENTIONED IN THE TEXT

Note: If you wish to contact someone to buy products, publications, or services discussed in the text (see index for specific page references), please mention this book in your communication with them. Some individuals profiled in the book are not listed here because they have nothing to offer individual buyers. Lack of a telephone number means contact is invited only by mail or through an individual's Web site, if one is listed. Although business-to-business networking is encouraged, please do not ask busy craft professionals to answer questions or give you free help or advice. Instead, refer to the many resources in this chapter, which will lead you to all the help or information you will need for success. *When writing to anyone for any reason, enclose an SASE for a reply.*

Nancy Bell Anderson, Northwest Craft Adventures, P.O. Box 2840, Gearhart, OR 97138; (503) 738-5206

Charlene Anderson-Shea, Anderson-Shea, Inc., P.O. Box 3154, Jackson, WY 83001; (307) 734-8207

SueAnn Antonini, P.O. Box 421, Sutter Creek, CA 95685

Rochelle and John Beach, Cinna-Minnies Collectibles, 615 N. Saginaw St., Owosso, MI 48867; (517) 725-2321

Jean and Steve Belknap, The Country Spirit, 104 Mellor Ave., Catonsville, MD 21228; (410) 744-6108

Laura Donnelly Bethmann, 110 Locust St., Tuckerton, NJ 08087; (609) 296-7219

Elizabeth Bishop, Seams Sew Creative Patterns, 212 E. St., Athens, AL 35611; (205) 233-3834

Karen Boden, Sable V Fine Art Gallery, P.O. Box 1792, Wimberley, TX 78676; (512) 847-8975

Lois Boncer, Aardvark to Zebra, 5219 El Arbol Dr., Carlsbad, CA 92008

Jan Bonner, Bonner Bears & Friends, 318 Caren Ave., Worthington, OH 43085; (614) 436-1571

Barbara Brabec, Barbara Brabec Productions, P.O. Box 2137, Naperville, IL 60567; (630) 717-4188; Web site: www.crafter.com/brabec

Donna Brady, Art from the Heart, 6057 N. NC 58, Nashville, NC 27856

Janet Burgess, Amazon Vinegar & Pickling Works Drygoods, 2218 E. 11th St., Davenport, IA 52803; (319) 322-6800

Carol Carlson (See Kimmeric Studio, Address List #4)

Maureen and Dan Carlson, Wee Folk Creations; Web site: www.weefolk.com

Renee Chase: Web site: www.crafter.com

Kathy Cisneros, Recreational Recycling, 9318 Bay Vista Est. Blvd., Orlando, FL 32836; (407) 352-2923; Web site: www.rainfall.com/caplady

Trudi Clark, Fire & Lace, 571 Crosskeys Rd., Sicklerville, NJ 08081; (609) 629-0211

Sue Cloutman, Color Me Creations, 530 Swamp Rd., Coventry, CT 06238

Karen Combs, Karen Combs Studio, 1405 Creekview Ct., Columbia, TN 38401; Web site: http://personalweb.edge.net/~kcombs/

Phillip Coomer (See American Craft Malls, Address List #4)

Sammie Crawford, The Fairy Gourdmother, 170 Russey Rd., Hot Springs, AR 71913-9781

Joy Crouch, The Sheep Station, RR1, Box 230, Eureka, IL 61530; (309) 467-4336

Eleena Danielson, Cranberry Junction Designs and E&S Creations, P.O. Box 68, Rexburg, ID 83440; (208) 356-6812

Barbara Deuel, Homebound Books, 413 Frederick St., Apt. A, San Francisco, CA 94117; (415) 731-1322

James Dillehay (See Warm Snow Publishers, Address List #1)

Kimberly Stroman Doffin, K&R . . . in the Country, RR 1, Box 200, Hoskins, NE 68740; (402) 565-4583

Dodie Eisenhauer, Village Designs at Grandma's House, 310 State Hwy. AA, Daisy, MO 63743; (573) 266-3642

Merrilyn Fedder, Hand Dids Needleart, 54 N. Main, Winchester, IL 62694; (217) 742-3660

Jacqueline Fox, Waxing Moon Designs, 609 Mechanic St., Osage, IA 50461-1311; (515) 732-4559

Charlotte Flygstad, Char's Folly, 23929 1st. Ave., Siren, WI 54872

Liz Fye and Maryn Wynne, Flytes of Fancy, P.O. Box 25545, Seattle, WA 98125-1045; (888) 558-9619

Jana Gallagher, Jana's Craft Connection, 30 Gould Rd., Newfoundland, NJ 07435; (973) 208-8882; Web site: www.wyomingcompanion.com/janacraft

Bob and Carol Gerdts, Bob & Carol's Egg-Art Ltd., 1604 N. Cayuse Trail, Greensburg, IN 47240; (812) 527-2997; Web site: www.craftmark.com/eggart/eggart.htm

Geoffrey Harris, Harris Collectibles, 116 Sunny Vista Dr., Lexington, SC 29073; (803) 356-0201

Eileen Heifner, Create an Heirloom, P.O. Box 480, Berlin, MA 01503; (800) 448-6173

Mary Lou Highfill, Sunbonnet Treasures, 31209 Memorial Rd., McLoud, OK 74851; (405) 386-3060

Joanne Hill, 2620 Tamarac Pl., South Bend, IN 46615; (219) 289-3526

Kay Hineman, Hineman Quilts, 5865 S. Runion Rd., Rushville, IN 46173; (317) 629-2586

Myra Hopkins, Brush & Needle, 776 Irongate Circle, Sykesville, MD 21784; (410) 795-7538

Bobbie Irwin, 1245 W. Gordon Creek Rd., Price, UT 84501; (435) 637-8476

Patricia Krauss, Showplace Marketing, 7046 Broadway #360, Lemon Grove, CA 91945

Carol Krob, Carol's Creations, 840 N. Summit St., Iowa City, IA 52245; (319) 351-7854

Patricia Kutza, 1450 Tuolumne St., Vallejo, CA 94590; (707) 552-0442

Sylvia Landman, Self Employment Consultants, 1090 Cambridge St., Novato, CA 94947; (415) 883-6206; Web site: www.crl.com/~studio

Annie Lang: Web site: See her books at www.easlpublications.com

Opal Leasure, The Apron Strings Lady, P.O. Box 758, Madera, CA 93639; (209) 675-9982

Sherrill M. Lewis, Eximiously Yours!, Rt. 4, Box 457, Stillwater, OK 74074

Sondra Lucente, Empty Nest Collectibles, 71 Farmcrest Ave., Lexington, MA 02173; (781) 861-8395

Shirley MacNulty, Stitches by Shirley and *Knitting News Newsletter,* 104 Travelers Ct., Wilmington, NC 28412; (910) 392-9449

Barbara Massie, Massies/The Magnolia Press, 127 Flathead Dr., Cherokee Village, AR 72529; (870) 257-3837

Betty Marx, 510 E. 77th St., #1008, New York, NY 10162

Anita Means, Cottage Crafts, 700 Bowne Rd., Wayside, NJ 07712; (732) 946-3229

Janet Middleton, Caned Canines & More, 913 W. Broadmoor St., Peoria, IL 61614; (309) 692-5006

Leslie J. Miller, 8346 Bear Creek Dr., Baltimore, MD 21222; (410) 282-9313

Sandy Mooney, Sandy's Wearable Art, 6293 River Rd., Flushing MI 48433

Julia Morrill, Designs by Julia, 307 E. Curtice St., St. Paul, MN 55107-3106

Nancy Mosher, NanCraft, 2804 Ryan Place Dr., Fort Worth, TX 76110-3127; (817) 921-6005

Mary Mulari, Mary's Productions, Box 87, 217 N. Main, Aurora, MN 55705; (218) 229-2804

Maria Nerius, Nerius House & Companies; Web site: www.procrafter.com/maria.htm

Susan Nelson, Cats 'N Stuff, 2316 13th Ave. N.W., Rochester, MN 55901; (507) 289-3503

Cathy Neunaber, Lasso the Moon Art Studio, 532 So. Broad, Carlinville, IL 62626; (217) 854-5108

Teresa Niell, The Topiary Garden, 5605 Terry St., The Colony, TX 75056

Sharon Olson, Northwoods Trading Co., 13451 Essex Ct., Eden Prairie, MN 55347; (612) 937-5275

Barbara Otterson, DreamWeaver, 429 Lee Ave., Kirkwood, MO 63122; (314) 966-8702

Deb Otto, Henri's, 618 Lake Ave., Storm Lake, IA 50588

Kay Owings, Owings Crafts and Gifts, 51523 Hwy. 443, Loranger, LA 70446

Adele Patti (See Front Room Publishers, Address List #1)

Julie Peterson, Minnesota Naturals, 10291 Mississippi Blvd., Coon Rapids, MN 55433; (612) 422-8889

Joyce Roark, Loving Thoughts, 5130 Spotsylvania Dr., Baton Rouge, LA 70817; (504) 751-4218

Norma Rudloff, Rose Petals, 117 Cross Rd., Lagrangeville, NY 12540

Barbara Schaffer, Calligraphy by Barbara, 264-60 73 Ave., Floral Park, NY 11004

Barbara Sharpe, 2921 Bedford Ave., Placerville, CA 95667

Jenni Sipe, Patchouly, Box 111, Stewartstown, PA 17363; (717) 993-6648

Marie Slovek, Prairie Moon Originals, 21551 Creighton Rd., Creighton, SD 57729; (605) 457-3330

Lynn Smythe, Dolphin Crafts, 5416 Cleveland Rd., Delray Beach, FL 33484-4276; (561) 496-7673; Web site: http://members.aol.com/dlphcrft/mailcat.htm

Rita Stone-Conwell (See *Crafts Remembered*, Address List #1)

Vicki Stozich, Personal Designs, P.O. Box 1709, Findlay, OH 45839; (419) 422-1389; Web site: http://members.aol.com/VStozich

Linda Markuly Szilvasy, P.O. Box 871, Metamora, IL 61548; (915) 757-9006

Tsia-Suzanne Sullivan, Touch the Sun Originals, 506 W. 7th St., Sioux Falls, SD 57104-3017

Ruby Tobey, Scribbles & Sketches Studio, 2305 W. 32nd So., Wichita, KS 67217-2044; (316) 942-5456

Lyndall "Granny" Toothman, 506 9th St., Apt. 403, Ashland, KY 41101

Genii Townsend, Genii Townsend Presents, 3710 W. Spinnaker Ln., Tucson, AZ 85742-9289; (520) 744-1071

Nancy Van Horn, Houseworks Ltd., 2388 Pleasantdale Rd. N.E., Atlanta, GA 30340; (770) 448-6596; Web site: www.miniatures.com

Pat and Niron Virch, Traditional Rosemaling, 1506 Lynn Ave., Marquette, MI 49855

Tiffany Wall, Tiffany's Treasures, 205 Arbor St., Bradford, IL 61421; (309) 897-8406

Yvonne Ward, Country Garden Designs, 913 Arnow Ave., Bronx, NY 10469; (212) 886-5485

Jane Wentz, From Wentz It Came, 112 LuAnn Ct., Lilburn, GA 30047

Maryn Wynne (See Liz Fye, above)

Susan Young, Peach Kitty Studio, P.O. Box 1202, Madison, AL 35758; (205) 895-0656

Ernie Ziegler, Custom Engraving, 8605 292nd St. S.W., Edmonds, WA 98026-9042; (425) 774-6398

ADDRESS LIST #4: GOVERNMENT AGENCIES, TRADE SHOWS, SUPPLIERS, AND OTHER BUSINESSES

The companies and organizations on this list either have descriptive listings in Sections I through IV, or have been mentioned in the text.

Action Bag Company: for a catalog, call (800) 926-6100

Aleene's Creative Living Show: Web site: www.aleenes.com

Amazon.com: catalog hotline: (206) 694-2952; Web site: www.amazon.com

American Craft Malls, Box 799, Azle, TX 76098-0799; Web site: www.craftmark.com

Annie's Attic, 103 N. Pearl St., Big Sandy, TX 75755

Better Homes and Gardens Crafts Showcase: (800) 688-6611

Betterway Books: to order a book on a credit card, call (800) 289-0963

Bureau of Consumer Protection, Division of Special Statutes, 6th & Pennsylvania Ave. N.W., Washington, DC 20580

Charm Woven Labels, 2400 W. Magnolia Blvd., Burbank, CA 91506; (800) 843-1111

Chiswick: for a catalog, call (800) 225-8708

Coomers, Inc., 6012 Reef Point Ln., Fort Worth, TX 76135; (817) 237-4588; Web site: www.coomers.com

The Copyright Office, Register of Copyrights, Library of Congress, Washington, DC 20559; (202) 707-3000

Consumer Product Safety Commission, Bureau of Compliance, 5401 Westbard Ave., Bethesda, MD 20207; (800) 638-2772

Design Originals, 2425 Cullen St., Fort Worth, TX 76107

Eas'l Publications, Box 22088, St. Louis, MO 63126; (314) 892-9222; Web site: www.easlpublications.com

Elderhostel, 75 Federal St., Boston, MA 02110; Web site: www.elderhostel.org

E&S Creations, P.O. Box 68, Rexburg, ID 83440; (208) 356-6812

Federal Trade Commission, 6th St. & Pennsylvania Ave. N.W., Washington, DC 20580; Web site: www.ftc.gov

Fetpak, Inc.: 1-800-88-FETPAK

Great Papers: (800) 287-8163

Industry Productions of America Inc., Beckman's Gift Show, Box 27337, Los Angeles, CA 90027; (213) 962-5424

International Quilt Market, Quilts Inc., 7660 Woodway Suite 550, Houston TX 77018; (713) 781-6864

Kimmeric Studio, P.O. Box 10749, So. Lake Tahoe, CA 96158; (530) 573-1616

Leisure Arts, 5701 Ranch Dr., Little Rock, AR 72212; (800) 643-8030; Web site: www.leisurearts.com

George Little Management, 10 Bank St., White Plains, NY 10606; (914) 421-3219

Market Square, Traditional Wholesale Shows, P.O. Box 899, Mechanicsburg, PA 17055; (717) 796-2377

Michaels Arts & Crafts Stores: Web site: www.michaels.com

MJ Designs Stores: Web site: www.mjdesigns.com

NEBS Small Business Catalog: (800) 685-5906

Office Max: (800) 788-8080

Office Depot: (800) 685-8800

Offinger Management Co., 1100-H Brandywine Blvd., P.O. Box 2188, Zanesville, OH 43702-2188; (614) 452-4541

On Paper: (800) 820-2299

Paper Direct: 1-800-A-PAPERS

Patent & Trademark Office, U.S. Department of Commerce, Washington, DC 20231; (800) 786-9199

Premier Papers: (800) 832-0414

Prima Publishing: to order a book by credit card, call (800) 632-8676; Web site: www.primapublishing.com

Queblo: (800) 523-9080

Quill Office Supplies: (800) 789-1331

The Rosen Group, Inc., 3000 Chestnut Ave., Suite 300, Baltimore, MD 21211; (410) 889-2933

SCORE: (800) 634-0245

Smidgens, Inc., 1938 Buell Ave., Lima, NY 14485; (800) 888-1486

Sterling Nane Tape Co., Box 1056, Winsted, CT 06098

Viking Office and Computer Supplies: (800) 421-1221

Widby USA, P.O. Box 53253, Knoxville, TN 37950-3253

Wood Cellar Graphics, 87180 563rd Ave., Coleridge, NE 68727; (402) 283-4725

U.S. Small Business Administration: (800) 827-5722; Web site: www.sbaonline.sba.gov

Index